In grateful appreciation
for the outstanding
support from a tremendous
Ready Room.

Robert W Barnett
cdr   USN
Co   Mar 78 - Jun 79

Division
Officer's
Guide

The leadership, supervision, and guidance that the junior officers and petty officers give, day in and day out, are the most important factors in achieving a high esprit de corps. The division officer is the core of the Navy's spirit—Arleigh Burke, Admiral, U.S. Navy, former Chief of Naval Operations, 1955–1961.

Division
Officer's
Guide

SEVENTH EDITION

By John V. Noel, Jr., Captain, U.S. Navy (Retired)
and Frank E. Bassett, Commander, U.S. Navy

Naval Institute Press
Annapolis, Maryland

*Dedicated with respect and admiration
to the officers and men of the fleet*

Foreword to the First Edition

Division Officer's Guide has been written for the benefit of division officers, who constitute the foundation upon which a ship's organization is built. The division officer is close to his men; he organizes, trains, and directs them according to the fundamental precepts of the Naval Service and with due regard for their individual development and personal needs.

This book is not a detailed study of each task to be performed by a division officer, but more a summary of what must be accomplished on board ship in the management of a strong, effective unit of men. Junior officers will find here many of the lessons usually learned only through long years of experience.

L. T. DuBose
Vice Admiral, U.S. Navy
(Chief of Naval Personnel, 1951–1953)

Preface to the Seventh Edition

The Navy has changed considerably since the publication of the Sixth Edition of the *Division Officer's Guide* in 1972, and the Seventh Edition now reflects these changes. Under the perceptive leadership of Admiral Zumwalt as Chief of Naval Operations, and continuing under Admiral Holloway, renewed emphasis has been placed on the moral and human aspects of naval leadership. Some of the minor but irritating customs and restrictions of the past have been eased, making the service more attractive to young men, yet true discipline has been preserved and even enhanced.

The *Division Officer's Guide* focuses on the Navy's single most important leadership objective: showing division officers and petty officers how best to understand, motivate, and inspire their men. In 1952 when the First Edition was published, the Navy was receptive to the doctrine that men must be understood and motivated before being directed and commanded. While much easier to profess than to accomplish, this basic precept in the management of men is still the foundation upon which a division officer builds an effective, efficient, and combat-ready team.

The long overdue recognition of the surface warfare officer is reflected in this edition. He must now formally qualify in the same demanding fashion as the aviation or submarine officer. Many of the professional qualification standards to be met by the aspiring surface warfare officer can be attained with the assistance of this volume.

A carefully selected trio of junior officers have played a major part in helping to produce this edition. They are Stephan J. Froggett, Lieutenant, U.S. Navy; John P. Villarosa, Lieutenant, U.S. Navy; John N. Petrie, Lieutenant, U.S. Navy. All of them are on duty at the U.S. Naval Academy.

Special thanks are due to Dr. Gregory J. Mann and Richard R. Wohlschlager, of the faculty of the U.S. Naval Academy, for their efforts on Chapters 8 and 10, respectively, and to Peter T. Deutermann, Lieutenant Commander, U.S. Navy, of the Bureau of Naval Personnel, for his overall review.

Comments and suggestions to the authors through the U.S. Naval Institute are always received with interest and appreciation.

John V. Noel, Jr., Captain, U.S. Navy (Ret.)
Frank E. Bassett, Commander, U.S. Navy

Contents

Qualification as Division Officer Afloat

The Personnel Qualification Standard (PQS) program for the division officer requires that he organize, plan, lead, and control the efforts of the personnel assigned within his division to support effectively the overall mission of the ship.

In order to qualify as a division officer, it is necessary to demonstrate a knowledge and understanding of the subjects below. Page numbers following the numbered topics serve as a handy reference to locate information in the *Division Officer's Guide* in these important areas.

Division
Officer's
Guide

1/Introduction

The ship's company is to be divided into as many divisions as there are Lieutenants and Masters allowed to the ship.—*Rules, Regulations and Instructions for the Naval Service of the United States, 1818.*

The departments of a ship shall be divided into divisions. These divisions are established in the organization structure so that they may be assigned as units within the components of the battle organization.—*Standard Organization and Regulations of the U.S. Navy.*

This guide has been compiled to help the division officer learn and apply those principles of leadership necessary for the successful management of the men for whom he is responsible—his division. It was designed to aid him in instilling obedience, confidence, respect, and loyal cooperation in these men—without which successful naval leadership cannot be accomplished. Leadership is an art whose practice, as the result of experience, is based on certain principles and attitudes rather than on abstract or inspirational concepts. In times past this art has been learned and the attitudes acquired only by means of a long apprenticeship at sea under experienced, seasoned officers, assisted by experienced senior petty officers.

But the expansion of our Navy, the introduction of modern sophisticated equipment, and the requirement of heavy operating schedules has forced junior officers into a position of immediate responsibility with no time for apprenticeship. This has disturbed if not destroyed this traditional system of the indoctrination of young officers. Therefore, after the techniques and principles of naval personnel management set forth in this guide have been mastered, the art of leadership can be cultivated on this foundation, the distilled experience of thousands of junior officers who have gone before.

Leadership

According to General Order 21 (as first issued) leadership is defined as "the art of accomplishing the Navy's mission through people. It is the sum of those qualities of intellect, of human understanding and of moral character that enable a man to inspire and to manage a group of people successfully. Effective leadership, therefore, is based on personal example, good management practices, and moral responsibility." It should be worthwhile to enlarge a bit on the above definition of naval leadership.

The first component mentioned above is personal example. Your men will reflect your sincerity, enthusiasm, smart appearance, military behavior, technical competence, coolness and courage under stress. To be an effective leader you must look and act like one; in your own way, of course, after your own fashion.

The second major component of leadership is effective management. Leaders, like musicians, surgeons, and scientists, do not spring forth full grown as masters of their art. They serve an apprenticeship during which they practice the disciplines of their profession. Management, common to almost all fields of human endeavor, is one of these disciplines.

This is a book on a particular kind of management, the management of a group of men known in the Navy as a *division*. To manage means "to bring about; to succeed in accomplishing; to take charge or take care of; to dominate or to influence; to handle, to direct, to govern; to control in action or in use." All of these meanings are relevant to the term "management" as it will be used in this book. *In learning to manage, you will take the first step in learning to lead.*

Third, but by no means the least important aspect of leadership, is moral responsibility. This may sound like an abstraction to you but it's quite simple. The difference between Hitler and Churchill was not only in their methods but in their motives. There is bad, irresponsible leadership that threatens, bluffs, deceives, and oppresses, and the morally responsible kind that guides firmly and honestly with every possible regard for human dignity. Both may obtain similar short-term results. Your division spaces could be brought up to excellent condition by threatening to punish every man if these results were not obtained. But in the long run your men would let you down and none would be encouraged to reenlist.

The basic unit of men in the Navy has always been the division. As long as the seagoing Navy was composed only of ships, there were no other units than the division; now there are men in aircraft squadrons, submarines, construction battalions, underwater demolition teams, air crews, and in departments of shore stations whose organization may differ slightly in detail or in terminology from the traditional division. For convenience, however, in this book the term *division* is used in a comprehensive sense to include *all* comparable basic units of men in the Navy. Similarly, while this guide will be addressed to a typical division officer afloat, it is also applicable, in all but a few details, to all officers and petty officers, male and female, whether afloat, in the air, or ashore, who deal directly with enlisted men and women.

In writing for *all* officers, it is recognized that many readers are noncareer or reserve officers whose eventual careers will be far removed from naval administration. However, few young men, at some point in their business or professional lives, can escape the need for knowing the fundamentals of human management. Organizing a group of men or obtaining productive effort from an organization already in operation are experiences that almost all of you who read these pages will have, whether or not you make the Navy your career. In almost every field of human endeavor, the men who are most successful are those who can coordinate the efforts of their associates and who motivate the work of their subordinates. Unless you become a writer or a research scientist, or follow some similar highly individualistic pursuit, you will, in some degree, in or out of the Navy, be an organizer and a leader. Thus the skills and the self-confidence that you will gain by learning to be an efficient division officer or petty officer will be of immense advantage to you even if you leave the service.

A division may consist of twenty specialists in a small ship or several hundred men in the E division of a large aircraft carrier. A division may be composed of highly trained and skilled technicians or may be made up largely of inexperienced seamen. Whatever may be the size, importance, or composition of a division, its supervision is a responsibility of the utmost importance. It cannot be run by remote control.

A division officer is one regularly assigned by the commanding officer to command a division of the ship's organization. Division officers are responsible to, and, in general, act as assistants to the department heads.

The division officer has always been recognized as a major link in the long chain of naval command. He operates at the core of the Navy spirit. He must understand the mission of his ship or unit, and at the same time he must concentrate on a great many specific details regarding his division. He performs his duties on a level where he must produce immediate results. No vague directives can be written by him for subordinates to work out the details. He must be capable and skilled in his profession, as well as approachable, in order to encourage the confidence of his men. The division officer must complete large amounts of paperwork, yet must find time for daily supervision of, and personal contact with, his men. *It is this supervision and guidance that must be recognized as your most important duty.* Men are obviously by far the most important factor in the success of any cooperative effort; it must be to your men that you devote the greater part of your time and attention. In small ships the division officer may also be a head of department, which gives him additional responsibilities and work.

The division officer, the assistant or junior division officer and that key man, the leading division chief petty officer, are the leaders who really make or break an organization. They are in direct, daily contact with the men. In carrying out the policies of the commanding officer, as amplified by the executive officer and the department heads, the division leader sets the pace and tone of the unit. His understanding, ability, and enthusiasm either produces smart, able, and efficient crews, or his lack of these qualities results in sloppy, poorly disciplined units. Just as a division is only as efficient as the sum of the efforts of the men in it, so a ship can be only as good as the sum of its divisions.

Purpose of the Division Officer's Guide

The *Division Officer's Guide* is not a complete manual for naval officers. It does not include all the information and all the directives that are found in standard official publications. It is designed as a companion volume to the well-known *Watch Officer's Guide*, which assists young officers in standing efficient deck watches at sea and in port, and to *The Naval Aviation Guide*, which provides guidance for young pilots and naval flight officers in their duties pertaining solely to aviation. The *Division Officer's Guide*, in a similar manner, will assist the younger officer and petty officer in discharging the remainder of his responsibilities in the administration of his men and their preparation for combat.

This book is applicable to all officers aboard ship, in aircraft squadrons, or ashore. It presents material not readily found elsewhere that applies specifically to the management of a division.

While aviation and submarine officers have their own particular problems in running their divisions, the differences from a surface ship situation as described herein are more matters of terms and details than matters of principle. Where major points of special application do exist, such as an aircraft squadron embarked in a carrier, for example, the matter is covered in detail.

A Division Officer's Day

For the benefit of those who have not yet been assigned to sea duty, there follows a description of a typical day for a typical division officer. Let us assume you have been assigned as OI (Operations Information) division officer aboard a *Brooke*-class guided missile frigate. Your immediate supervisor is a senior lieutenant, the operations officer, and your division is part of the Operations Department.

Breakfast is served in the wardroom from 0630 until 0730 and you turn out early enough so that you can finish eating by 0700, for two reasons. First, there is not enough room to seat all officers at once; second, by finishing at 0700 you give yourself sufficient time before quarters to organize your day and read your message traffic, which you will pick up at Radio Central.

Planning and flexibility are the real keys to effective management aboard ship. The Plan of the Day, the Plan of the Week (which is published on Friday for the following week), your message traffic, yesterday's notebook page, and the word which comes out at quarters are the ingredients of your day's work. Although everything seems to be laid out for you, flexibility to reorder your priorities to accommodate the ever-changing demands of shipboard life will be necessary.

Quarters is normally held at 0740. Officer's Call is held at 0745. Your men will begin to gather at their assigned muster area at about 0730, which is when you should arrive. During the next ten minutes you can discuss business with your chief and the leading petty officers and refine your plans for the day. At 0740 the leading first class petty officer calls a formal roll. The chief gives you the muster sheet and makes his report, and you proceed to the starboard side amidships, where all the ship's officers are forming up. You give the muster sheet to the personnelman and report to your department head that your division is all present or accounted for (if you have no absentees).

The executive officer takes formal reports from the department heads, and puts out whatever word he might have for the various departments or for all officers. He then dismisses the officers, who meet with their respective department heads for any amplifying instructions. You then return to your division to pass on the word. Your chief has read the Plan of the Day to the division so that they are waiting for your announcements and an inspection of their uniforms and personal appearance. It is important, if at all practical, that you speak to all of your men each day. Whether it is to stress an item in the Plan of the Day, or make an announcement brought from officer's call, or just to comment on some item of interest to the entire division, it is to your benefit to stand in front of the entire division and reinforce the fact that you are their division officer. Quarters is generally the only time you will get to do this. After making your announcements, have the chief dismiss the division from quarters.

At this point, as the men proceed to their working spaces, you will gather your senior petty officers, receive any special request chits, discuss them if need be, and agree on the work for the first hour of the morning. You will then take the special request chits directly to the department head for action; if you hand-carry them, he will act on them right away. A special request chit is very important to the man who submits it; even if the matter seems trivial, you should respect the importance which the man places on it. Action, even negative action, which comes right away lets the man know his desires were considered and decided upon, not simply ignored as insignificant.

As soon as you have taken care of the special request chits, head for your division spaces. The presence of the division officer gets things going and shows he is interested in the progress of the work. You need not stay long, but you should be seen there. This will also give you an opportunity to check the material condition of your spaces. After you have determined that the day's work is on track, you will drop by the departmental office to clear your incoming basket of paperwork. The simplest way to handle paperwork is to take each item and do it. Quite often there will be some research required, or consultation with your technicians, or you will have to rough-draft a letter for the department head. You will spend between one and two hours on a typical day's paperwork, after which you might stop by the wardroom for a cup of coffee, and then back to your spaces, to spend an hour or so with your division.

Work will begin shortly after 0800 for your men. By 0900 they should all be completely involved in their work (preparation for some jobs could make work slow in starting). The hour from 0900 to 1000 is the best time for individualized instruction and on-the-job training or field day and maintenance work. You should try to be available to your petty officers as they direct the men and to directly supervise some evolutions. By 1030 your department head may have generated some more projects for you. You will most effectively spend the hour before 1130 lunch working on these new tasks.

The day resumes at 1300, and, again, you head for your spaces. The afternoon is the best time for team training, since group activity is easier to get moving than individual work in the afternoon, particularly after lunch.

Team training will typically last until 1530, after which you begin to wrap up the day. It's time for a clean-up, stowage of equipment or classified material, tools, paint brushes, etc. By 1600 your men will be heading for the compartment to prepare for liberty. You will make another pickup of your message traffic, and then your paperwork, just before liberty call. You will examine your projects; if they are going to pile up you will have some "after hours homework," typically about an hour's worth, after which you'll probably hit the beach for liberty yourself.

The preceding routine is more accurately described as that of an ideal day rather than a typical day. Daily quarters are not always possible, particularly underway, because of intensive operations and demanding watch requirements. There is seldom a "routine day" and this, of course, is one of the most satisfying characteristics of life in the Navy.

Men as a Major Challenge

A naval officer must meet daily a broader spectrum of challenges than almost any other professional man. One moment he may have the conn, handling the ship at high speed; at another he might be engaged in a damage control drill. He may be called upon to resolve a technical question about the repair of a radar, or he may find himself advising one of his men whose wife has just threatened divorce. At his desk he might be struggling to balance the wardroom mess accounts, to write a directive, or to prepare a recognition lesson for the lookouts. Obviously he cannot give all his attention to his duties as a division officer, yet it is through his men that he can accomplish his major goal to be an effective, efficient, and respected naval officer.

Commanding officers recognize that exacting requirements in performance, conduct, and appearance of the crew can be met only when intelligent supervision is exerted down through the most junior petty officer to the last man on board. This process of complete and effective participation by all leaders is not automatic; it takes planning, organization, knowledge, and skill. This book will show how the process can be set in motion and maintained.

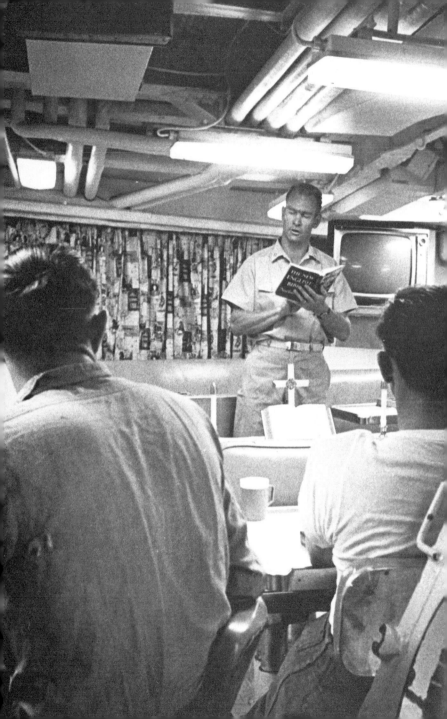

2/Capabilities and Needs

A Division Officer shall keep himself informed of the capabilities and needs of each of his subordinates.
—*Standard Organization and Regulations of the U.S. Navy.*

Management is based upon the understanding of human motivations, sensitivity to the means of securing human responses, and skill in supplying human satisfactions.—Lawrence A. Appley, President, American Management Association.

The Navy is a social as well as a military organization. It is concerned not only with ships and aircraft and weapons; it is concerned also with the human beings who operate these machines. The Navy is interested in all its men—their hopes and fears as well as their capabilities and their needs. It is interested in them as individuals and (this is much more complex) as *groups* of individuals who influence each other and are influenced in turn by the group.

Executives in industry have learned, particularly in recent years, that problems in human relations have a tremendous effect on efficiency and profits and are often more complex in their solution than those presented by technology or economics. Efficient machinery can be purchased; human cooperation must be earned. The Navy faces quite similar problems. Weapons can be made, repaired, modernized, or scrapped, but men are not subject to the same logical, legal, or mathematical laws as electronics or metallurgy. The physical plant of a ship can be restored to first-class fighting condition by an extensive shipyard overhaul, but its crew, exhausted and perhaps demoralized by long periods away from home under conditions of danger and hardship, requires the skillful attention of leaders who understand *and who can take steps to solve* the human problems involved.

Man is a social being whose behavior is subject to feelings and sentiments that are not always rational or logical. Stop a minute and grasp this idea and never lose sight of it. Man is *not* a completely logical, rational, reasonable being; he is subject to conscious and unconscious feelings which stem from his childhood or his immediate past, as well as his culture and environment. You cannot say of a group of workers: shorten their hours, feed them better, pay them more, and their efficiency and productivity will increase. It might increase, but it might decrease instead. Within limits, man's productivity depends on his attitudes, his emotions; if these favor greater output, then no mere change in his physical environment will affect him. Here is the key which can unlock a storehouse of power, energy, cooperation, devotion to duty, and courage. To employ this key requires, on the part of a division officer, a certain amount of heart, understanding, patience, and emotional maturity. Above all, it requires the acceptance of the principle that men are social beings whose behavior may or may not be guided by logic, but is largely governed by feelings or sentiments. It is your job to encourage the feelings that further the caliber of work desired, and to dissipate those feelings and attitudes that destroy collaboration and cooperation.

In dealing with physical energy or output, you cannot create it; you must, in accordance with the law of the conservation of energy, convert it or else release it. But in human relations, in dealing with the feelings and attitudes of a group of men, there is almost no limit to the energy, devotion to duty, and effectiveness that can be elicited. Men in combat will go to hell and back for someone or something they believe in. In the more prosaic atmosphere of a division of men working in peacetime, this concept of almost limitless human resources is just as relevant. If your men are with you, they will gladly work around the clock to get a job done. If your men, on the other hand, are disturbed, bitter, confused, insecure, or resentful, they will have to be driven every minute and will do as little as possible just to get by.

Understanding of men and their behavior in groups is not *absolutely* essential in the Navy. If you are an average, honest man, and normal in your relations with others, you can get along in a low-powered way and may gain a reputation for being a well-meaning if not particularly effective officer. You can also manage a farm or drive a car in the same way—not really knowing much about farming or automobiles, but going through the motions with moderate success. You can drive a car, for example, for years without any attention or service except gasoline, oil, and water. But the car's performance will be poor and its gasoline mileage low. The big point here is that, with a little understanding, you can do a much better job in handling men as well as in operating machinery. Thus you see that it is as important to try to understand what goes on in the minds and hearts of men as it is to understand the intricacies of a radar circuit or a fire control system.

Lyndall Urwick, an international authority on management, declares that: "Without a constant sensitivity to what is going on below the surface—a sensitivity which can be improved and refined by theory, but which is ultimately dependent on an instinctive grasp of how other individuals react to him and to each other—the administrator is not likely to get far. Tact and judgment are the keys to effective leadership. Successful practical men rightly devote much of their lives to exercising them. They know that all the logic in the world, an irrefutable array of facts and arguments, is worth less than nothing if the sentiments of those they lead leave no chink for the light of reason to enter."

This equal emphasis on the human aspects of management is not applicable to naval situations alone. A group of sailors doing a job aboard ship is quite comparable to a similar group working in an office or factory ashore. The interactions within the groups will be basically the same even though the roles of the organizations may be vastly different. The skills and techniques you, as a young naval officer, develop in managing a division will be of the greatest value to you in almost any other supervisory situation in which you find yourself in later years. Even though you may never again be in a position where you directly manage a group of men, your understanding of, and skill in, group leadership will be of inestimable value in almost any activity you pursue. It will also help you to understand yourself and your relations with those for whom you work or with whom you are associated.

Human Capabilities

In recent years science has learned a great deal about people—how they feel about their work, and why they act as they do. This has not necessarily changed the relationship between men and their leaders, but it has removed much of the necessity for dealing with people by trial and error. Years ago, to get an automobile engine tuned up, you hired a mechanic, who fiddled around and listened to the engine and tried adjusting the carburetor and then cleaned the points and plugs and perhaps replaced the coil. If he was a good mechanic, he eventually found the trouble and fixed it. This is just the way leaders in the past usually managed their men. If they were good leaders, they had gained most of their experience by trial and error, or by observation, and their units were well organized and efficient.

Now let us see how your car is handled in a modern garage. Science has provided complex and efficient instruments which reveal at once by flashing lights or moving indicators just what the trouble is. Adjustments are made, parts replaced if necessary, and you leave with a smoothly running car.

You may be bored with this illustration by now, but let's finish it. Science has not developed machines that you can attach to people to discover what is wrong with them, but it has provided information, gained through careful research, that will help you as a division officer immensely. The important points to understand are that there is plenty of straightforward, easily-understood knowledge about men's behavior; and this knowledge must be applied with a certain amount of common sense. The principles of human behavior are not as rigid and exact as those of ballistics, for example. We are dealing with that very complex mechanism, man. It must also be remembered that there are a few people whose feelings and behavior are very much different from the average. These abnormal people are, fortunately, rare in military circles; the people you deal with should be quite normal and average. But even with these normal men, you will not be able to apply your knowledge of people with 100 percent success. However, your chances of dealing with human problems effectively are improved by using the guides that science can offer.

Intelligence

The capabilities of the men in your division depend on many factors. One of these is intelligence, generally defined as the capacity for understanding, and for adapting to, changing conditions. It is a quality with which a man is born and which may be developed by his environment. In any large group a few people will be very intelligent and a few very dull, with most of us somewhere between the two extremes. We will divide intelligence into three parts: abstract, manual, and social intelligence.

Abstract Intelligence

The first of these, abstract intelligence, is, roughly speaking, the capacity of a person to learn to reason and to solve problems. It means only what he can do, his potential, not necessarily what he is doing. It is measured in the Navy by general classification tests, given during recruit training. Some men may want to take the test again later in their enlistments. Unless there is a language problem, as with many Filipinos and Chicanos, or a strong cultural difference, as with men from certain geographic regions or members of some ethnic groups which maintain a strong subculture, experience shows that their scores will rarely improve significantly. The mark a man makes on this test (his GCT) is a fair approximation of his abstract intelligence. But it is extremely important that you understand that this is only an approximation and is *not* a measure of his value to the service or his ability to advance. For a large group of men, the use of their GCT scores will predict those who will be successful at electronics school, for example, and for this reason the Navy must set up somewhat arbitrary standards in the interest of overall efficiency and economy. The requirement of the Bureau of Naval Personnel that a man have a GCT of 60 to be eligible for a certain school may seem unreasonable and may rule out a few men who could complete the course, but experience has shown that lowering the requirements would waste time and money because of many failures. This does not mean, however, that as a division officer you should discount a man with a low GCT. In the last analysis, a psychological test only reveals the grade a man made on that particular test—it is not necessarily a measure of the man's potentiality for success in a particular job. If you took the trouble to investigate, you would most likely find that a large proportion of the most respected and capable petty officers on the ship have GCTs under 50. As you may have observed, GCTs are listed in the men's records, and run from about 30 on up, with 50 being the median. The significance of the score is whether it is decidedly below 50, about 50, or considerably higher than 50. This indicates, with fair reliability, whether most men are somewhat below average, average, or above average in abstract intelligence.

Manual Intelligence

Another measure of a man's capabilities is his score in arithmetic, mechanical, and clerical aptitude tests. These tests are a rough measure of his manual intelligence. A low mechanical score and a high clerical aptitude score would certainly tag a man as being better material for a yeoman than for a machinist's mate. We must be careful, however, not to take these scores too literally. A man with average scores in his GCT, arithmetic, and mechanical tests might have a high clerical aptitude score but might detest office work, particularly typing. If he is sincerely interested in learning to be a quartermaster, it would be advisable to give him a trial with the bridge gang. Personnel tests are valuable tools in selecting men for jobs and special schools, but they should be used as guides primarily, and with some flexibility. Motivation (which means whether a man wants to do something) is the most important factor. A highly motivated man of limited ability will often be more successful than a talented person who really doesn't care or who cannot concentrate on learning.

Personality (Social Intelligence)

Personality may be defined as the effect that a person has upon others. It is a measure of his social intelligence. It is closely related to a man's capabilities. Science is developing tests that measure some of the traits that make up personality, but these tests are still too complicated for general use by division officers. The best that can be done is to discuss as examples some common traits and their applications. It must be remembered that few men exhibit the extreme characteristics that will be described. Most people are in between these limits. It is foolish to make snap judgments of people and to base job selection on first impressions of their personality traits.

Some men enjoy the company of other people; they like to be one of the gang; they seem to be natural leaders. Other factors being equal, these men make good boatswain's mates, for example. Other men are quiet, retiring, studious—traits which would be suitable for an electronic technician or a radioman. Some men are naturally more polite, more tactful than others; these men should be placed in jobs where these qualities are needed. The captain's yeoman would be one such job. Some men are naturally steady and sober, always on the job, never in trouble. Other men of equal intelligence, ability, and industry are often amusing to some and irritating to others. They may get into trouble ashore, and show a tendency to have good days and bad days aboard ship. Some men might be conscientious and work to the limit of their abilities, while others might be embittered or disappointed and produce only a minimum of work. Some of these personality traits are fixed in a man, but others can be modified if you can discover the major reason for the particular attitude—but that is another subject which will be discussed in a later chapter. The important point here is that in judging a man's capabilities, which simply means trying to figure out what he can do in the Navy, you have to take into consideration all the information you can gather. This includes his official record, his personal history, his reputation among his shipmates, and his general appearance and attitude.

You should be alert to the possibility that some of your men are not aware that the different races have the same capabilities. Apparent differences are not the result of racial inferiority but rather the symptom of the belief that racial inferiority does exist. Our history has unfortunately presented us with a situation in which large portions of some ethnic groups have received an inferior form of education and were offered limited opportunities in other aspects of personal development. Furthermore, cultural differences at times make it easier to see how some people are different rather than what all people have in common. These areas can be very sensitive; if you sense a lack of understanding within your division you should take prompt action to ensure that your men become better educated in the facts of the situation. Each man should know he will be evaluated primarily on the performance of his assigned duties. Once he is sure this is the case he will feel secure knowing you are a fair man. You must be cautious in your dealings with your men never to upset that trust by inconsistency. This will prove invaluable in offsetting racial tension. Because of the sensitivity of these situations you may want to seek advice and assistance from your department head or the executive officer. The Navy presently has several programs to assist in this area and your superiors will be able to advise you as to the best solution.

Personal Needs

In the quotation from the *Standard Organization and Regulations of the U.S. Navy* at the beginning of this chapter, *needs* are grouped with *capabilities* as particulars about which the division officer "shall keep himself informed."

At first we might pass over the word *needs* without much notice, assuming that the needs of men are rather simple and well known. But there is a great deal to be considered here.

Clothing

The most obvious physical needs are proper clothing, food, a place to live and sleep, and medical attention. American sailors are fortunate in obtaining, for the most part, these requirements. But there are some aspects of these items that division officers should consider. The satisfaction of these needs is more or less relative, and a little forethought and ingenuity on the part of the division officer can often result in great improvement.

There is little that division officers can do about the uniform that is specified, but assistance should be given in procuring small stores, in stowing clothes, in cleaning and repairing them, etc. All men in the division should be required to maintain a full bag as a matter of routine. The sooner you establish this practice, the better and easier life will be for you and your petty officers.

Be alert to the needs of your men for foul weather or cold weather clothing. The remainder of the crew may be comfortable, but if your men are signalmen who stand watches at night in exposed areas they may need cold weather jackets. Do not hesitate to make these needs known to the executive officer through your head of department. Perhaps your division must stand out in the rain, as the anchor detail does, for extended periods. See that they all have rainproof clothing available.

Storage space for foul weather gear, raincoats, peacoats, and such items as safety shoes, always presents a problem. If gear must be stowed on bunks it tends to go adrift. Since the men all stencil their gear it is not difficult to trace the owner of stray clothing. Note, however, that the stray clothing of a careless owner may not be easy to trace if found by someone who is less than honest. During your daily inspection of living spaces, insist that the petty officers in charge see that men stow their gear properly.

With the advent of policies allowing most enlisted personnel the privilege of keeping civilian clothing on board and the new officer-style enlisted dress uniforms, the stowage problem is increased, and, in some cases, may become insurmountable. Your genuine interest in attempting to solve these very real problems will go a long way towards convincing your men of your concern for their welfare.

In addition to stowage, the repair and cleaning of uniforms presents a few problems. Naturally, uniform repair facilities are beyond the power of a division officer to acquire, but you *can* find out what facilities are available and what the prices are. If your men's dress blues, for example, begin to show signs of wear, you can find out where repair can best be done and at what cost and so advise your men. Or perhaps their ribbons or shoes are beginning to look shabby—you should take action without waiting for something to be done by the executive officer.

Laundry pickup and delivery is often dismissed as routine, but there is a right way to handle your division laundry, and a wrong way—which usually results in lost clothing. Appoint a capable laundry petty officer and make him responsible for collection of laundry in the compartment, delivery of dirty clothes to the laundry, and, most important of all, distribution of clean clothes upon return of the week's wash. Most of the clothing claimed to be "lost in the laundry" has really gone adrift through sloppy distribution. Unless supervised, the distribution of clean wash in the compartment will consist of throwing the men's clothes in the general direction of their bunks, with no real concern for the owner who may be on liberty or on watch.

Food

Good food is another obvious need for all men and is also something that is largely beyond the control of most division officers. There are certain refinements, however, that can mean a great deal to your men. Division leaders should make it a point to visit their men occasionally at meals and to be familiar with the menu and the meal-serving routine. All serious complaints about the food should be thoroughly investigated.

Living Spaces

Another important factor in filling the needs of men is the provision of adequate living quarters. This is always a problem on board ship, where the addition of new gear and extra men tends to fill the living spaces to the bursting point. The alert and aggressive division offcer can often relieve this condition somewhat by talking to the men and finding out what minor changes or additions might help. Improvements in lighting, ventilation, and bunk and locker space can often be achieved by work that is within the capacity of the ship's force. Do not make major changes, technically known as alterations, however, without proper authority. Lights can be shifted, fans relocated, bunks can be removed and extra lockers installed, bunks can be rearranged and canvas or metal dust shields erected—all items within the capacity of the ship's force. It will take a well-worded work request on your part and a bit of pushing, but something can usually be done if you try. If the work request is not approved, try again at a later date; at least your men will know you are trying.

Cleanliness always improves habitability and is gained by regular attention and, sometimes, pressure on your part. Make it a habit to visit the living spaces of your men periodically and ensure that bunks are made up, trash picked up, decks cleaned, etc.

Other Basic Needs

This discussion so far has touched on some of the more obvious physical needs of men and must not be assumed to be complete.

The important point to remember is that all the details of the men's environment are the intimate concern of their officers. In the following paragraphs we will outline some of the more important basic needs, and these you will find a little more complex.

To make it short and simple, we will include the remainder of men's needs under five headings. These are *security, information, self-respect, group approval,* and *attainable objectives.* This will not be a lecture on psychology; it contains facts about people. We are not only concerned with the moral aspects of treating your men in a considerate and humane manner; we are concerned as well with the concrete need to lead men efficiently.

Security

There is no more important necessity in a man's relations with others than a feeling of security. Not just physical security, but rather the assurance that he will be well treated and fairly judged by his leaders. By questioning thousands of workers in different factories over a period of years, scientists have found that first on their list of complaints is not low pay, not long hours, but arbitrary and inconsiderate treatment by their supervisors.

Your men are dependent on you twenty-four hours a day for most of the little things that make up their lives. To make your men feel secure you must first of all be consistent. Don't drive them for a few days and then let them loaf, unless they know the reason for the special effort. Don't demand the impossible one day and ignore the same matter the next. Don't be overly strict on some occasions and then try to make it up to the men later by being indulgent. Men can only feel secure if they know what to expect from their leaders.

Another important aid to security is an atmosphere of approval. Courtesy, tact, good humor, and a pleasant manner all contribute to such a feeling of approval and are all very useful tools to obtain efficient and wholehearted cooperation. A leader must be firm, exacting, and sometimes tough and hardboiled, but he can usually be pleasant at the same time. Again it must be emphasized that there are practical reasons, as well as humanitarian ones, for recommending an atmosphere of approval. Men who feel they have been slighted, scorned, threatened, or abused are generally diverted from their jobs by thoughts of their misfortune; they tend to brood over it, and their performance of duty suffers. Thus, a hostile and overcritical attitude on the part of supervisors will ruin the morale of a unit. Men should feel that their conscientious efforts will meet with approval.

You may have a profound effect on the attitudes of your men by being aware of the way you relate to them. You know that if you see someone you know and they say "hello" and call you by name you may feel a little better than just moments before. If the same person had passed you, said nothing, and gone on his way even though he had seen you standing there you might feel a bit offended. Your men are subject to these same feelings and you may affect them even more significantly in that you are in a position of authority over them.

It is particularly important for petty officers and junior officers, who work directly with the men, to encourage an air of friendliness in their divisions. A word of praise when earned, the liberal use of men's names, a friendly and confident bearing— these are all marks of approval and security by good leaders. Showing an interest in the men and praising them for work well done are techniques that should be more than acknowledged by division officers. They should be developed and practiced. Special events, such as marriages, the birth of children, promotions, and athletic success should be the occasion for congratulations. Similarly, unfortunate occurrences, such as death or illness, should be noted and dealt with sympathetically. Sending flowers, attending funerals, or writing a man who is in the hospital are recommended. Assistance in getting away on emergency leave and help in obtaining funds from Navy Relief will make a man feel that his officers and shipmates really care about him. The future performance of duty of the man who has been helped is usually improved.

None of the above is to suggest that all must be sweetness and light; there are often occasions when only blunt and direct words and action are called for. The smart leader discloses the steel hand in the velvet glove only when necessary, and attempts to keep his relationships with his men free from emotion. Consider your own feelings after being reprimanded peevishly—your natural resentment occupies your thoughts for some time. Men are very sensitive to the words and feelings of their leaders and work and efficiency is bound to suffer when emotions run wild. Good humor and consideration for others is a priceless lubricant in the complex gears of human relations.

Men often require advice and assistance in their personal problems. Be sure you are approachable, encourage them to come to you, help them when you can and be sure you do not attempt anything you are not qualified or authorized to do. If you attempt to solve problems that are too big for you matters may only get worse, no matter how good your intentions. The mere talking to someone in authority will usually help them even if nothing else comes from the interview. If nothing specific can be done for your men, try to make them see why. Remember that many people are shy about bringing up personal matters and will often not ask for a talk with you unless it is an emergency. However, by speaking to the men as you meet them casually while working, you can often get them talking about matters that are on their mind.

So far in this chapter we have described men's basic needs, both physical and psychological. Men also have certain moral and spiritual needs. They need to believe in something, their Creator, their Country, the American way of life. You, as their division officer, must not only recognize this need, you must do your best to fill it. You can do this best by your own attitude and example. Make it clear, for example, that you believe in serving your country. Your men will not only tend to share your patriotism, they will gain the profound satisfaction of being led by someone in whom they can believe.

A leader's sense of values is communicated to his men by everything he does and says. This is why leadership must be essentially moral.

Information

Closely related to security is information. Men who are informed about their jobs, their futures, their ship or station, are more efficient than those who spend time worrying and talking about matters that puzzle them. They are far less likely to become disciplinary problems. Keeping the men informed must be an organized, methodical, and continuous part of their training. The methods used depend on the size of the unit and the ingenuity of its leaders. Group discussions led by an officer or petty officer are probably the most effective method. Others are mimeographed handouts and bulletin board displays. Daily quarters for muster, in ships for which this is practicable, should be the principal means used for keeping the men informed.

Information about their own unit and its organization is of great importance to the men. They can often do their jobs better if they know how the work and responsibility are divided. This means that the ship's organization and pertinent ship's notices and instructions, as well as the *Standard Organization and Regulations of the U.S. Navy*, should be available to the men—particularly to petty officers and prospective petty officers.

Information about ship movements, for example, is of particular interest to all hands. Plans for movements of a ship or aircraft squadron are rarely secret in peacetime and should be released as quickly as possible. Time of return to port after a stretch at sea, whether or not there will be an inspection, and the time that liberty commences—these are all items of importance. The petty officers should be informed first, so that their prestige and authority may be increased. The men will then be encouraged to come to them for information.

News of national or world affairs is also of importance to men when that news is related to the operations of the ship or squadron, or is related to such things as the cost of living or veterans' benefits. The Chief of Information broadcasts a weekly newsgram which may be obtained from Radio Central if it is not already routed to you. This will be of particular interest to the men, especially when deployed. The ship's library is a major source of information; its use should be encouraged.

In order to inform your men, it is obvious that you should always have the word yourself. This means reading your mail and the literature and correspondence routed to you with some care. Be alert for items of interest or of value to your men. *All Hands*, a monthly magazine published by the Bureau of Naval Personnel, is perhaps the single best publication for a young officer to make a point of reading every month. In it the latest directives of Navy-wide interest are compiled and explained.

Self-respect

The average man needs a certain amount of self-respect in order to be well adjusted to his work. In order to do the job well, he must feel that what he is doing is of some importance. Among men who all do the same job, such as the signal gang, this is no major problem, but in a division from which messmen must be assigned, for example, this need for self-approval should be considered.

In general, the men with the lowliest jobs require the most personal attention. Just to listen to their troubles occasionally, and to remark favorably on a job well done, is usually enough to show your men that you think their job is important.

Never underestimate the power that can be released by a word of praise. The following quotation could well be memorized by every officer:

> The harsh word of criticism flies on eager wings. It requires no skill, anyone can be an expert. But it causes bitter resentment wherever it falls. The kind word of correction is far more effective. We accept correction without loss of pride, which is the most sensitive trait we have. However, it is much better to use the magic word of appreciation. Every heart is hungry for appreciation. We double our efforts when someone sees the good in us. Stimulate a man's pride in himself and he will need but little correcting.

Group Approval

In addition to self-approval, a basic need for most people is the approval of the group in which they work. If a man feels that he belongs, then this need is filled. Most men in a military unit have this sense of belonging.

It is particularly important to recognize this need when the unusual occurs, when a man does not seem to fit. It sometimes happens that a man is not accepted by his group because of something different in his manner or appearance, or because of his antisocial habits or behavior. A familiar example is the new man in a small ship who cannot seem to keep himself clean. His appearance and odor make him the object of jokes and horseplay, and soon you have an outcast in your group. To get any work out of this man or to train him, it is first necessary to get him back in the gang.

Usually a frank talk and the special attention of his petty officer for a few days is enough to get him squared away. Often, however, you have to search for the reasons for a man not being accepted. Even if you find the cause, you may only be able to assign the misfit some duty requiring less cooperation from his shipmates.

Group approval can often be accented for particularly outstanding men by turning their names in, with a proposed commendation, for commendatory mast. This is an excellent example of the positive approach to discipline. Just as you must report a man who commits a serious breach of discipline, so should you be prompt to report a man who is markedly superior to his shipmates in zeal, initiative, actions during an emergency, or other characteristics of an outstanding Navy man.

Attainable Objectives

The last of our five basic needs is the provision of attainable objectives. A man must have something to shoot at in order to perform at maximum efficiency. Men lose their desire to cooperate and work together if they feel they are just going through empty motions. To operate as a team, men must have an objective in sight. A gun captain may want to have the cleanest gun and the best shooting crew in the ship. A yeoman may want to make chief someday and be qualified as a court reporter. Those are long-range objectives.

In order to make these aims attainable, they should be divided into short-range objectives. The gun captain should be encouraged to coach his gun crew for an important antiaircraft practice, or should point toward an inspection where the appearance and material condition of the gun will be judged. The yeoman should be encouraged to perfect his typing and to increase his speed to some definite standard. Men perform their work more efficiently when it is divided into units which can be completed. Competition is often a useful device to provide short-range objectives; it is discussed in the chapter on Administration.

A word of caution is necessary concerning the important facts about people stated above. Do not confuse a vital concern for morale and concentration on good human relations with ignoring the need for high standards of performance. You, as a leader, must have the moral courage and the sense of responsibility to demand the most from your men. Remember that combat readiness is the primary reason that military organizations exist. Someday you may have to lead your men into battle. This is where the naval profession differs from the usual civilian occupation or profession. There may be times when the needs of your unit are more important than the needs of a single man. An example could be the question of granting emergency leave—the man is important but the military mission comes first.

Special Problems of Young Men

There is one final point to consider in this chapter on needs. About half the men in the average division will be in their adolescence. This means that they are in the process of changing from boys to men. Adolescents are those developing from puberty (the age of 14 years in common law at which boys are considered capable of procreation) to maturity, a process which is longer than most people suppose and which is not fully completed until their twenty-fifth birthday.

Adolescent young men are no longer children but they have not yet figured out how to act at all times like men. Of course, they are all a little different. Some at 17 seem to have steadied down, while some men at 22 and 23 still act like children. The point here is that while you cannot speed up their process of becoming mature, you can make your own job more simple by understanding it. Showing off, excessive profanity, skylarking, and leaving gear adrift are a few examples of the behavior of every young man. On the other hand, men between 17 and 23 are usually looking for a model to copy, and will quickly follow an officer or petty officer who gains their confidence and respect. Young men, for all their superficial and somewhat loudly expressed cynicism, are really idealists and can be influenced by men they like and admire.

Drugs and alcohol have received increased attention as special sources of trouble to Navy personnel. You should be aware of the problems that drug and alcohol abuse create and the symptoms that will alert you to an abuser. The Department of Defense and the Navy have several worthwhile rehabilitation and treatment programs which include both voluntary and referral activities. If a man has a problem you may be able to help him by pointing out how it detracts from his performance. If counseling fails, special evaluations noting his impaired or unsatisfactory performance may help. Disciplinary action is not inappropriate when a person fails to seek assistance or respond to counseling. You should bear in mind, however, that the problem may be medical rather than motivational. SecNav Instruction 5300.20 (series) gives basic guidance on alcohol abuse and is amplified at the various echelons of command. Drug counseling and rehabilitation is also available on a voluntary basis. The legal problems involved make this a bit more complicated but your department head or the executive officer can provide you with the latest information and procedures should one of your men need this assistance.

The matter of officers and petty officers setting an example for their men cannot be too strongly emphasized. It is one of the principles of military leadership that is most powerful and obvious, yet one that is often violated through carelessness and negligence. To make your men look smart and observe military courtesy, *you* must look smart and be military in your manner.

Similarly, a division officer can often minimize the bad influence of some of his "characters." New men, usually the young ones, will often attach themselves to, and attempt to follow, the nonregulation troublesome "old hands" in the mistaken belief that these reprobates are admirable and salty. Very often the petty officers will note such misguided hero worship. It is usually practicable to separate the new men from the undesirable models by changing their sections and perhaps their cleaning or duty stations.

Senior Petty Officers

Most of your nonrated men will be young and even junior petty officers these days are not old salts. Senior petty officers, however, are likely to be men of some years, substance, and experience, and they provide a special challenge. These men are your juniors in rank but, of course, have a wealth of professional experience and maturity in dealing with people that you must recognize and profit by. Your senior petty officers must perform the immediate supervision of the men. It has always been a widespread complaint in the Navy, on the part of senior petty officers, that the junior officers are usurping their duties. Some of this is justified; eager young officers often step into details of supervision that can offend the old chiefs who then are tempted to retire to the CPO mess and drink coffee. There is a fine line here which you, as a division officer, must learn to follow if you are to achieve both efficiency and a relationship of close cooperation with your senior petty officers. Accord them the same special "trust and confidence" that you expect from senior officers and, above all, support them fully in public. At the same time do not turn over your division to your leading chief. You have the final responsibility for the performance of your division so it follows that you must retain the final authority. Be skeptical of reports, check references, ask questions; your petty officers will respect your desire to learn.

This chapter has summarized, in a simplified way, the capabilities and needs of your men. Understanding these concepts is the first step toward the successful organization and administration of any group or military unit.

People are the most important tools an officer works with. Influencing them is an art whose cultivation can be one of the most rewarding experiences in life. Not only will you find your work easier and your personal relations with your men more pleasant as you gain understanding of them, but you will gain immeasurably in understanding yourself and developing that maturity of character that is one of the real goals in every man's life.

It is as true now as in the days of Frederick the Great, who said, "The Commander should appear friendly to his soldiers, speak to them on the march, visit them while they are cooking, ask them if they are well cared for, and alleviate their needs if they have any."

3/Organization

The requirements for battle shall be the basis for organization of units. This provision shall also apply, as appropriate, to noncombatant units. A unit's organization for battle consists of functional groups headed by key officers who are at specified stations and control the activities of personnel under their direction.—*Standard Organization and Regulations of the U.S. Navy.*

The difference between a whaleboat full of naval recruits all shouting directions and pulling at random and an eight-oared Navy shell rowing strongly down the river is, first of all, a difference in organization. Certainly training, experience, and other factors play an important part, but the first objective of any one teaching the recruits how to row is to get them organized. In the case of the whaleboat, appointing a coxswain and a stroke would be the first step in establishing a chain of authority and responsibility.

Importance of Organization

An officer or a petty officer should be concerned with organization in any job he must perform. In taking over new duties or in seeking to improve the efficiency of his unit, an officer in the Navy should learn early that the best way to start doing the job is to examine the organization. Even assuming that you have no authority to change it, it is important to understand your organization thoroughly. In addition to providing the obvious framework which distinguishes a division from an unorganized group of men, organization provides the members of a group with a strong sense of unity. It is this powerful group feeling, discussed more fully elsewhere in this book, that is an important result of efficient organization. Knowing how your division is organized is the first step in taking charge of it. If you happen to be a department head in a small ship, this question of organization is even more important. In this chapter, as in the rest of the book, the words "division" and "department" can usually be used interchangeably.

Basic Principles

One of the meanings of organize is, "to prepare for the transaction of business." That is a good way to look at your division or department. Are you well organized to accomplish the business of daily living, of training, and of fighting? We are not concerned with abstract theories here, but there are a number of well-established principles that are important to observe in the organization of any unit. After going over these principles briefly, illustrating each one in terms of a naval situation, the specific duties of a division officer will be described. Examine the following ideas in their relation to your job. This examination should result in a good understanding of your organization.

Organization can be defined objectively and without reference to persons or individuals. Note that a ship's Battle Bill contains no names; it is a list of duties. The process of organizing consists of determining what activities are necessary for any particular major purpose or mission, and then arranging the corresponding duties in a pattern that permits the efficient flow of responsibility and authority through the individuals who are subsequently assigned.

The very first principle of organization is that *every job given your division, every duty for which your division is responsible, must be assigned to one or more of your men.* Let us assume that the Special Sea Detail Bill assigns the telephone talker on the bridge as part of the special sea detail from your division. It is not only necessary to assign, by name, one of your men for this job, but it is also essential to give some petty officer the responsibility of instructing the talker in his duties. Replacing the talker with a trained man in the event of his absence or transfer is another consideration.

The question may present itself: Where can I find the duties and responsibilities assigned to my division? The answer is: in your *Ship's Organization and Regulations Manual* (including the Battle Bill). Check through all the bills methodically, searching for the obscure assignments that may be effective only on rare occasions, but which must be made and kept up to date. For example, your ship may operate for months in clear weather without having to station fog lookouts, but when the occasion arises and the word is passed, the lookouts must be posted instantly. You will quite properly be held responsible if your division is supposed to provide fog lookouts and the men fail to appear because assignments have not been made or are not up to date.

The second principle is that *all the responsibilities assigned to your men must be clear-cut and well understood by them.* This is where your division organization manual is used. Each of the duties and functions for which your division is responsible must be clearly assigned to one of your men. If the job is a big one, he will need help, of course; but one person should be responsible. If your division, for example, is required to assign a signalman to the duty motor whaleboat, you must make certain that a qualified signalman in each watch and section is instructed to man the boat when it is called away.

Each piece of machinery or equipment for which your division is responsible must be assigned to a man who *knows* that the upkeep and maintenance of that particular item is *his* responsibility. Within the Planned Maintenance Subsystem (see Chapter 9) each piece of equipment is assigned to an individual. In addition, "responsibility cards" are posted in each space or compartment to denote divisional responsibility for the upkeep and maintenance of that space.

A third principle of organization is that *no specific responsibility should be assigned to more than one person.* Closing certain watertight doors, for instance, should not be left to a group of compartment cleaners who happen to work in that area. One man should be given the responsibility and should check the doors each time closures are made. Others may, of course, do the closing, but his should be the responsibility. You may not consider it necessary in all cases to follow this precept; some duties may seem so obvious that there appears no need to spell out the specific responsibility. But beware of falling for this easy rationalization; the man you trusted may be transferred or may be on the binnacle list. Suddenly you find a job not done, and all your inquiries are met with excuses and evasions, because no one, in fact, was assigned that responsibility. For example, when sweepers are piped after working hours in port, it may be normal procedure for the duty petty officer to see that your spaces are swept down. Unless, however, the responsibility for this detail is made known in writing to the division petty officers of each section and not just passed along haphazardly by word of mouth, a petty officer new to your division may fail to insure that a sweep down has been performed. The subsequent inquiry (after a reminder from the officer of the deck, let us say) will only further embarrass you, because the new petty officer can say with perfect logic that he did not know what his responsibilities were.

A fourth basic principle is that *each member of the organization, from top to bottom, should know to whom he reports and who reports to him.* In other words, who is in charge of whom, and when? Do the stewardsmen work for the supply officer or for the wardroom mess caterer? Circumstances often require unusual arrangements, but the important point is that every man should know his responsibilities and the limits of his authority. It is also important that, insofar as possible, no man have more than one boss. This is another precept that appears obvious, but few naval units are completely free from confusion on the lower levels of supervision in regard to who reports to whom. If a deck division is not carefully organized, down to the last seaman, there is likely to exist a mild form of chaos on the lowest levels. A large number of the nonrated men may compose a sort of pool from which any petty officer can draw the hands he needs for a particular job. This always leads to confusion and inefficiency. These men, having no recognized boss, will seize every opportunity to melt away into some unproductive activity (such as the barber shop or soda fountain or small-stores line) and a very minimum of useful work will be accomplished by the division.

A fifth principle is one that is frequently violated: *responsibility must be matched by authority and accountability.* If you hold your gun captain responsible for the efficiency of his gun crew, then give him freedom to assign and drill his men. Let him recommend drill schedules, for example, and take his recommendations into consideration in assignment of semiannual marks. Insofar as possible, let him consider the crew his own. Permit him to endorse or reject special requests by his men. If he can only supervise the work of his men, with no power either to reward them or to show his dissatisfaction, then his authority is being unnecessarily hampered. It should be clear that the petty officer is accountable for the success or failure of his men.

A sixth basic principle is *not to have too many men report to one leader*. The number of men who can properly be administered by one supervisor is known to students of organization as the "span of control." This number varies, of course, with the nature and complexity of the work. Let us suppose that you have a large division and one outstanding chief petty officer. You can place this chief directly in charge of all your division spaces and men, or you can divide the division into three parts with a responsible petty officer in charge of each section. The petty officers would report to the chief. This latter arrangement would conform to Navy usage and would be the best arrangement in a division because each petty officer, while not as experienced as the chief, could handle his own section. The chief then could concentrate on the more important matters and not waste his talents on small details. If he were personally responsible for every compartment and every man, these responsibilities would exceed his optimum "span of control."

It is a common organizational failing in deck divisions which include specialists such as gunner's mates, to concentrate all the seamen into one or two large groups and then expect one or two harassed boatswain's mates to look after and supervise all the seamen. Petty officers are naturally inclined to want to specialize, and thus to develop skills useful in their naval and perhaps postnaval careers. Being human, they are not averse to neglecting at the same time their military responsibilities. A division officer must use *all* his petty officers, including the specialists. One petty officer cannot properly control more than 12 or 15 men if he is responsible for their appearance at inspection, their work assignments, and all the many other details of their day-to-day supervision.

Another important principle of organization is to *exercise control on your proper level* and not get lost in a maze of trivialities which properly belong to a lower echelon. Unless you take the trouble to make certain that your petty officers know their jobs, and then leave them alone to do these jobs, you will never be free of the thousand and one minor details that can prevent you from doing your real work of supervision.

You should not have to see that Brown gets a haircut before inspection or that Jones draws small stores. You must delegate the details to your assistants in order to leave time for the planning and overall supervision and inspection that no one else but you can do. This, of course, does not mean that you should not take the time to talk to your men individually, or that you should be too busy to check important items, such as the alignment of your guns, for example. It is a question of selecting the most important things to do, yourself, and delegating the others to your assistants.

A final principle of organization is to *divide the work load fairly among your subordinates*. Often the easy way to get something done is to give it to your most efficient assistant. This common practice of piling the work on the strongest back can have two most unprofitable results. The first is to encourage the less productive men to do and learn nothing, because very little is demanded from them. The second result of uneven distribution of the work load is the development of almost indispensable subordinates whose detachment will temporarily wreck your unit. Make certain that all officers and petty officers carry their share of the load to avoid penalizing the most competent men. The additional effort involved usually pays off in the long run.

The chances are that you will find an organization already set up and working when you take over. Don't be too hasty to change things, even if you have the authority and even if some of the above principles seem to be violated. Few problems in the field of human relations can be solved according to strict rules. Circumstances and personalities may lead to logical exceptions. But knowing the principles can often result in a greater understanding of an existing organization and should lead to making certain well-considered changes, if circumstances so require.

Basic Directives

Standard Organization and Regulations of the U.S. Navy (Op-NavInst 3120.32), issued by the Office of the Chief of Naval Operations, is the basic source for material relating to the organization of naval units. This publication is the guide for type commanders who originate a standard organization manual for their own type of unit. Each unit, in turn, either adopts the standard organization manual as its own, or makes relatively minor changes in it, as may be required by nonstandard equipment, shortage of personnel, or changes in equipment or armament. In all these basic commands (ships, stations, facilities, and aviation squadrons), the men are organized in divisions. Their division officers are all governed by the applicable portions of OpNavInst 3120.32 quoted in this guide.

Chapter 3 of this instruction contains a description of the duties, responsibilities, and authority of the division officer. The guidance included is general in nature and applies to a division officer and his assistants in all types of units.

This is true despite the fact that special relationships may exist, as between the patrol plane commander and his crew. Another special situation occurs when a squadron is embarked on a carrier. There, for purposes of naval justice and for matters concerned with the administration of the carrier (daily routine, emergency drills, etc.), the men in the squadron come under the commanding officer of the carrier. The same situation does not exist when a squadron reports to a Naval air station or a Naval air facility. There, the squadron commander retains all of his command functions, although his men are governed by station regulations. It must be emphasized that these jurisdictional variations, which are only a sample of those throughout the Navy, do not affect the basic duties and responsibilities of division officers.

Ship's Organization and Regulations Manual

A ship's organization is made up of two parts: the administrative organization (described in the following pages) and the battle organization set forth in the Battle Bill. For units under Ship's Manning Document (SMD) or Squadron Manning Document (SQMD) that publication also serves as a battle organization manual and Battle Bill. The Battle Bill is described in NWIP 50-1 and lists the stations manned during Condition I, II, and III. Note that it lists stations, not names. It is based on the ship's equipment and the armament to be manned, together with the personnel assigned to the ship.

This is a good place to define three terms which are often confused. *Organizational Manning* is the authorized officer and enlisted strength of a fully ready unit or activity as determined by the Chief of Naval Operations from established organizational manning requirements. *Conditional Manning* is an authorized reduction in organizational manning resulting from, or accomplished by, a commensurate reduction in the required operational capabilities prescribed by the Chief of Naval Operations for a fully ready unit. *Reduced Conditional Manning* is not official terminology; however, it equates to a level of manning that is constrained by operating funds or other operational or fiscal constraints and is equal to or less than conditional manning. It equates to present fleet squadron manning, and full wartime operations cannot be performed beyond a 30-day period.

The organizational manning of a unit is developed as a result of researching and tabulating the workload involved with all facets of operating and maintaining a fully ready unit, and translating that workload into manpower requirements. These manpower requirements are displayed in the Ship Manning Document (SMD) for each ship class, and Squadron Manning Document (SQMD) for aircraft squadrons.

A division officer is not concerned with the construction of a Battle Bill, but he is required to conform to it when making out his Watch, Quarter, and Station Bill. Another feature of the Battle Bill is that it lists the stations to be manned, not only at General Quarters, but also during the various conditions when less than all hands are required. Definitions of Condition Watches I through V are found in OpNavInst 3120.32 and NWIP 50-1. It should also be noted that the Battle Bill indicates in most cases the duties that are to be performed at each station, as well as the succession to command in the event that casualties are suffered.

Administrative Organization

A comparison of the administrative organization and the battle organization indicates that the division of personnel in administrative departments closely approximates that found in the major battle components. However, to meet the requirements of sound organization principles, the administrative organization structure must allow for the carrying out of certain functions which have no place in battle. In the day-to-day routine, the needs of training and maintenance are emphasized, and certain support measures are necessary for administrative reasons.— *Standard Organization and Regulations of the U.S. Navy.*

The first major subdivision of the ship's organization manual is administrative and is usually as outlined in Chapters 2 and 3 of OpNavInst 3120.32 series. This includes the ship's organization charts down to the division level. Functional guides for each key officer are also included.

The second subdivision of the ship's organization is the watch organization, described in Chapter 4. Both the underway and inport watch arrangements are specified.

A third major aspect of a ship's organization are the organizational bills—administrative, operational, and emergency. Chapter 6 of OpNavInst 3120.32 contains standard unit bills to be used either as they are written or as a guide to assist Type/Unit commanders in formulating bills for their units. A "bill" is naval terminology for a written procedure to meet a need (as for berthing) or an emergency (such as fire). A bill is a directive which lists the things to be done, the material needed, and who is to take the prescribed action. Note that none of these bills contain names. Personnel requirements will be indicated by division, rate and rating, which the division officer will translate into specific personnel when he makes out the Watch, Quarter, and Station Bill for his division. The Berthing and Locker Bill, and Formation and Parade Bill assigns living compartments, lockers, and areas for divisional masters for each division. The Cleaning, Preservation and Maintenance Bill assigns responsibility for spaces, machinery, and equipment to departments. The Personnel Assignment Bill assigns officers and enlisted personnel to billets within the ship's organization.

These are all examples of administrative bills. Operational bills are developed to establish standard procedures for conducting recurring shipboard evolutions. The Replenishment Bill describes the stations to be manned and the duties to be performed during underway replenishment. The Special Sea and Anchor Bill assigns personnel to stations and duties when the ship is being handled in restricted waters. There are a number of others, such as the Rescue and Assistance Bill, and the Heavy Weather Bill. Emergency bills are written to provide for proper shipboard personnel response to emergencies that may occur, such as collision, grounding, or man overboard.

Basic Definitions

This is a good place to pause and offer some basic definitions. A *billet number* is merely a device for assigning personnel. While men come and go, a billet number remains fixed and can thus be used to designate a bunk, a locker, a rate, and any number of special duties and details on various administrative and emergency bills. The first letter or digit represents the division, the second digit is the watch section, and the last two digits show the position within the watch section. Billet 2-301, for example, may be listed for the petty officer who is in charge of the third section of the Second Division. A particular bunk and locker in the division compartment can be tagged with that number. If the senior petty officer available for this section is a BM2, then he would be assigned this billet. It should be noted that billet numbers may not always be convenient to use in assigning personnel; each ship determines whether or not to use them, depending on circumstances. As a division officer, you should know how to use billet numbers if the ship's policy requires their employment.

It might be profitable here to distinguish between *rate* and *rating*. *Rate* is associated with a particular pay grade; for instance, boatswain's mate, third class, is a rate. *Rating* is both a classification and a group of rates; for example, boatswain's mate is a rating, as is gunner's mate. These are also *general ratings*. Most, but not all, general ratings are expanded and subdivided into *service ratings*. As an example, a general rating would be Fire Control Technician (FT) and service ratings within that category are FTG (Gunnery), FTB (Ballistic), and FTM (Missile).

It has been noted that billet numbers are assigned to sections within the divisions. The primary unit of a ship's company for purposes of liberty, watch standing, messing, and berthing is the *section*. The number of sections within the division may vary, and will depend on the number of watch sections within the individual unit. Each section includes adequate ratings and numbers to man all required stations in emergency bills. During normal peacetime inport conditions, a ship is generally required to keep one-sixth of her crew aboard in a duty status. Her underway watch bill will normally provide for fewer than six sections, depending upon the number of personnel assigned. The ship's divisions will be organized into sections that allow an easy transition from inport to underway status, and billet numbers are assigned accordingly.

Ship's Regulations

Usually bound with the *Ship's Organization and Regulations Manual*, and contained within Chapter 5 of OpNavInst 3120.32, are the ship's regulations. These should be made known to all your men. A recommended method is to maintain in your living spaces, shops, and offices, wherever your men congregate, a special binder in which are inserted copies of the ship's regulations, as well as the ship's Watch Bill, Cleaning, Preservation, and Maintenance Bill, and any other parts of the *Ship's Organization and Regulations Manual* that are of direct concern to your men. Division officers and leading petty officers should have similar binders for daily use and consultation.

Division Organization

The departments of a ship shall be organized into divisions. These divisions are established in the organizational structure so that they may be assigned as units within the components of the battle organization. Divisions shall be organized into watches, or sections, or both.—*Standard Organization and Regulations of the U.S. Navy.*

The careful and efficient organization of your division should be your first concern in assuming the duties of a division officer. One of the tools the division officer has at his disposal is the *Division Organization Manual*. This manual will be an expansion of the guidance provided by the department head, and will normally be contained within the *Department Organization Manual*.

The *Division Organization Manual* serves principally as a means of delegating the authority of the division officer down to the lowest supervisory level (the junior petty officers). It should not be used for prescribing division procedures. Such procedures—like handling special requests, for example—should be issued as division instructions or notices. *Division Organization Manuals* should be approved by the head of department concerned.

The division officer should assign certain assistants to aid in efficiently controlling his division. If a junior division officer is assigned, he will assist you in coordinating and administering the division. He will also normally be assigned duty as division training assistant. In this capacity he will assist the division officer in the administration of training within the division, and coordinate the program with the departmental and overall training program of the ship. If a junior division officer is not assigned, the job of training assistant may fall to the division petty officer.

A division petty officer, normally the senior chief petty officer or petty officer in the division, should be a valuable assistant. He will normally assist in the preparation of such items as watch and liberty lists, cleaning station assignments, supply requisitions, and general supervision of section leaders' performance.

A division damage control petty officer should be assigned, under the division leading petty officer, to perform various damage control functions of the division. His duties will be described more fully in Chapter 9 of this guide.

You should organize the personnel assigned into work centers for the maintenance of installed equipment, under a work center supervisor. These assignments will cut across section lines, since each watch section normally includes only a percentage of the men in each rating. The work center supervisor will oversee the performance of corrective and preventive maintenance, and the operation of the 3M system. He will report to the department's 3M assistant, via the division officer, for 3M system operation within his work center.

Chain of Command

Organization charts and functional guides are important, but they represent, for the most part, a theoretical ideal. A group of men, such as a division, will rarely operate exactly along the lines of a chart that is drawn for them. It is one of your jobs, as a division officer, to see that your organizational directives are followed within reason, making necessary allowances for the characteristics and abilities of the men involved.

In general, the chain of command should be followed. A seaman should have his special request for early liberty approved by his immediate superior, the petty officer for whom he works, and so on up the line. There are times, however, when this orderly procedure will not be followed. A man having serious marital troubles, for example, will usually go straight to his division officer.

Assignment of Personnel

The assignment of men to tasks within the ship is accomplished in three steps:
1. Assignment by name to departments and divisions as outlined in the ship's Personnel Assignment Bill.
2. Assignment to watches, stations, and duties within the department and division. These assignments are made by the division officer in accordance with the various ship's bills.
3. Dissemination of information on assignments of individuals. This is accomplished in the main by posting the Watch, Quarter, and Station Bill.

The division officer has the major role in assigning personnel. He must adjust his men to the changes in manning level, on-board count, division assignments, and operating conditions. In making these adjustments he must perform the following:

1. Assign his men to sections, maintaining rates and numbers of men in each section as nearly equal as possible in conformance with the Personnel Assignment Bill.

2. Arrange the rates in each section in order of seniority from top to bottom. Watches, duty stations (cleaning, maintenance, etc.), and liberty are assigned on the basis of sections.

3. Make a list of divisional responsibilities contained in each ship's organization bill, and indicate the number of men required to be furnished for each station of duty.

4. Assign men from appropriate sections and of appropriate ratings or abilities to each station and duty listed in paragraph 3 above.

5. Fill out the Watch, Quarter, and Station Bill by following provisions of paragraphs 2 and 4. Post the completed bill and *insure that all your men know* their assignments and duties. This is particularly important after considerable personnel changes have occurred. It is recommended that a methodical effort be made, after any long stay in port, to insure that *all* new men have, in fact, been instructed in their assigned duties.

Watch, Quarter, and Station Bill

> The Watch, Quarter, and Station Bill is the division officer's summary of assignments of personnel to duties and stations within each of the unit's bills. Its primary purpose is to inform division personnel of those assignments.—*Standard Organization and Regulations of the U.S. Navy.*

The *Ship's Organization and Regulations Manual* has been described in enough detail so that by referring to a copy as you read this you should understand the major directives on which your own organization is based. As a division officer (or department head of a small ship), you now come to the heart of the matter—your Watch, Quarter, and Station Bill, which is your summary of assignments of personnel to duties and stations speci-

WATCH, QUARTER

BILLET NO.	RATE			NAME	CONDITION I	CONDITION II	CONDITION III	SEA WATCH DETAIL	SPECIAL SEA DETAIL
	COMP.	ALLOW.	ACTUAL						

COMPLEMENT   ALLOWANCE   ON BOARD

Figure 3–1. Typical Watch, Quarter, and Station Bill.
(Some details will vary in different types of ships.)

fied within the Battle Bill and each of the other ship's bills. Its primary purpose is to inform division personnel of those assignments.

The Watch, Quarter, and Station Bill is standard for all ships of a type, and a supply of blank forms is usually maintained on board each ship. The standard bill is bulletin-board sized—that for a cruiser includes 31 columns—and too big to be reproduced here. A smaller mechanical form in common use is shown in Figure 3-1.

The bill allows one line for each man in the division, and shows his billet number, name, rate, compartment number, bunk and locker number, and cleaning and maintenance assignment. Under Battle Stations it lists duties for all Condition Watches applicable to the particular ship. Next it lists stations and duties for Special Sea Detail, Replenishment at Sea, Rescue and Assist-

& STATION BILL

		DIVISION						LAST CORRECTED	

PORT WATCH DETAIL	CLEANING STATION	FIRE		COLLISION- UNDERWATER DAMAGE	ABANDON SHIP		FIRE & RESCUE		LANDING FORCE	REMARKS
		STATION	PROVIDE		STATION	PROVIDE	PARTY	PROVIDE		

ance, Visit and Search, and Boarding and Prize Crew. The final section covers General Emergencies: Securing and Salvage, Abandon Ship, Fire, and Man Overboard.

The first step in making the bill for your division is to obtain from the ship's Personnel Assignment Bill the billet numbers for each section. Then, the battle stations to be manned are taken from the Battle Bill, and similarly the other assignments in emergency and miscellaneous bills are filled in from the *Ship's Organization and Regulations Manual.*

The next job is to assign a man to each billet number. Selection of personnel for the various billets is guided by the experience, training, and known capabilities of the individuals. This is your first major opportunity to exercise your judgment and your knowledge of your men. Of course, certain billets call for certain rates, but there are many ways in which you can organize your men. You should anticipate eventually losing your key men by transfer. For this reason, it is always wise to have your most promising younger petty officers in positions where they can learn more responsible jobs, and gain the practical experience necessary to qualify for duties such as those of mount captains, section leaders, etc.

There are, of course, other considerations that will also influence your assignments. Often two or more men together make a strong team if they each have special qualifications. Let us assume, for example, that you have a mount captain who is a fine leader: aggressive, cool in emergencies, and full of competitive spirit during practice firings. If he is only fair on maintenance you can back him up with a junior petty officer who is a natural mechanic, keen on checks and upkeep. This, of course, is an extreme case, but there are many opportunities in every unit to do something similar on a smaller scale.

The important point here is that, in assigning your men, you do not look upon them as just bodies to fill billet numbers. Recognize and take the utmost advantage of their individual capabilities. If you have not served with your division long enough, or if you are not yet familiar with the new men in a large division, then ask your petty officers for advice and recommendations. It is often a good idea to do this anyway as a check against your own estimates. Never put your faith in snap judgments of people.

Battle Requirements Govern

There are several other aspects of the Watch, Quarter, and Station Bill that are worthy of note. As quoted from the *Standard Organization and Regulations of the U.S. Navy* at the head of this chapter, "The requirements for battle shall be the basis for the organization of the ship." An obvious way to comply with that is to have Condition II and III stations. The men's cleaning stations should also, if practicable, be related to their battle stations. This not only facilitates training, but also helps in reducing the time needed for your men to get to their general quarters stations. It is particularly important to have all duties and assignments of the key men related to their battle stations in order to develop their battle efficiency. Men whose duties change, such as mess cooks and compartment cleaners, should be given relatively routine battle stations, such as handling ammunition.

Cleaning Bill

In assigning cleaning details on the Watch, Quarter, and Station Bill, the division officer has more leeway than in filling out the other bills. Only the spaces are assigned to each division; it is up to the division officer to keep them clean with the men he has.

It should be noted that there are certain accepted practices in sharing the work where the responsibilities of two divisions meet. Some of the more common ones follow:

The insides of hatch coamings are cleaned by the men whose station is in the compartment *into which* the hatch leads. The outside of the coaming and the knife-edges are cleaned by the topside personnel. Doors are cleaned by men into whose compartment they open. Ladders are cleaned by men who keep up the space at the foot of the ladder.

In addition to listing each man's cleaning station opposite his name on the Watch, Quarter, and Station Bill, it is important for the division officer to make up a separate cleaning bill for the division, listing each compartment and space along with the names of those who work there and the name of the man in charge. Also, in each compartment or area of deck space there should be posted the names of those who are detailed there for cleaning. This may seem at first glance to be just more paperwork, especially when these cards have to be kept up to date, but the results gained make it very worthwhile. It drives home to all your men, without the possibility of a doubt, the exact nature and extent of their duties and responsibilities in regard to cleaning.

A final thought on organization may be helpful. There is no "one" organization in a command. A man may report to one senior for military matters and to another for cleaning and maintenance. At general quarters and while on watch or standing a day's duty, he may have other seniors. Every activity of a ship such as fueling, rearming, etc., requires him to adjust to a different chain of command.

4/Administration

Every officer must enhance the operational readiness of his unit within his area of responsibility. To be prepared to carry out this duty, he must have a clear understanding of the meaning of administration and the responsibilities involved.—*Standard Organization and Regulations of the U.S. Navy.*

Administration is the act of managing, supervising, and controlling. It is a broad term and, applied to a division, it includes all the activities of the men: their training, their inspection, their discipline, and their welfare. Since these specific subjects are covered in detail in following chapters, this chapter will include only a brief treatment of the methods of administration. A young officer need not know in detail the theories of administration; on the division level he is really a supervisor, concerned with the most efficient methods of getting his division work done and his men trained for battle. A grasp of the essential principles of administration, however, should help a division officer in developing the art of efficiently supervising his men.

Policy

Administration from a division officer's viewpoint is accomplished in three general ways: by *policy*, by *procedure*, and by *personal supervision*. Policy is a statement of intent, a statement of what action will be taken under certain circumstances. Most of the important policy in the Navy is established on a higher level. However, in many small ways, a division officer can establish his own. A regular and well-understood system for granting leave is an example of policy. Perhaps it has been announced, for example, that two weeks' leave for half the division at a time will be approved for the Christmas holidays. Policy should, whenever practicable, be in writing and should be made known to all hands, particularly to new officers and men. Carefully written and well-understood policies, covering many of the day-to-day questions and problems of working and living, will go far toward a division officer's goal of having a happy and efficient unit. When policies are clearly stated, the men will know where they stand and what the accepted rules of the game are. This tends to eliminate many minor misunderstandings and bickerings. When a petty officer can make a decision based on a well-known division policy, there will be no question of its ready acceptance by the men. Policy must not be inflexible; circumstances often change and individual questions often require special answers. The division officer will do well to remember that he is dealing with men and not machines. Neither must policy be so flexible as to render it useless.

Procedures

Procedure is concerned with *how* the division is managed. *How* will a man or a group of men perform a particular task? What will their responsibilities be? In what order will they act? Established procedure, like policy, simplifies the daily problems of managing a group of men. Instead of problems to be solved each day, the matter becomes routine if established procedures are known. The men are inclined to feel secure; they are protected, in a sense, from the minor vagaries of their petty officers. It is assumed, of course, that the division has first been properly organized. Procedure should be simple yet complete, and should be stated in writing. An example of division procedure would be the steps necessary to qualify a man in his practical factors for advancement in rating. Procedure, in contrast to policy, should be rigid, and exceptions to established procedure should rarely be permitted. Since procedure establishes individual responsibility, failure to observe the procedure may deprive some individual of the opportunity to discharge his responsibility. If many exceptions to the routine become necessary, the procedure should be examined and revised.

Personal Supervision

The third way in which a unit is administered is through personal supervision. This is by far the most important method and is the one most often neglected by division officers who confuse paperwork with leadership. A division officer must, first of all, maintain contact with his men, know where they are, and what they are doing. He must know their attitudes, feelings, hopes, desires, fears, and worries. He must know these things, not so much individually as collectively. Men may behave quite differently as a group from the way they act individually under the same circumstances. These human factors are a division officer's primary administrative responsibility. The demands of making reports, filling out forms, and answering correspondence will often appear so overwhelming that a division officer is tempted to concentrate on his paperwork and neglect his men. Certainly, the complexities of the modern Navy result in a staggering burden of letters and directives, not only for the division officer, but for his superiors as well. Whatever the answer may be, it must not be neglect of your men. You must divide the paperwork among your assistants and seek every legitimate shortcut. You must concentrate on items of importance. You may at times have to do your paperwork after working hours—particularly when you have the day's duty—if you cannot otherwise devote the proper time during the day to the personal supervision of your men. *The Armed Forces Officer*, a manual promulgated by the Office of the Secretary of Defense, contains a very pertinent passage on this subject.

> They dupe only themselves who believe that there is a brand of military efficiency which consists in moving smartly, expediting papers, and achieving perfection in formation, while at the same time slighting or ignoring the human nature of those they command. The art of leadership, the art of command, whether the forces be large or small, is the art of dealing with humanity. Only the officer who dedicates his thought and energy to his men can convert into coherent military force their desire to be of service to the country.

In stressing the need for personal supervision, it cannot be emphasized too strongly that a division officer must comprehend the direct nature of his task in regard to understanding his men. The point has been made above that an officer must be concerned about the feelings of his men as a group, as well as their feelings as individuals. Men in a group react upon each other, and develop group attitudes and sentiments in a way that is often quite difficult to understand. Very often these group feelings are not all logical or reasonable. Nevertheless, their existence must be acknowledged, since these feelings directly affect the efficiency and productivity of the group. A division officer must always keep group feelings in mind when he makes decisions. For example, one of your less efficient men comes to you with a special request slip for early liberty. He has been in a few minor scrapes and his section leader has quite properly disapproved the request. The man has business to do at the bank, and you may be tempted to be kindhearted and let him go ashore early before the bank closes. But stop and consider the effect on his shipmates. They know his lazy habits only too well and may be embittered beyond all reason to see him go ashore early when there is no known emergency: they must stay aboard and do his work as well as their own.

Group feelings are, of course, not all negative; it is just as easy to arouse strong, positive, cooperative sentiments in a group of men—and here lies the real key to effective management. The major purpose of this book is to help you release in your men this great potential for cooperation and efficient work.

Control

Closely associated with supervision, the third method of administration described above, is the idea or philosophy of control. It is a most important concept and one that is vital for the success of any administrative effort. After a unit has been properly organized and its administration has been properly initiated by policy, procedure, and supervision, there becomes apparent a need for something else that is sort of an extension of supervision. This additional factor is *control*. By exercising control, a manager insures that his policies and procedures are actually working. It is all very well to detail a group of men to clean and paint a compartment, but to make sure that the job is done properly requires supervision (by a petty officer) and inspection by the division officer. In this example, control is being exercised by inspection. Or perhaps your division provides a number of lookouts, and you have organized this detail and detailed a petty officer to assign the men and instruct them. Sometime later you should exercise control; check on these men on watch, see if they know their job. If your engineering division provides the man for "steering aft," drop back there every week to see if a qualified man is on watch and if he is alert. Failure to exercise control over division assignments and responsibilities means that sooner or later one of the men, being human, will let you down; and someone, perhaps the captain, will ask some embarrassing questions.

Young officers too often accept at face value the reports made to them. Has the requisition for an important spare part actually left the ship? Is that critical equipment really beyond repair without tender assistance? Are your sentries, patrols, lookouts, etc., really alert and on their toes? Be skeptical and tough-minded; the best of men are only human and can, despite the best of intentions, let you down.

Delegation of Authority

The preceding chapter on organization contained a few pointers on how to utilize junior division officers. As these officers learn the division and become acquainted with the men, the division officer should give them increased responsibility and authority. It must be understood that delegation of authority to a subordinate does not relieve from responsibility the person who does the delegating. The senior, in delegating, really creates new responsibilities which he places upon the shoulders of his subordinates. The senior's responsibilities to *his* seniors remain unchanged. This is a point worth stressing. Suppose that you, as a division officer, delegate the authority for maintaining a motor launch to one of your petty officers. You cannot then assume that the motor launch is no longer your responsibility; since it is assigned to your division, it will always be your concern to insure that it is maintained properly. If the executive officer notices that your boat needs repainting, he may call it to your attention via your head of department. You, in turn, will check on your petty officer. This point may seem obvious, but one of the greatest shortcomings of inexperienced division officers is delegation of authority without continuation of supervision and control.

It should be obvious that when things go amiss and a division officer is reminded that a job has not been done or has been done improperly, excuses should not be made that reflect on a subordinate. A division officer should never make excuses to his department head along the lines of: "Well, I told the chief to check those fittings before Friday." This will only irritate the department head, who has several divisions to worry about, who cannot become intimately involved in details of division administration, and who will not appreciate the division officer's efforts to evade his responsibilities by passing the buck.

A good officer (one who can delegate authority effectively) absorbs criticism from his superiors without passing it down to his subordinates. He acts as a buffer and provides, if necessary, a less troubled and emotional atmosphere in which his people can perform most effectively. He knows his subordinates, particularly how far each can be trusted to act on his own initiative, and he is willing to let them make the kind of mistakes by which men benefit.

The words of John Paul Jones are pertinent here, and just as applicable as they were two hundred years ago: ". . . be quick and unfailing to distinguish error from malice, thoughtlessness from incompetency, and well-meant shortcomings from needless or stupid blunder." A meaningful delegation of authority implies that the division officer must be willing to accept some level of mistakes. This is not to excuse or justify error, simply to point out its probability of occurrence, and to suggest that the division officer plan accordingly.

A final thought on this subject of delegating authority. While you must retain your responsibility and must thus continue a certain amount of supervision, be free and comprehensive in your delegation; give your subordinates a big work load. Men learn and develop by doing, and are happier and more efficient when given a job to do that they feel is important and is theirs alone. As your assistants in your division learn to handle their men, give them more and more authority. Nothing is more shortsighted on the part of a superior than a reluctance to let go of some of the reins. It takes a nice sense of judgment to delegate efficiently and safely to the maximum extent, but mastering this technique will earn you much peace of mind and allow you the time for planning that is most important.

It might be well to discuss here a small, but often vexing problem. What does a division officer do when his head of department, the first lieutenant, the executive officer, or some other senior officer bypasses him and goes directly to one of his men with a complaint, admonition, or order? The solution is not always simple, but in general you should direct your men to inform you of such incidents and to comply, of course, with any orders. If such incidents are rare, the best thing to do is to overlook them; the officers concerned are busy and sometimes take direct action to save time both for themselves and for you. But if it seems to be a habit on the part of some officer to bypass you, then it is advisable to remonstrate, respectfully and good-humoredly. Be polite but firm, for repeated incidents of this nature tend to undermine your authority over your men.

There is another violation of the "chain of command" that sometimes plagues a division officer. That is the practice of men bypassing their immediate superiors and bringing a special request directly to you. Do not let them get away with it. Insist that their immediate supervisor, the petty officer for whom they work, recommend approval or disapproval of any special requests. Unless your petty officers have real prestige and authority, they cannot be expected to assume full responsibility for their men. This may seem at first glance to be a small matter, but it is vital in your relations with your petty officers that they feel secure in their authority over their men. Petty officers of long service are understandably quite sensitive to any actions of a newly commissioned officer that could be interpreted as undermining their authority. Chief petty officers deserve special mention—they are a division officer's strong right arm. Give them as much responsibility as they can handle and consult them frequently. Often they will be your only assistants and may act as junior division officers.

Planning Work and Drills

An important aid in administration is the planning of work and drills with care and foresight. Within the framework of the ship's organization, and limited by the Plan of the Day, a division officer always has the detailed planning to do to get his work done and his men trained for combat. There is no substitute for experience in developing the mature judgment needed to decide how much work to do and how long to train. There are certain general principles, however, whose understanding will help to develop that judgment. These principles have been derived from years of study and experimentation in industry with groups of workers: measuring their output, while hours of work, rest periods, lighting, noise, and other working conditions were changed.

The first principle is that productivity—the relationship between amount of work done and time spent on the job—depends largely on the attitudes of the workers, and not on working conditions alone. In spite of high pay, short hours, and lots of rest periods, a group of workers may produce less if they are distracted by some controversy or disgruntled with the leaders or foremen. The reverse is also true; working conditions may be bad, but if the workers believe that their duties are important, and if they have been inspired to accept their hardships, their output will be high. The application of this principle to the work of the men in a division is obvious. Within reasonable limits, the men will do any amount of hard work under the worst conditions if they have the right kind of leadership. Men will perform prodigiously for supervisors who plan the work intelligently, who go to bat for them when required, and who share their work by staying on the job. This statement is somewhat simplified, of course, as there are usually many other factors to consider. The big point here is that there is no easily determined limit to what men will do if they want to do it. A naval air station may get sudden orders to send all its planes to a hurricane refuge. Three-fourths of the men may have planned to go on liberty that evening, but all hands will turn to willingly all night to service the planes and secure the station.

This is an obvious example. Much more often you will have to use lots of ingenuity and common sense to show your men that a tough, unpleasant job needs to be done. It may be particularly difficult to keep the men interested in doing the routine chores of shipkeeping, and it is usually impossible to find any dramatic reason, like an approaching hurricane, for making a big effort. In such a situation, careful planning and personal supervision are the only answers. Show the petty officers and men that to you, at least, the work they are doing is important. A division officer can usually find some small way to show his interest and enthusiam. Frequent contact with the men is, of course, the best, and for this there is no substitute. Special marks of interest, such as getting permission for a certain hard-working detail to sleep in during the morning after working all night, or arranging for cold soft drinks on a hot day, are always worthwhile.

Long Hours

A second principle, particularly applicable to drills, is that when the men's interest in a job is exhausted and cannot be revived, they will learn nothing further that day. In fact, their performance is likely to suffer if drilling is pushed beyond the interest point. Long hours are not a substitute for intelligently conducted drills. Here, again, it is a question of thorough planning and forceful, aggressive leadership. Men should never be permitted to loaf along or to skylark at drills; their performance should usually be intense and relatively short.

Competition

A third principle in planning work and drills is that competition is an important means of increasing efficiency. This is true, however, only up to the point where the competition becomes an end in itself.

While competition is now well regulated in our modern Navy, it is still possible to observe instances of the "tail wagging the dog." There is only one logical basis on which competition should be judged. Does it increase in any way the fighting efficiency of the unit? A division officer and his men are always engaged in some form of competition, because during peacetime there must be some substitute for the rigorous demands of fighting. In peace you shoot for a score, in war you shoot to destroy the enemy and to protect yourself. It is important for all officers to understand what competition strives to accomplish—which simply is to increase the fighting efficiency of the unit.

Cooperation Between Divisions

A final general principle in planning the work and drills of a division is that cooperation with the other divisions is essential. No matter how well an officer runs his division, if he only gives lip service to the coordinating efforts of the executive officer he is not pulling his weight in the boat. This is not so much of an issue when a division is made up entirely of maintenance men, or radar-men, or other specialists whose duties are clear-cut and confined to one space on the ship. But the healthy softball rivalry between two gunnery divisions or between a deck and an engineering division on a ship must not spill over into squabbles over cleaning assign-ments or other administrative matters. Just as the Navy is much more important than a single ship of the fleet, so are the interests of a ship, squadron, or station more important than the interests of a single division.

The ship should be viewed as an entity, a combat system com-posed of interrelated and interdependent subsystems. Each divi-sion provides a necessary service, and generally does so without much difficulty. It is at the interfaces between subsystems, divi-sions, that coordination problems may arise. The division officer must recognize that mutual support between divisions is not only reasonable, but necessary. Occasionally one division may have the technical expertise that is needed by another division to efficiently repair important shipboard equipment. For example, an Electron-ics Technician may be able to help the Fire Control Technician solve a particularly knotty problem, but only if the two division officers recognize the potential benefit. In other words, all of the ships resources should be employed in a mutually supportive manner. This does not mean that one division should habitually do another division's maintenance, but rather that the division officer should recognize both the ship's needs and her assets. The best shortcut to harmony between divisions is a thorough under-standing by the division officers of the work and responsibility assignments laid down in the ship's organization.

Directives

A requirement for the efficient management of a division is famil-iarity by the division officer with the current directives that apply to the duties of the division and to the men of the division. No attempt will be made here to list all of these publications, but the important ones will be mentioned. *U.S. Navy Regulations, 1973*, should head the list of important directives, followed by the *Standard Organization and Regulations of the U.S. Navy*, the *Bureau of Naval Personnel Manual*, the *Uniform Code of Military Justice*, and your own ship or station regulations.

The various Systems Command manuals are most important, particularly the *Naval Ships Systems Manual*. If your duties involve gunnery (weapons) or supply, then the *Naval Ordnance Systems Manual* or the *Naval Supply Systems Manual* are important aids.

Most of the remaining directives are in the form of instructions and notices. The object of this Navy directive system of instructions and notices is to group together under a common subject number the directives from different commands concerning the same subject, to differentiate between directives of a continuing or permanent nature and those designed for brief use, and to improve general naval administration by using throughout the service a uniform format and numbering system. The system includes all directives, from those issued by the Chief of Naval Operations to those issued by a division officer aboard ship. See Chapter 10 for details on instructions and notices.

For special occasions when, for example, a man makes inquiries concerning a hardship discharge, a division officer should find the answer either in the *Bureau of Naval Personnel Manual*, or in an instruction or notice on file in the personnel office. It is important that a division officer be informed on such matters as requirements for advancement in rate, shore duty eligibility, overseas shore duty, humanitarian shore duty, transfers between ships, etc.

A division officer who takes the time and effort to obtain the answers for his men, or who has his leading petty officer obtain them, will not only gain the respect and confidence of his men but will probably find that he will receive much more cooperation from the personnel office, disbursing office, etc., than does the division officer who sends his men to these offices for answers to questions such as "When will I be eligible for third class?" "Do I rate a Good Conduct Metal?" etc.

Division Personnel Records

The *Standard Organization and Regulations of the U.S. Navy* require that a division officer "maintain a division notebook containing personnel data, training program data, a space and equipment responsibility log, the watch and battle stations required to be manned, and such other data as may be useful for the orientation of an officer relieving him, and for ready reference."

Keeping the records of the men in a division is a standardized routine throughout the Navy, using the Division Officer's Personnel Record Form (Figures 4-1 and 4-2). These forms, filled out for each man and assembled in a binder, constitute a division notebook, a most important tool for efficient personnel management.

Note that much data is taken from the man's official, permanent record kept in the personnel office. This data is required, for example, when you assign men their duties and stations, when you consider leave, allotments, and special requests, and when you review job classifications. Additionally, the form provides space in which to record semiannual marks as a continuing record of performance without referring to the Enlisted Performance Evaluation record (page 9) filed in individual service jackets. The back side of the form provides blanks for logging training accomplishments.

Their application is obvious. The largest part of the responsibility for training rests upon the division officer. He must keep adequate data on file to help discharge this responsibility. Some of the important items, such as the completion of a training course, are reported to the personnel office (sometimes via the training and/ or personnel officer). There the information is entered in the man's service record.

In addition to the division officer's notebook, the division officer should maintain an informal division book in which Watch, Quarter, and Station Bill assignments are listed as well as muster lists for various drills and evolutions. The leading division petty officer and the section leaders should keep books for their own sections. These notebooks serve as a muster list at quarters and as checks for proper procedures at all drills. In addition to checking

DIVISION OFFICER'S PERSONNEL RECORD FORM
NAVPERS 1070/6 (REV. 10-73) S/N 0106-017-0601

Figure 4-1. Division Officer's Personnel Record Form (Front).

DIVISION OFFICER'S PERSONNEL RECORD FORM
NAVPERS 1070/6 (REV. 10-73) (BACK)

FORMAL EDUCATION							
HIGH SCHOOL				MAJOR SUBJECTS			
9	10	11	12				
COLLEGE							
1	2	3	4				

BASIC BATTERY SCORES							
GCT	ARI	MECH	CLER	ETST	SONAR	RADIO	FLAT

GED					
☐ HIGH SCHOOL ☐ COLLEGE	PART 1 SCORE	PART II SCORE	PART III SCORE	PART IV SCORE	PART V SCORE

NAVAL EDUCATION AND ADVANCEMENT RECORD

ITEM	TITLE	DATE COMPLETED	MARK	TITLE	DATE COMPLETED	MARK
SERVICE SCHOOLS						
MILITARY CORRESPONDENCE COURSES						
OTHERS						

PRACTICAL FACTORS		SERVICE-WIDE RATING EXAMINATIONS		
RATE	DATE COMPLETED	DATE	RATE	RESULTS

FIRST AID	SWIMMING	TEL. TALKER	FIRE FIGHTING	DRIVER	TRUCK DRIVER	BUS DRIVER	COX'SN	BOAT ENG.				

REMARKS

☆ U.S.GPO: 1974—713-658/5331 2-1

Figure 4-2. Division Officer's Personnel Record Form (Back).

the assignments of the men at drills, the books can be used to record minor deficiencies that might otherwise remain uncorrected.

To assist the division officer and his assistants in keeping up with the ever-changing training required by or desired by his men, the *Standard Organization and Regulations of the U.S. Navy*, Chapter 5, provides guidance and sample formats for scheduling and maintaining a divisional training schedule, a group record of training and skill qualifications, and a record of qualifications at battle stations. Chapter 5 also describes the use of the Personnel

Qualifications Standards. Several types of general record forms are illustrated, showing the flexible use of such forms to set down this vital training and qualification data. These forms are available in the Supply System and are used to assist in maintaining a comprehensive training and readiness status within the division.

The important point is that a systematic procedure must be used to assist in qualifying your men on various stations and on various pieces of equipment. If you have determined and listed the schools and training courses available through the fleet training centers and other facilities, it will be easier for you to schedule your personnel for such training. If practical factors records are available to each man together with lists of source books for each rate, your men will be positively informed of the study requirements for promotion. Lastly, your men will realize through these efforts that you are aware of their progress and, most important, that you are interested in their training.

Other Personnel Records

Service Record

The enlisted service record reflects the career history of each enlisted man and is the property of the U.S. government, not the man. The records are maintained in the ship's or activity's personnel office. These records are always available for review by the individual and anyone with a need to review them. They cannot, however, have entries made to them except by personnel specifically authorized to make service record entries—usually the executive officer or personnel officer and his personnel staff.

The division officer should become intimately familiar with each of his men's service records and take the personal responsibility of ensuring that they are fully correct at all times. Any discrepancies should immediately be reported to the executive officer or the personnel officer.

The service record can be an extremely useful tool for the division officer both in taking care of his men and in learning about his men. When reviewing a service record a division officer will be able to find such information as: time left in current enlistment; test scores; basic talents; educational level; record of schooling; leave record; record of transfers; summary of evaluations; and special remarks and qualifications.

The Enlisted Service Record consists of a flat-type folder with Pages 1 through 15, as necessary, on the right-hand side of the folder. Other official or unofficial papers are filed on the left-hand side of the folder in chronological order.

Page 1: *Enlistment Contract*. This is the contract a man signs upon joining the Navy.

Page 2: *Dependency Application/Record of Emergency Data*. This page is one of the most important ones in a man's record, and it should be kept up to date. This form is used by all naval personnel to provide the Navy with necessary information about next of kin, dependents, or other people who should be notified in case of death or other emergency.

Page 3: *Enlisted Classification Record*. This contains pertinent information relative to a man's aptitude, test scores, civilian education and training, personal interests and civilian experience. This information is prepared from the data obtained by the naval training centers during the routine testing and interviewing of recruits. Page 3 shows the basic battery test scores, such as the General Classification Test [GCT], the Arithmetic Test [ARI], the Mechanical Test [MECH], and the Clerical Test [CLER]. These tests are used to help select the best rating and type of duty for the man.

Page 4: *Navy Occupation/Training and Awards History*. This page provides for ready reference a complete chronological record of the man's enlisted classification codes, Navy schools attended, Navy training courses, performance tests, changes in rate or rating, decorations and other awards.

Page 5: *History of Assignments*. The purpose of this page is to maintain a record of the ships and stations to which the man has been assigned, and a record of enlistments and extensions.

Page 6: *Record of Unauthorized Absence*. This page is used to record unauthorized absence in excess of 24 hours.

Page 7: *Court Memorandum*. This is designed to report all court-martial action where a guilty finding is made and approved.

Additionally, it reports any nonjudicial punishment which affects pay.

Page 8: *Enlisted Leave Record.* This provides a means of recording data concerning leave and time not served.

Page 9: *Enlisted Performance Record.* This page is used to record chronologically the evaluation of performance of enlisted members on active duty.

Page 10: *Record of Personnel Actions.* This page reports changes in rate or rating by any means except as a result of disciplinary actions.

Page 11: *Record of Naval Reserve Service.* This is to provide a history of the man's reserve service, if applicable.

Page 12: *Transfers and Receipts.* This page is used administratively by the personnel office to record details of a man's transfers between previous duty stations.

Page 13: *Administrative Remarks.* This serves as a chronological record of miscellaneous entries which are not provided for elsewhere.

Page 14: *Record of Discharge, Release from Active Duty, or Death.* This is prepared when a man's active duty is terminated.

Page 15: *Armed Forces of the United States Report of Transfer or Discharge.* This page provides documentary evidence of active naval service.

*Enlisted Performance
Evaluation*

One of the most important duties a division officer must perform is the periodic evaluation of his men in such areas as professional performance, leadership and supervisory ability, military behavior and appearance. These marks are used to determine a man's eligibility for reenlistment, honorable discharge, good conduct medals, advancement, assignment to special duties, and for special education programs. An indication of the importance of accurate evaluations is that they are weighted at least as heavily as the advancement examination when determining whether a man should be promoted. Consequently, the division officer's evaluation must not be allowed to become casual or routine. The evaluation should be carefully made, considering the discussion that follows the descriptions in BUPERS Manual, and by comparing a man with his peers, rate for rate and rating for rating. Be objective and discerning to ensure that only truly outstanding individuals receive outstanding reports, with adequate justification. Be sure that shortcomings or deficiencies which signify unreliability are reported. After the evaluation is completed, it is a good idea to put it away for a few days, and then reread it. When you are satisfied with it, then bring the man in to review the evaluation with you. The whole procedure should be used as a leadership tool in counselling your men. The individual reported on shall be given an opportunity to review and sign the completed report. If he doesn't agree with the report, he has the option of submitting a statement concerning his disagreement, through the chain of command.

Because of the importance of these evaluations, and perhaps a feeling of inexperience, there is a common tendency among new or careless officers to give all men who do their work satisfactorily a 4.0 across the board. This defeats the system and makes no distinction between an average man, a good man, and an outstanding man. Extreme care should be exercised that marks are correct, strict, and fair estimates of the man's ability, character, and worth. Only if this is done can the Navy select people efficiently for schooling, special programs, and promotions.

Enlisted personnel in pay grades E1 through E4 are evaluated twice a year, using NavPers Form 1616/5. Normally the rough evaluation will be made by the division officer and then submitted to the commanding officer or executive officer (in some cases the department head), for review and approval. The traits evaluated on the NavPers 1616/5 are professional performance, military behavior, leadership and supervisory ability, military appearance, and adaptability. The following discussion will be useful in making out the NavPers 1616/5.

Professional Performance. This is how well the man does his job. It's a matter of how well he knows his job, how skillfully he can perform what he has to do, and how industrious he is.

Ask yourself: Does this man do his jobs quickly, efficiently, correctly? Do I have to tell him what to do, or how to do it? Can I depend on him, or do I have to keep after him or keep checking his work?

A word of warning. Be sure to *compare each man with the other man in his own rate.* As you read each description, add to yourself: "for a third class," "for a seaman," etc.

Military Behavior. A man's conduct record doesn't really tell the whole story. Most men have clean records, yet there is a lot of difference in the way they respond to discipline and regulation. Some men are really enthusiastic and loyal, observe regulations to the letter, and are unusually respectful. Others are half-hearted, or resentful of authority, or are always violating regulations in small ways, or griping. They seem to be trying to get away with as much as possible without getting on report. Sometimes they get into lots of trouble. But most men are somewhere in between, accepting authority and discipline in their stride, without resentment. They aren't troublesome. They aren't perfect. They're good, average men. These are the kinds of differences among your men that you should show on this trait when you mark it. Whenever a mark of less than 3.0 is assigned in the trait of military behavior and the man has not had disciplinary action recorded against him during the marking period, substantiating remarks must be made on the evaluation sheet in order that a service record page 13 entry of explanation can be made by the personnel office.

Leadership and Supervisory Ability. You can sometimes tell a good supervisor by his results. Is he able to organize a detail of men to get a job done efficiently? Or do his men get in each other's way? How good a supervisor is he in an emergency? Do his men complain, goof-off, "go over his head"? Do you—or someone else—have to step in to settle supervisory problems, or can you depend upon the man to handle these affairs himself? Does he know his men? Do his men respect him or do they "walk all over him"? Does he show loyalty to his men and does he get it in return?

This trait is not limited to petty officers alone. If the assignment requires it, even a seaman may supervise. Supervisory ability doesn't refer to *how much* supervising a man does, but to *how effective* he is in whatever supervisory jobs he is given. Compare each man with men of his own rate.

Military Appearance. Consider the man's everyday appearance. The man who "polishes up" for liberty or inspection, but who is somewhat bedraggled at other times, doesn't deserve perfect marks here. How does the man look when he shows up for watch, for work, for meals, or for recreation? Does he keep his shoes clean, his hair cut, his face shaved? Are his dungarees neat and clean? Of course, the man on liberty or review is important, too. It's particularly important how a man looks when he is in public.

Adaptability. Navy men have to get along together, work, play, and live together. And the Navy way calls for teamwork and cooperation. Some men are particularly good men to have around. They're very well liked and they like working with their shipmates. They're happy themselves, and they help the morale of the crew in general.

Then there are others who always seem to be dissatisfied. They are generally a source of trouble—are belligerent, inconsiderate. Or they may be "lone wolves" who won't join in.

Most men are somewhere in between, are just ordinary, friendly "good joes" who get along OK without standing out in the crowd. They are good men to have in a crew or a detail.

Not observed. This box is reserved for a check mark to indicate that the rater has been unable to observe the trait and cannot give a fair evaluation of the man. This should be used sparingly.

Performance evaluations for E5 and E6 are required once each year, and are submitted on NavPers 1616/18. This form requires slightly different information; it reflects more closely the leadership position of a Second or First Class Petty Officer. You will evaluate these men in the areas of directing, counseling, individual productivity, flexibility, reliability, conduct, personal appearance, cooperation, equal opportunity achievement, intercultural relations and overall performance. The petty officers rated here are generally career people, and as such the Navy needs a greater amount of information on them. These people are more apt to apply for special programs and schools, and may eventually be recommended for Chief Petty Officer.

You will use NavPers Form 1616/8 to evaluate your E7, E8, and E9 personnel. You will probably find these men the most difficult to evaluate critically and accurately, but just as before, you must base your evaluation objectively on the man's demonstrated performance and abilities as compared to established Navy standards, and the performance of his contemporaries. You will be rating these men in the areas of performance of duty, personal appearance, cooperativeness, reliability, initiative, conduct, resourcefulness, potential, leadership, verbal expression, and finally an overall evaluation.

The implication of the above for a division officer who may need every possible means to persuade his men to behave should be clear. If you are troubled by an excess of shore patrol reports concerning drunkenness and fighting, or if the venereal rate in your division increases, one of your most effective means to encourage your men to tread the straight and narrow path is to let them know that their bad behavior will be reflected in low periodic marks in leadership and in proficiency in rate. This will not influence the few really "bad eggs" you may have, but it will be very effective for the majority of your petty offenders whose professional pride is reasonably well developed.

Conduct marks are assigned by the division officer and checked by the personnel officer. Two cases of nonjudicial punishment during a marking period would normally require a mark of less than 3.0 to be assigned. The marks are reviewed by the department head and by the executive officer. The completed evaluations will be signed by the commanding officer, except that he may authorize the executive officer or department head to sign provided they are of the grade of lieutenant commander or above.

Men's periodic marks and petty officer evaluation sheets are highly important in their relation to discipline, and they must never be considered as just another item of administrative paperwork. Marks are one of the most effective means of rewarding good men, especially if the men realize the importance of the marks. Giving a man poor marks when he deserves them is an effective means of indicating your disapproval, and, in some cases, spurring him on to improve himself. Unless a decided difference is made in the marks given to poor, average, and good men, there will be no means to insure the promotion of efficient petty officers. The common complaint that "we have few good petty officers" is not a reflection on the American sailor or on the system of advancement, particularly in regard to training and somewhat in regard to periodic marks. If all officers were conscientious in training and marking their men, the Navy would, in time, have all the efficient petty officers it could use. There is no easy way to develop a large group of able petty officers; the only sure way is for every officer to develop all the men under him to the full extent of the men's capabilities.

In filling out the periodic evaluation sheets for chief petty officers and first class petty officers, it is particularly important to be fair and just in following the standards laid down in the *Bureau of Naval Personnel Manual*. There is a strong tendency for a young officer to mark all his men too high. This misguided loyalty may backfire in later years, and you may find yourself saddled with an incompetent chief petty officer who has reached his position because many officers gave him a high mark every time because he was a "good guy" and tried hard. It is not fair to the really good men to mark everyone high just because they have not pulled any real boners these last six months.

The Enlisted Distribution and Verification Report

The Enlisted Distribution and Verification Report, BuPers Report 1080-14, serves as a rate or NEC (see below) summary of the current and future manning status onboard a ship, in an air squadron, or at a shore activity. This report is distributed monthly. BuPers 1080-14 will give the division officer a summary of his allowance for personnel in numbers and by NEC, a view of his prospective gains and losses, and a common point of reference in any discussion of manning status. The division officer should review the 1080-14 and ensure that it is correct for his personnel. Since this report is used in assigning personnel to the unit, errors in it may result in the failure of needed personnel to be assigned to the ship.

Navy Enlisted Classification [NEC] Coding

The purpose of the Navy Enlisted Classification system is to supplement the enlisted rating structure in identifying special skills and knowledge requirements. The use of NECs expresses both the special requirements of ships and stations, and the attainment of these skills by enlisted personnel. Navy Enlisted Classification coding has been integrated with the rating structure and enlisted distribution system in assigning personnel to ships and stations.

All organizations employing large numbers of people use some system for identifying and relating the skills of people with the skills required for all jobs. In military organizations, however, because of far-flung operations and constant training effort, large numbers of personnel are transferred periodically from job to job and from one type of command to another. The identification system used, therefore, must be developed to serve more purposes than a similar one employed in a more static civilian organization.

The Army and Air Force use numerical systems to classify both men and jobs, but the Navy relies first of all upon its traditional rating structure because each man must become as versatile and broadly qualified as possible. Only a given number of men can be berthed on a ship, yet all jobs must be accomplished—including the all-important one of manning battle stations.

The key word in the Navy system is "rate." Navy *rates* are combinations of (1) ratings and pay grades (example, RM3, Radioman Third Class) or (2) apprenticeships and pay grades (example, SA, Seaman Apprentice). There are six apprenticeships: seaman, fireman, constructionman, airman, hospitalman, and dentalman. Each have three pay grades, E-1, E-2 and E-3, thereby comprising 18 *rates*. Then at pay grades above E-3 there are approximately 68 general service ratings, which subdivide into *rates* at each pay grade.

Taken together, these *rates* provide a broad occupational classification system for identifying both job requirements and personnel. Since all personnel are advanced in pay grade under this system, the aim of versatility and broad qualification is basically attained.

On the other hand, many jobs are extremely specialized in nature. Some require long and expensive training; others are simply not numerous enough to warrant training everyone in a given rate. Classification of this type is attained by using NECs, Navy Enlisted Classification Codes, to identify both the job and the man able to do it. While NECs have nothing to do with your men's advancement in pay grade, they often have a lot to do with their next duty assignments or their opportunity for advanced schooling. By referring to BuPers Report 1080-14, you can determine the rates, ratings, and the NECs that are allowed your ship. You should verify that your allowance contains the necessary NECs. This will go a long way toward insuring that the right number of men are trained in key specialties and that your ship receives a qualified replacement when your trained man is transferred.

When you open the *Manual of Navy Enlisted Classifications*, NavPers 15105 series, you will see codes are arranged in three major categories: Entry Series Codes—these are essentially for learners; Rating Series Codes—these amplify rating information; Special Codes—these may apply to any one of a number of ratings. Whenever possible, codes are listed under specific ratings. This is because the distributor, the command that parcels out personnel as evenly as possible among fleets and districts, and among type commands, can work from only one set of books. If the NEC he is dealing with is allied to rate, he can assure the right number of specialists in each broad area. Then the detailer, down the line, has made available to him his proper share of the right people to fill his specialized billets. In cases where the specialty crosses a number of ratings, however, as in the case of Special Series Codes (9901 series is an example), the distributor must treat these numbers as if they were rates in themselves and handle the personnel in special categories.

It is easy to shrug off NEC coding as the responsibility of someone else—the personnel man, the department head, or even the type commander. You are in the key position, however, and have a major responsibility both to your men and to the Navy.

You must ensure that your men are correctly identified; the best times to do this are when you receive a new man, transfer a man, and when one of your men completes a school for which an identifying NEC should be assigned. To do it correctly requires service record review, personal interview, and observation of duties performed. Failure to insure a correct NEC assignment for each man is inviting loss of proficiency pay or a later checkage if payment has been made because of an incorrect entry.

Watch, Quarter, and Station Bill

Another important task that confronts a division officer is keeping his Watch, Quarter, and Station Bill up to date. In the preceding chapter on organization, the steps in making out the bill were described in detail. An equally important task is making the bill familiar to all hands and keeping it up to date. One of the simplest ways to do the former is to have the section petty officers make a copy of the bill for their section and then use it for instructing their men. Having each man initial the posted bill near his name is recommended. Some division officers prefer to make out billet slips for each man, and to deliver these to the man (Figure 4-3). Whatever the method used, it is important to have the men familiar with the Watch, Quarter, and Station Bill. The abbreviations used on the bill because of space limitations must be defined. The bill should be checked at frequent and regular intervals, particularly before getting underway, to insure not only that all new men have a listing, but that the departure of old hands has been recognized and compensated for as well.

An important feature of a Watch, Quarter, and Station Bill is permanence. Once you have considered all the factors and have written up your bill, do not change it. Nothing is more conducive to uproar and confusion than a Watch, Quarter, and Station Bill that is always being revised. Training comes to a halt when different personnel are assigned different jobs every time the ship goes to sea. Changes should be made only for really important reasons.

The idea of a semipermanent Watch, Quarter, and Station Bill should not preclude the rotation of personnel at regular periods as a means of helping their training. For example, all yeomen strikers might be rotated through enough battle stations and condition watch stations to prepare them for the important duty, some day, of captain's talker. Rotation for training is a necessity that should never be confused with the constant and aimless revision that is a symptom of poor administration. Remember when men are rotated it is your responsibility to ensure that they are qualified for the new job.

In making up the Watch, Quarter, and Station Bill, it is recommended that all items be printed, typed, or written in ink except the men's names and some cleaning stations that are changed peri-

BILLET SLIP

Name	
Rate	Division
Billet No.	
Bunk No.	
Locker No.	
Condition I (General Quarters)	
Condition II	
Condition III	
Condition IV	
Condition V	
Collision	
Rescue and Assistance	
Abandon Ship	
Scuttling and Destruction	
Survivor Rescue	
Fueling Transfer	
Boarding and Salvage	
Prize Crew	
Fire	
Landing Party	
General Emergency	
Visit and Search	
Special Sea Detail	
Cleaning Maintenance	

(Items will vary in detail depending on type of ship.)

Figure 4-3. Personnel Billet Slip.

odically. This procedure will assure greater permanence and more careful construction. Another recommendation is to avoid ditto marks. Fill in all items to assist the men in seeing their assignments plainly. Vertical insertions, written up and down the column, such as "See Station Notice 1-54," are also frowned upon since they tell the men nothing. Such shortcuts indicate a poorly run division.

Security

No chapter on administration in the Navy would be complete without discussing security. The division officer may have custody of classified publications, charts, blueprints, or pictures. He is also likely to be responsible for classified equipment and ordnance. Thus, a division officer is largely concerned with matters of safeguarding classified matter. His first act should be to become familiar with the basic directives. These are *U.S. Navy Regulations, 1973* (Chapter 11), the Department of the Navy Information Security Program Regulation, OpNavInst 5510.1 (Series), and the Security Bill contained in Chapter 6 of the *Standard Organization and Regulations of the U.S. Navy.* Amplifying instructions may be issued by fleet, type, and squadron commanders, to mention a few examples. For those division officers who are designated as custodians of registered publications, there are additional CNO instructions and notices in the 5510 series.

The second step in insuring security in a division is to set up a systematic procedure for the stowage and use of classified publications. Blueprints and manuals must be given the proper stowage, required by their degree of classification, as specified by regulations, and when removed from that stowage should be signed for on a card or in a book. This emphasis on security must not, of course, result in hiding classified matter from those who should use it, either for their job or for their training. Good judgment must be applied here by the division officer.

In regard to classified equipment or ordnance, such as radars or new antiaircraft weapons, the division officer should be vigilant at all times when visitors or guests are aboard ship. He should insure that critical spaces, such as CIC, are locked or guarded, and that classified gear on deck is covered. Further guidance on general visiting and ship security in port is contained in section three of OpNavInst 5510.1 (Series).

There are times when the ship must be secured against the wholesale disappearance of everything that is not welded down. One of these occasions is when a ship enters a shipyard for overhaul. Before entering the yard, a division officer should either stow all his tools and other portable equipage in a compartment where no work will be done, or should pack the gear in boxes to be stowed ashore. Among the hundreds of thoroughly honest workmen there will always be a few who cannot resist taking a tool or a souvenir. Over a period of weeks or months such persons can effectively strip a ship. This condition becomes more acute, of course, in times of naval expansion when many new workers are joining the shipyards.

Another occasion for special precautions is when the ship is open to large numbers of civilians, whether invited guests attending a ceremony or visitors during an Armed Forces Day open house. Similar precautions must be taken during the mass evacuation of civilians. Under these circumstances, a division officer can only keep some of his men on watch in all spaces, with instructions to discourage, courteously but firmly, the collection of souvenirs. At such a time men must also be instructed to enforce no-smoking regulations, observe safety precautions, and keep visitors out of restricted or classified areas.

It is the practice in many shipyards for the workmen, while working on a ship, to leave their tools on board in locked tool boxes, usually stowed topside. Occasionally, sailors will break into these tool boxes. This infrequent, but embarrassing, occurrence can often be avoided by a forehanded division officer, who not only instructs his men about leaving the workers' tools alone but also suggests that the toolboxes be stowed where the quarterdeck watch can see them.

When in foreign ports, a ship must be particularly alert to prevent theft, not only by casual visitors, but also by ship's personnel. Where black market prices ashore are very high for medical supplies, electronic spare parts, etc., it is a great temptation for the men to take material ashore. This can be greatly aggravated by the presence aboard ship of civilians representing themselves as foreign merchants and tradesmen, but who may really be on board for less honest reasons.

The division officer should not overlook the vital importance of information security. He should caution his men to refrain from discussing anything of a classified nature either ashore or afloat—except, of course, in the pursuit of their duties.

All of the above is, of course, only a bare outline and a suggestion of the many aspects of security that will affect a division officer. The big point is that every person in the Navy must be security-conscious. He should be suspicious of everyone and trust no one, including himself, when it comes to matters affecting the security of the United States. Sometimes, a conscientious observance of this principle becomes tedious and time-consuming. Any shortcuts, however, in matters of security are a reflection on an officer's sense of responsibility.

Administrative Details

There are several aspects of administration that are deserving of discussion as the conclusion to this chapter. *U.S. Navy Regulations, 1973*, Article 0727, directs commanding officers to "afford an opportunity, with reasonable restrictions as to time and place, for the personnel under his command to make requests, reports, or statements to him, and shall insure that they understand the procedures for making such requests, reports, or statements." The division officer carries out the last part of the above directive in that he insures that his men understand the procedures to be carried out, when they desire to make a special request of any kind. He should also advise the men about the subject matter and manner of making a request or statement. Even if the division officer believes that the only result may be that of wasting the captain's time, it is important for the men to feel free to exercise their rights as stated in *Navy Regulations*. The usual procedure is for a man to write out his request on a special request form, available in the personnel office, and to submit it through his division officer.

The same article in *Navy Regulations* which was partly quoted above, directs the commanding officer to "insure that noteworthy performance of duty of personnel under his command receive timely and appropriate recognition, and that suitable notations are entered in the official records of the individuals." It is thus clear that division officers should bring such noteworthy performance of duty to the attention of their commanding officer for possible public recognition at Meritorious Mast, and that they should be meticulous in having such a commendation entered in the man's service record. The *Bureau of Naval Personnel Manual* contains detailed instructions on this subject.

The chief master-at-arms derives his authority from Article 303.3 of the *Standard Organization and Regulations of the U.S. Navy*, which reads: "In units, there will be assigned under the executive officer a chief master-at-arms [MAA] and such other masters-at-arms [MAAS] as may be required as his assistants, for the maintenance of good order and discipline." Division officers are often called upon to furnish the assistants referred to above. All hands in a division should be informed in regard to the authority of the masters-at-arms. There should be no basis, through ignorance, for a feeling on the part of your men that masters-at-arms were invented to harass them. The duties and responsibilities of these important assistants to the executive officer should be familiar to all the men in the division. They are listed in the *Standard Organization and Regulations of the U.S. Navy*.

The importance of well-understood leave and liberty policies is obvious. While these matters are primarily the responsibility of the executive officer, nevertheless division officers can often do much within their unit to stabilize leave and liberty. If men are led to believe they will have a certain amount of leave at a certain time, nothing but a real emergency should deprive them of that leave. A firm and fair policy is often more important than any particular number of days allowed each man.

In regard to liberty, it is a great advantage for the division officer to have some discretion in granting liberty which has been authorized by the commanding officer. Many well-managed ships now have a policy of commencing liberty at a certain time *at the discretion of the division officer.* Liberty, then, is not an automatic right, it is dependent on the necessary work being finished. A division officer may then keep certain men on board who have not finished their work. A ship that follows this policy is usually able to grant almost continuous early liberty while in port and yet get the same amount of work done. The men have a goal; they know that if they turn to and get the work done, they can earn early liberty. By the same token, men who have not been pulling their weight in the ship can be kept aboard.

In actual practice, division officers seldom have to deprive any of their men of part of their liberty, but the very existence of this prerogative serves to remind the lazy and less efficient men that if they do not produce they are liable to be delayed in getting ashore.

Another administrative matter of some importance is relieving or being relieved as a division officer. When taking over a division for the first time you have every right to expect that the men have a full bag, are up on their training, have their machinery and spaces in good shape, and that all division paperwork is in order. The men's progress in being prepared for advancement in rate should be noted. The Administrative Inspection Check-off Lists, available in every ship, should be used as much as possible to cover administrative details. Remember that when you have taken over the division you will be in no position to explain deficiencies that might become apparent to your seniors unless you have noted them in writing as part of the turn-over procedure.

5/Training

A division officer will . . . train his subordinates in their own duties and in the duties to which they may succeed, and encourage them to qualify for advancement and to improve their education.—*Standard Organization and Regulations of the U.S. Navy.*

In peace and war, training is a primary naval objective, surpassed in wartime only by the necessity for victory, for which it is the essential preparation. A ship's state of training is a major factor affecting her ability to carry out assigned operations. Her personnel must be able to operate and maintain all of the installed equipment and systems. They must also be able to function continuously as a combat team, as a cohesive group. As ships, aircraft, and weapons become increasingly sophisticated, the need for training becomes more critical, and, as a parallel, more difficult to conduct. But computers and space-age weapons are useless without skilled hands and well-trained minds to operate them. It is clear then, why the division officer must train his subordinates.

Shipboard training can be viewed as a composite of several kinds of training. First, there is individual in-rate maintenance training, conducted ashore before assigning a man to a fleet unit. Individual in-rate operator training, also traditionally conducted ashore, prepares a man to operate the equipment he will be called upon to work with aboard ship. Once a man reaches his ship, he will participate in watch-station training designed to teach him to function as part of a watch team. Finally, systems training (such as ASW and AAW team training) for both individuals and watch teams is conducted both ashore and on board ship. Normally the basic training is done ashore, and advanced training to maintain proficiency is performed on the ship. However, a great deal of advanced training, especially in combat systems, can be accomplished at fleet schools. The importance of advanced training ashore must be kept in mind when at-sea time is limited.

As far as the division officer is concerned, the various types of training—whether specifically for advancement in rate or just shipboard training in general—are practically the same thing. That is, they have the same objective, which is to get the man to operate better in the billet in which he is assigned or to which he may be assigned. The fact that the Chief of Naval Personnel has set forth the requirements for advancement in rating in a manual does not make it a different kind of training. The division officer's problem is to conduct training so that his personnel operate his division at maximum efficiency.

The real value to the Navy of every man preparing himself for promotion is that it improves combat readiness. Thus a division officer is not just "looking after his men" when he closely supervises and encourages their preparation for promotion; he is at the same time improving the efficiency, performance, and readiness of his ship or crew.

Training Definitions

Military Standards. The general naval qualifications, both knowledge and practical factors, that Navy men are expected to have concerning discipline, ceremonies, uniform regulations, first aid, responsibilities under the Uniform Code of Military Justice, etc.

Occupational Standards. The skills and knowledge expected of a man in his specialty, his rate and rating; for example, typing for yeomen, signalling for signalmen. Both military and occupational standards will be found in the *Manual of Qualifications for Advancement* (NavPers 18068), known as the "Quals Manual." (The older term for occupational standards was "technical requirements.")

Rate Training. Training designed to teach men professional qualification for a specific rate.

Individual Training. Any training (including all rate training) which improves a man's usefulness to his unit.

Functional Training. Training in a specialized task or function, such as teaching men to operate a specific weapon or machine.

Team Training. Training groups of men and officers to work together in CIC, ASW, etc.

Enlisted Technical Schools. Schools which provide individual technical training. They have the following designation and functions:

Class R - Recruit training. This is the basic training that each new enlistee undergoes to accomplish the transfer between civilian life and the Navy.

Class A - Provides basic apprentice and job entry level training to prepare personnel for the lower petty officer rates (pay grades). An NEC may be awarded.

Class C - Provides advanced technical knowledge and skills required to prepare personnel for the higher petty officer rates, or may provide training in a particular skill or technique. An NEC may be awarded.

Class F - Provides team training to fleet personnel who are members of ships' companies, or individual operator and maintenance training of less than 13 days' duration.

Group or team training is provided by the following types of schools or programs:

Functional Schools. Provide training to personnel, often in a group or team situation which includes both officers and enlisted men, in the performance of specialized tasks or functions which are not normal to rating training of enlisted personnel nor to professional training of officers. They also provide training on weapons of new or advanced design which have not reached fleet usage.

Fleet Schools Ashore. Shore-based fleet training activities, assigned to fleet commanders, which provide refresher and team training to fleet personnel who normally are members of ships' companies.

Refresher Training. An intensive training period, of about six weeks' duration, in which the Fleet Training Group comes aboard a ship and works that ship up in every phase of naval operations, culminating in an all-day battle problem conducted at sea. Usually follows a yard overhaul.

Ship's Qualification Trials. An intensive training period, usually of two weeks' duration, in which the ship's weapons systems are thoroughly wrung out and all associated sensors are tested to determine that they are compatible and operable. Usually precedes Reftra, with one week in port, one week at sea.

Off-Duty Training. A training program which assists individuals in enrolling in Navy correspondence courses, foreign language study, or prepares them for eventual enrollment in the Naval Academy or NROTC programs.

Training Services. Various organizations in the fleet are set up to provide training services to fleet units, such as tractor aircraft (for AA gunnery) drone control (for missile exercises), fleet tugs and towed targets (for surface conventional gunnery), towed submarine targets, shore fire control parties (for naval gunfire support training), etc.

The Training Program

The ship's training officer is responsible for organizing and executing a vigorous training program. In doing so, he is working for the executive officer, and with the department heads, first lieutenant, damage control assistant, personnel officer, and educational services officer, as members of the Planning Board for Training.

When developing the training program, his first step is to establish long-range goals which cover the ship's competitive training cycle, with a series of intermediate short-range goals that recognize the ship's operational commitments. These goals must then be meshed with personnel resource requirements, that is, the required personnel and NECs, shore-based training, watch stations, and systems qualifications. Finally, he must establish a schedule for ship training which meets his goals and allows specific, measurable accomplishments. He will assemble what is known as the ship's long-range training program, which normally covers one year and schedules an integrated set of standardized exercises for that period. It is important to note that these exercises are normally major evolutions, involving the entire battle organization of the ship, or at least a major portion of that organization. Thus, the long-range training program is the framework around which the departments, and subsequently the divisions, construct their individual training programs.

The long-range training program is not made up in a vacuum; the training officer will meet with the executive officer and the other department heads in the Planning Board for Training. This committee is the coordinating body for all training. The required exercises are well defined, but do not cover all the training which must be accomplished over the projected year. The advancement-in-rate program, team training, fleet schools, the operational schedule and maintenance workload, and overseas deployment plans will be considered, and each department will have training requirements which are unique to that department's role in the overall combat system. As a result, the training officer will prepare a Quarterly Training Plan (Figure 5-1), which consists of one page of the long-range plan, updated to reflect the latest information on the ship's employment and containing more detail on the training intentions during a given quarter. The Planning Board for Training will sit down with this document at the beginning of the month and prepare a Monthly Training Plan (Figure 5-2) showing all unit training, evolutions, and operations scheduled in the Quarterly Training Plan. From this plan the division officer will build his own training plan.

With the Monthly Training Plan, you have a leg up on your own divisional plan. You will need to add some material to the monthly plan; specifically you must determine what training is required for your watchstanders, what instruction is needed for equipment maintenance, and what professional and military training will be necessary to meet the standards in the Quals Manual. For example, the OI division officer will probably decide that his operations specialists need instruction in surface and air plotting, radiotelephone procedures, security of classified publications, radar operation and preventive maintenance, the Uniform Code of Military Justice, and so on. He will have determined this by considering what jobs his men need to do, what equipment they do it with, and what military knowledge they should be conversant with. His sources of information are the *Manual for Qualifications for Advancement*, his division's responsibilities under the Battle Bill, the ship's operating schedule, and the list of General Military Training contained within OpNavInst 1500.22 series. (GMT will be discussed in greater detail later in the chapter.)

Within the framework discussed above, your training responsibilities as a division officer are basically concerned with *organizing your division's time* in order to get all the required training done. Two rules should apply: the first is that you need to make

LONG RANGE TRAINING PLAN

FIRST QUARTER AFTER REGULAR OVERHAUL: JULY (CALENDAR YEAR); SEPTEMBER (CALENDAR YEAR)

CONFIDENTIAL (WHEN FILLED IN)

PREPARED ____

Employment	JULY			AUGUST			SEPTEMBER			OCT
	1 7	14	21 28	4 11	18	25	1 8	15 22	29	6

Employment	Regular Overhaul	LBEACH	Sea Trials on 14th	RFS	TYT WESTPAC (MOT)	REFRESHER TRAINING SDIEGO	

Major Maintenance Projects, Trials and Tests: Paint portside Complete OVHL 1 SS GEN — Dock Trials on 8th — Lower decks (mg) work) on 11th — (Note: Much of the information in this section of the Long Range Training Plan should be drawn from PMS schedule)

Inspections and Examinations: P.O. load exam on 2nd — Pers Insp on 26th — E+e Exam on 5th E-5 on 7th — E+e Exams on 12th E-7 on 14th — Dep) Heads School to XO Complete RFT Check-off — TRE by FTG

Operational Readiness Exercises (Compet): 2-24-G on 12th 2-21-G on 11th — Z-24-G on 12th Z-21-G on 11th

Team Training Ashore: ASW Team Training ASW School — ASW Team Training ASW School — RFT Scol week (see ship's RFT sced sked) — RFT Scol week (see ship's RFT sced sked)

School Training Ashore (Individual): AIC (ENS & RDC) — ENGR Off Scol (LTJG)

General and Operational Drills: OOD Scol (2 ENS). CDO Conduct Z-27-D daily except Sunday with the Duty Section when in port: Z-10-D & Z-11-D 25th, 29th & 31st. Z-21-G; Z-24-C; Z-29-C; Z-3-E; Z-5-E; Z-6-E; Z-23-E; Z-24-E; Z-9-E; Z-28-E; Z-43-E; Z-83-E; Z-10-D; Z-11-D; Z-12-E; Z-25-D; Z-26-D; Z-29-D; Z-52-D; Z-7-N; Z-9-S; Z-5-S; Z-11-S; Z-14-S; Z-78-S; Z-10-CX; Z-11-CX; Z-11-D; Z-12-C; Z-24-C; Z-7-C; Z-94-C; X-13-C; Z-1-ET; Z-2-ET; Z-5-ET; Z-7-ET; Z-14-ET. Drills and Exercises in accordance with FTG Weekly Schedule

Professional Training: OPS / NAV / WEPS / SUP / ENGR
(Note: The details of this section of the Long Range Training Plan should be completed by Department/Division Officers from the Division or Department instruction schedule)

General Military Training: First Aid — General Safety — Physical Fitness — Maneuver Board — Veterans Benefits — UCMJ — Safe Driving — Personal Health — VD Prevention — Leadership Discussion — I.D. Ship Handling — Piloting — Tactical Comm

Officer Training: Load Stores 21st Load Ammo. 24th

Miscellaneous Activities

SAMPLE PAGE - - - UNCLASSIFIED

Figure 5-1. Long Range/Quarterly Training Plan.

MONTHLY TRAINING PLAN

1973

JULY

SUNDAY	MONDAY	TUESDAY	WEDNESDAY	THURSDAY	FRIDAY	SATURDAY
OPPORTUNE: Z-26-S (R) Z-29-S (O) Z-13-CC	1 G.Q. Z-10-D NBC Lecture Intelligence Briefing UNREP: 3 DER	2 DIVISIONAL SCHOOL J.O. School Cryto Drill UNREP: 2 MSO	3 DIVISIONAL SCHOOL J.O. School INREP: An Thoi	4 Hand grenade & small arms training all day for Deck and Ops	5 Field Day	6 G.Q. Battle Prob Z-6-D Z-11-S (R) Z-10-D Z-14-S Z-24-D Z-27-D Z-52-D Z-111-E (R)
7 Arrive Subic Z-27-D	8 Z-20-C (O) Z-27-D (Sec I)	9 GMT III DIVISIONAL SCHOOL J.O. School Crypto Drill Z-27-D (Sec II)	10 GMT III DIVISIONAL SCHOOL J.O. School Z-27-D (Sec III)	11 Lookouts lecture (Steaming Watches) Z-27-D (Sec I) PAY DAY	12 0500 Depart SUB G.Q. Gun Shoot Z-20-S Z-14-CC (R) Z-1-AA(R) Z-1-N(R) Z-3-AA(O) Z-5-N(O) Z-29-G (R) Z-110-E (R) Z-21-S (O) Z-1-E(R)	13 SF-1, 6-M (R) for all departments GQI.T NBC Lecture Training Board Z-27-D (Night)
14	15 Mil/Lead Exams E-3 Exams	16 Arrive YOKO DIVISIONAL SCHOOL J.O. School Z-27-D (Sec II)	17 DIVISIONAL SCHOOL J.O. School Blood Donations Z-27-D (Sec III)	18 Z-27-D (Sec I)	19 Field Day Z-27-D (Sec II)	20 DEPART YOKO C. O. Pers Insp. C. O. Zone Insp.
21	22 G.Q. Battle Prob. Z-6-D Z-10-D Z-24-D Z-27-D	23 DIVISIONAL SCHOOL J.O. School Crypto Drill	24 DIVISIONAL SCHOOL J.O. School	25 Telephone Talker Drill (GQ talkers) PAY DAY	26 Field Day SF-2, 5-M (R) for all departments	27 GQI.T NBC Lecture Training Board Z-27-D (Night)
28 Arrive PEARL Z-27-D (Sec III)	29 COMSERVPAC visit G.Q. Z-10-D NBC Lecture Z-27-D (Sec I)	30 Depart PEARL DC Lectures DIVISIONAL SCHOOL J.O. School Crypto Drill	31 DC Lectures DIVISIONAL SCHOOL J.O. School	1 AUG Hand grenade & small arms training for Supply & Engineering	2 AUG Field Day	3 AUG C. O. Zone Insp. C. O. Pers Insp. 5 AUG Arrive SFRAN

Figure 5-2. Sample Monthly Training Plan.

each man proficient, first at his particular job and then as a member of a combat team. The second is that "doing" is the most effective method of training. Both of these imply a certain progression.

Your training program will begin with individualized instruction under the supervision of petty officers. Each man will be assigned a particular billet and station on the Watch, Quarter, and Station Bill of the entire division. If an operations specialist is assigned to operate an air-search radar console, his training must show him everything he needs to know to operate the console. To accomplish this, the petty officer will use his own knowledge, the Navy Training Course for operations specialist, console operating instructions, and the CIC doctrine book. His shipboard training probably will be supplemented by a week at a fleet school in one of the specialized courses. You, as division officer, will see to it that the man gets the required console time and is assigned the right petty officer as an instructor. You will have to schedule this in coordination with that man's watchstanding and cleaning duties, and all hands evolutions such as working parties, all of which combine to complicate your training program. Your senior petty officers might tell you that it takes three weeks of daily instruction for an average operations specialist to become proficient at this particular job; you must see to it that he gets this time in spite of interruptions and that this is made a matter of record.

When the man is proficient, he is ready to advance to team training, in which he becomes proficient at coordinated operations of the CIC team. This type of training will require that your entire division be training at the same time. This would be difficult for you to accomplish in a scheduling sense, but this is the point where your Monthly Training Plan comes into play. The monthly plan has already scheduled team training, by division, during the quarter: you simply take advantage of this scheduling, and work up your CIC team training sessions accordingly. Remember, your responsibility as a division officer is to get *all* the training done, and the monthly plan should give you an opportunity to do just that if you are prepared to participate.

In addition to that training which is peculiar to your own departmental combat systems, there will be other training, such as a first-aid lecture or military indoctrination, which will be scheduled in the ship's quarterly training program. Since, however, your monthly plan was constructed around the ship's quarterly plan, time will already have been allotted for this kind of training. Your responsibility here is to see to it that your men attend these sessions. Remember that practical factors and military standards for advancement-in-rate include many aspects of training which your specialized divisional program may not cover, but which the ship's programs *do* cover, and this factor gives your people a visible incentive to make effective use of both kinds of training opportunities.

One rule which holds true all the time aboard Navy ships is that things are always changing, which implies that the best-laid plans may have to be altered on a continuing basis. To keep the training program for the ship current, the training officer, in cooperation with the executive officer and other department heads, will publish a plan of the week, which is usually attached to Monday's plan of the day. It should list "all hands" evolutions planned for that week, and will contain significant changes to the ship's schedule or training plans. Its value to you as a division officer is that you can update your own training plans at the beginning of the week, so that your training sessions are not disrupted by an evolution which you could not or did not anticipate.

The most difficult aspect of training is how to measure your program's effectiveness while it is in progress. You will have to employ a variety of resources to get a feel for how the training is going. Your chief or first class petty officer will be able to give you a very good idea of the program's strengths and weaknesses; they have been in the training business for a long time. The attitude of the men is another measure. If they are challenged by the training program, it will show in their interest and the seriousness with which they apply themselves. The smoothness of team training will give yet another measure: an efficient combat team will perform its jobs quickly, quietly, and correctly the first time around. When you think the division is up to speed, ask your department head to sit in and observe; if you are having problems, go to him and ask for help.

Training Records

The record-keeping requirements for a successful training program are not elaborate. It is more important that your records be functional and effective than impressive. Chapter 8 of the *Standard Organization and Regulations of the U.S. Navy* describes the necessary records.

The division officer should keep a Division Drill/Instruction Schedule (Figure 5-3), a Record of Available Formal School Training (Figure 5-4), and a Division Officer's Personnel Record. The Group Record of Training and Skill Qualifications (Figure 5-5), will be maintained by the division chief or leading petty officer. Finally, the individual in charge of each watch or general quarters station not manned during periods of normal peacetime cruising will maintain the Record of Qualifications at Watch/ Battle Stations (Figure 5-6).

The Division Drill/Instruction Schedule is used both to schedule and record all of the operational drills, team training periods, and instruction periods applicable to a single division. It includes the training required by the ship's Monthly Training Plan, and as well, the additional training the division officer wishes his division to receive. The Division Drill/Instruction Schedule is kept on both sides of OpNav Form 1500-32. Entries on the front side are coded, and explained on the reverse. Normally two or three letter abbreviations and serial numbers are used, for example, BM1 (Hoisting and Lowering Boats), and T50 (Telephone Talker Drill). If standard lesson plans are available, they should be noted on the reverse side. Drills or lectures that support one of the requirements for advancement listed in the *Manual of Qualifications for Advancement* should be noted in the legend. The schedule should be made out in pencil, and as the training is

DATE PREPARED OR PERIOD COVERED: FROM   TO

TITLE

Legend of Coded Drills/Instruction Periods Type Drill/Instruction	Code	FXP or Tycom No.	NAVPERS 18068 Rqmts & References, Films, etc.
Hoisting and Lowering Boats	BM1	Z-11-S	SN C.2.31
Boat Crew Drill (IN Port	B2		E3 D.1.31 & SN C.1.32 BM3&2
Telephone Talker Drill	T50		E3 W.1.32 Navpers 14005A
Handling & Firing .45 cal.	A13	50-G SF-9-M	E4 V.1.41 E3 L.1.34 & 2.35
Fractures & Splints	F9	SF-10-M	GM3&2 NAVMED P-5056
Gen. Mil. Training- Unit I	I1		OPNAVINST 1500.22
DC Material Readiness	D10	Z-10-D	E3 P.2.31 Battle Bill
Security Orientation	I5		E3 E.2.32
Career Appraisal Team Pres.	I9		E2 K.2.24
UCMJ Apprehension/Restraint	U7		E4 C.2.29h UCMJ Art. 7-14
Financial Planning, Pt. I	I13		Base Legal Officer
Traffic Safety Presentation	I70		Calif. Highway Patrol
Narcotics Presentation	I86		SDIEGO Police Dept.

Figure 5-3. Division Drill and Instruction Schedule.

GENERAL RECORD (Type III)
OPNAV FORM 1500-32 (10-60)   PERIOD COVERED: FROM 1 JAN 76   TO 31 DEC 76

TITLE

Second Division Drill/Instruction Schedule

MONTH		JAN	FEB	MAR	APR	MAY	JUN	JUL	AUG	SEP	OCT	NOV	DEC
DAY OF THE MONTH	1		SUN	BM21									
	2	BM1		I70									
	3	SAT											
	4	SUN	BM9										
	5												
	6			SAT									
	7		SAT	SUN									
	8	I5	SUN	BM18									
	9	T50											
	10	SAT		D3									
	11	SUN		D4									
	12												
	13			SAT									
	14	D10	SAT	SUN									
	15	D5	SUN	B2									
	16	BM7	HOL	I45									
	17	SAT											
	18	SUN		I86									
	19												
	20			SAT									
	21	BM9	SAT	SUN									
	22	PF20	SUN	T50									
	23	BM30		BM6									
	24	SAT		BM4									
	25	SUN											
	26	I9											
	27			SAT									
	28		SAT	SUN									
	29		SUN										
	30												
	31												
WEEKLY OR BIWEEKLY	1ST												
	2ND												
	3RD												
	4TH												
	5TH												
MONTHLY													
QUARTERLY													
SEMI-ANNUAL													
ANNUAL													

0107-701-1000   (See reverse for instructions and/or explanations of entries)

Division Drill and Instruction Schedule (Continued).

GENERAL RECORD (Type 1)
OPNAV FORM 1500-30 (10-60)

CONTINUOUS

PERIOD COVERED: FROM   TO

TITLE

AVAILABLE OFF-SHIP TRAINING, "R" DIVISION

COLUMN CAPTIONS COURSE IDENTIFICATION	CLCVN DATES	COURSE LENGTH	REQUIRED/ DESIRED	QUOTA RQMT
SHPBD FIRE FIGHTING K-780-442, FTC, SDIEGO	MONDAYS	5 DY	ANNUALLY REP. PAR.	10
DC (BUTTERCUP) CASUALTY EX A-780-023, NAVSCOL, TI	AVAIL UPON REQUEST	1 DY	ANNUALLY REP. PAR.	25 (REP III
CAREER INFO & COUNSELING K-500-007, FTC, SDIEGO	1st,2nd,3rd MONDAYS	5 DY	1 PO PER 15 MEN	2 PO2/PO1
ADVANCED WELDERS T-16, SFBNS HUNTER'S PT	7, 21 OCT 4 NOV	2 WK	DESIRED: ALL PO3	2 PO3
Course prerequisites are found in applicable catalog and BUPERS Manual.				
TEMADDINS information is found in TYCOM instruction _____ .				

Figure 5-4. Available Off-Ship Training, "R" Division.

GENERAL RECORD (Type II)
OPNAV FORM 1500-21 (10-60)

(date started)

PERIOD COVERED: FROM 12 JAN 73 TO CONTINUOUS

TITLE

Group Record of Practical Factors for Signalmen (SM)

COLUMN CAPTIONS

Page 1 of 3

Date assigned to div.
Date transferred.
Date last advanced in rating
Date qual. next rate level.

Paste cutout sheet from
NAVPERS 1414/1 for each
rating on the card.

MILITARY STANDARDS

D. INTERNATIONAL AGREEMENTS

.81 Explain the general purpose of the Status of Forces Agreements concerning personnel of the Armed Forces in foreign countries. — E-8

.91 Explain the usual provisions of the Status of Forces Agreements concerning personnel of the Armed Forces in foreign countries. — E-9

| Date & Initial | Date & Initial |

I. DRILL

.51 Command a squad in close-order drill. — E-5

J. UNIFORMS

.39 Identify the following U.S. naval officer designators:
    a. Corps devices. — E-4

L. FIRST AID AND PERSONAL HYGIENE

.41 Transport an injured person by fireman's lift and tied-hands crawl (Men Only). — E-4

O. NUCLEAR, BIOLOGICAL, AND CHEMICAL (NBC) WARFARE

.41 Act as a member of a monitoring team, other than monitor (Men Only). — E-4

Recommend that all entries in this form be written in ink. When a man is transferred, simply cross out his column.

.42 Use a self-reading pocket dosimeter. — E-4

.51 Use radiac instruments and perform monitoring and surveying operations on surfaces exposed to chemical, biological, and radioactive agents (Men Only). — E-5

Number all pages of this record:
Page 1 of 3
Page 2 of 3
Page 3 of 3

.61 Supervise an NBC decontamination team and personnel decontamination facility, observing safety precautions (Men Only). — E-6

.71 Supervise an NBC monitoring team (Men Only). — E-7

.81 Describe procedures to be followed in preparation against attack as set forth in the Nuclear Warfare and Biological and Chemical Warfare defense bills (Men Only). — E-8

Q. SMALL ARMS (Men Only)

.41 Field-strip, clean, and assemble the service pistol (Not applicable for Groups X and XI personnel in accordance with 1949 Geneva Convention). — E-4

.42 Fire service pistol, observing safety precautions (Not applicable for Groups X and XI personnel in accordance with 1949 Geneva Convention). — E-4

Figure 5-5. Group Record of Training and Skill Qualifications.

GENERAL RECORD (Type II)
OPNAV FORM 1500-21 (10-60)

(date started)

PERIOD COVERED: FROM 1 July TO continuous

TITLE

Record of Qualifications at Battle Stations for Crew of Mount 31, 3"/50

COLUMN CAPTIONS

Page 1 of 1 page

Date assigned to Mt 31								
Date transferred from Mt 31								
Date his previous 3"/50 qual entered this record								

HAS STUDIED AND KNOWS THE BELOW LISTED ITEMS:

Hangfire-misfire procedure		Date						
Identification markings of 3" ammo. (OP4)		Initials						
Safety precautions								
Ammo service to guns								
All duties of 3"/50 gun crew given in Ship's Gunnery Doctrine								
Ship's Spotting Doctrine - (Mandatory only for Mt Capt)		Date & Initials						

KNOWS HOW TO REPAIR FOLLOWING COMMON CASUALTIES:

(a) Broken firing pin								
(b) Broken firing lead								

HAS QUALIFIED TO PERFORM THE FOLLOWING DUTIES:

(1) Mount Captain ((GM only)		Note: Since this record covers a gun crew, the only applicable practical factor is the qualification as a Mount Captain for gunner's mates.						
(2) Pointer								
(3) Trainer								
(4) Sightsetter								
(5) 1st loader								
(6) Fuzesetter								
(7) Passer								
(8) Hot shellman								

Figure 5-6. Record of Qualification at Watch/Battle Stations.

completed the penciled entries can be inked over to become records of training.

The record of available formal school training is used to assemble, for easy reference, information on all Navy schools of interest to the division. Information on available schools is published in the Catalog of Navy Training Courses (NavEdTra 10500). The ship's SMD and BuPers 1080-14 lists the NECs that you should have within the division, and the type commander may specify some additional formal school requirements. As a division officer it is up to you to take advantage of these schools. You should determine what your requirements are and request school quotas from the ship's training officer. You should arrange for schooling needed to qualify on board reliefs for personnel who are due for detachment.

The division officer's Personnel Record is kept in NavPers 1070/6, and records a number of items of interest. Space is provided for administrative information, such as date reported, expected loss date, personal data, previous duty stations, semiannual marks, awards, educational achievement, advancement, and general remarks.

The Group Record of Training and Skill Qualifications is a record of individual training accomplishments. It reflects the subjects listed in the Division Drill/Instruction Schedule, noting attendance or qualification. It also contains a list of the practical factors that must be completed for advancement, and notes qualification with the date and petty officer's initials. A glance at this record at the beginning of each quarter will assist the division officer in scheduling individual instruction during the next three months.

The Record of Qualifications at Watch/Battle Stations shows the knowledge and skills required of men who are assigned to battle stations, such as gun crews and repair parties, which are manned only during general quarters or condition watches. The officer or petty officer in charge of the battle station needs to record the items of desired knowledge, each man's qualifications, and each man's proficiency in carrying out certain important machinery casualty procedures.

Training Principles

The division officer must determine when, where, how, and by whom his training plan will be carried out. There are several general principles that are well to observe here. First and foremost, the instruction should be "on the job" as much as possible. During general quarters, condition watches, and routine underway and inport watches, at cleaning and maintenance stations, and at drills, there is time to conduct most of the required individual and team training. Petty officers must be taught how to take advantage of every opportunity for the training of subordinates. This point cannot be stressed too heavily; it is the key to efficient and relatively painless training. Many inexperienced young officers look upon training as something separate from day-to-day duties and then complain because they have no "time" for training. Training is an integral part of all the activities of your men. While cleaning, repairing, and maintaining spaces and equipment, your men, if properly supervised, should learn as they work. In addition, during the frequent, inevitable "standby" periods, instead of letting your men doze or just "rap," seize the opportunity for important training. For example, your division is standing by, at ease, for personnel inspection and may do so for some time before the inspecting party arrives. Do more than just read them a section of the *Uniform Code of Military Justice.* Organize a question and answer session on topics of interest to the men—such as the loss of veterans' benefits that accompany a bad conduct discharge, or the procedure for appealing a sentence at mast. There are dozens of topics that can be profitably discussed at an impromptu session of this sort, from the authority of shore patrol to next quarter's employment schedule. Damage control, NBC defense, federal housing loans for men on active duty, and the benefits and advantages of a naval career are just a few of the topics on which your men either should be informed or would like to be informed. Much of the knowledge gained by your men this way will pay off directly—as, for instance, in a future battle problem when all your men will be expected to know the rudiments of nuclear defense. If your men are standing by under less formal circumstances, such as a deck division during replenishment while the ship's approach is made, you can conduct first aid and resuscitation demonstrations and have each man checked out in certain minimum requirements. It is not hard to get the men interested in this sort of training by appealing to their self-interest, and it is far better to have them learn something useful than just to lounge around being bored. An alert, opportunistic attitude on training by a division officer need not be an annoyance for his men if their interest is aroused and if their leisure time after normal working hours is respected.

Each petty officer must be responsible for the training of the men under him during watches, on battle stations, and in all other situations where he exercises command. It should be made clear to the petty officers that training is one of their most important duties, and that their performance in this activity will be reflected in their marks for proficiency in rate and leadership in their evaluation sheets.

A second principle is that training must be planned, organized, and controlled. Instruction must be orderly and complete. To accomplish this, the division officer must first devote his time to a plan of instruction and to the proper indoctrination of the petty officer instructors.

A third principle of training is that it must not be rammed down the throats of the men; it must be presented logically, reasonably, and with a certain amount of salesmanship. The position of the division officer is sometimes a difficult one, since he is usually on the receiving end of a long and elaborate series of directives. If he permits himself to become stampeded by this pressure, he will defeat himself. Men can comprehend and retain just so much, and the amount depends to a large extent on their attitudes. If the reasons for the instruction are not obvious, explain them to the men. It is not difficult to relate all training to some need in battle, to necessary economies in material or labor, or to such matters of self-interest as personal survival. It is understandable that in the fast pace of day-to-day operations this need to keep the men informed is sometimes overlooked.

A fourth principle of division training is that the plan should be realistic and not too ambitious. It must be coordinated with the employment of the unit. Inexperienced officers sometimes try to do too much in order to have a comprehensive plan on paper to impress their superiors. This form of self-deception is rarely effective, even for a short time, and in the long run it is far less worthwhile than a modest plan well executed.

Effective Training

A successful division training program depends on a division officer who knows what he is trying to achieve and is enthusiastic about training his men. Enthusiasm is always infectious, and if you are really interested in molding a group of people into an effective fighting unit, they will respond. You can best display your interest by being present at as many training sessions or lectures as possible. You will have many duties aboard ship, but you have the advantage of being able to arrange your daily schedule to a great extent, so it is possible to get around the problem of your being called away from a training session by some foresighted planning.

One problem you will face in initiating a training program is the fact that you may not know as much on a particular subject as some of the men being trained under your direction. This is not as significant a problem as it might first appear. Your senior petty officers represent a reservoir of technical knowledge. Your job is to tap that reservoir and to apply their experience and know-how to the education of the less experienced men.

When you are assigned as a division officer, examine the training program already in effect. Satisfy yourself that it is effective, and that your people are getting better at their jobs as a result of the training. If your predecessor had a vigorous and successful program going, don't discard it out of hand just to change things. Sit down with the chief or leading petty officer and examine the whole program. See if it is complete, i.e., if it covers the requirements of the ship's training program. Does it complement the division's advancement-in-rate program? Is it going at the right pace, or should it be slowed, accelerated, or discarded altogether?

Ask yourself: are the men really interested or has their training become monotonous and mechanical? Size up your petty officers: do they really know more than their subordinates or are they out of their depth? Is the program attempting to cover something for which there is a specific formal school which might be better equipped to do the job? Search the catalog of Navy training courses for course descriptions which fit your area of training and compare what the schools offer with what you can accomplish on board.

These measures will get you involved, and the existing program will slowly become your program. Your departmental head has been there before you: discuss training with him and show him your proposals. In one sense you are competing for school time, and if you have an integrated and well balanced training program your chances are much better for convincing your department head that your men should get the school quotas.

Effective Speaking

Speaking to his men is something no division officer can escape. There will be a number of occasions when, in the course of the division training program, the division officer will wish to personally deliver a lecture or briefing. This can be a source of satisfaction or a source of embarrassment, depending on the officer's personality and experience. Speaking comes harder to some officers than others, but all can teach themselves to do a reasonably good job. The important point is to be relaxed, friendly, and natural. Look upon your speech as a sort of conversation, and talk in an easy manner directly to your men. At first, talk to and look at one man, forgetting the others. Then learn to address individuals in turn, shifting from one to another. Do not bother with introductory remarks or closing salutations. Do not tell jokes unless you are very sure of yourself, but do bring in all the humor and light touches that you appropriately can. Humor relaxes your audience, and their relaxation will relax you. Say what you have to say simply and sincerely, and you will get across. Avoid the pitfalls of profanity; most men may laugh at it, but they do not respect an officer who can only express himself by swearing. Above everything, avoid being trite and long-winded.

Speaking, like writing, is a basic way to communicate with people and is important to success in any profession. The surest way to learn to speak easily and effectively is to take every opportunity to do so. There are many opportunities to practice speaking in training situations. Lectures must be introduced and drills must be explained, and how well a drill goes may depend in large part on your ability to arouse motivation and interest. Your real opportunity to speak comes during the critique of an operation or event, where your words can impart the lessons learned in such a way that the time spent will not have been wasted.

All but the shortest and most informal talks should be outlined with notes made on the key points to be covered. It is good practice to rehearse the talk, but do not attempt to memorize it; refer freely to your notes. Rehearse it by writing it over two or three times. Try out your talk on a recorder if you have the time.

Training Instructors

The selection of instructors, and their training and supervision, is most important. The best designed training will be a resounding failure if poor instructors are inflicted upon your men. Choose petty officers who seem to be able to communicate. If they have not been to instructor training school, check them out as much in detail as possible yourself, using the *Manual for Navy Instructors* as a text. Remember that your men must be persuaded to learn; it takes a great deal of skill sometimes on the part of instructors to hold the interest of a group of men and teach them anything.

Imagination in Training

One important part of a division officer's training duties is divisional and departmental drills. Here your men must work as a team whether your group is involved in weapons, engineering, or tracking drills. The existence of a team allows you, as division officer, to use another technique of instruction, that of imagination to improve the degree of realism in drills.

If a feeling of vivid imagination can be caught by every last bluejacket in the organization, it will bring a dull drill to life. With this comes a spontaneous enthusiasm which affects every man it reaches, so that he tackles his job with a will that can come to him in no other way.

As actors respond with vivacity to an inspired director, so can the officer who leads with energy, enthusiasm, and a vivid imagination bring his drills to a state of reality which, even though temporary, can double their effectiveness. Beneath the truly inspired touch of such a leader, wholly imaginary enemy aircraft can maneuver in groups and singly, attack and retire, or fall in flames. Even lower handling-room crews will, in all seriousness, go about their jobs in two feet of simulated water.

An officer who takes up his job this way may find for the first few times that his men regard him as slightly eccentric. Once caught, however, the idea will spread, and progress will improve in proportion.

Group Discussions

An outstanding technique developed in the Navy for leadership training is known as group discussions. Small groups of men gather informally under a discussion leader such as the division officer, and talk over subjects of importance.

A topic is suggested and men are asked their opinions and reactions. Gradually, by pertinent questions and unobtrusive control, the leader encourages the men to come to some meaningful conclusions on the topic under discussion. The men's interest is aroused through their participation and, since they come to certain conclusions themselves, they tend to remember their conclusions and the lessons implicit therein.

This thumbnail sketch of a major training tool can only give you a vague idea of what it is. See the leadership material issued by BuPers. It may take some practice on your part as a division officer, even when using prepared material, to guide successfully a discussion group, but it is well worth learning. Men usually remember ideas they have expressed themselves or heard their shipmates express. Guided discusssions can be used to get across anything from the pitfalls of alcohol to the techniques of preparing for personnel inspection. Often on-the-job training-guided discussions are the most effective training method.

Weapons Exercises

Weapons exercises are probably the most important general drills conducted aboard a warship. They are held both in port and at sea, usually in a progression from walk-through rehearsals in port to live firings at sea. The ship's long-range training program schedules the exercises to be conducted; your job as a division officer is to see to it that your men are prepared individually and as members of their combat team to handle the drill and the eventual live firing.

The conduct of drills is particularly susceptible to effective management, in which the division officer is the key man. He knows best the state of training and readiness of his people and thus he is in the best position to organize weapons drills. In most ships the distinction between weapons and operations departments has blurred significantly. The operations department handles target detection, tracking, identification and finally, designation to a particular weapons system for engagement. The weapons team then acquires, tracks, solves the fire control problem, and launches weapons against the target. The management of this whole progression is in CIC; thus weapons exercises and the drills which prepare you for them are usually run in combination with operations drills, even when they are extremely rudimentary.

A good drill takes careful preparation. The division officer needs to know what he is trying to accomplish; i.e., know what his training objectives are for each man participating and for the team as a whole. There are many complex machines involved in weapons exercises, but men still run the machines and make the important decisions; they must know what your training objectives are, and what the drill is supposed to accomplish for them. You must explain what will take place, and describe the exercise. If it is being graded or evaluated, you must describe the evaluation points to your team. Above all, you as division officer should know the exercise thoroughly.

There are many training aids available which are useful in increasing the realism of drills, including audio tapes for sonarmen, video tapes for search and fire control radars, and complete battle problem scenarios for many different combat situations. Your department head makes a good adversary when you feel that your team is ready to handle unrestricted drills, for he can impose equipment and personnel casualties as your men run through the drill, so that an exercise which they know fairly well becomes quite realistic and challenging.

The basic rule of training still applies in actual drills—each man must know his own job before you can put the team together.

Emergency Drills

While emergency drills are scheduled by the ship or unit, the division officer has important responsibilities related to the performance of his men at these drills. As in almost every other activity in the Navy, successful drills are a product of intelligent and careful planning. If each division officer not only assigns his men accurately, but follows up to see whether or not the men really know their assignments, then even the first emergency drills held should be moderately successful. From here on, the division officer continues to instruct his men at their stations, and, most important of all, keeps his assignments up to date. As men are detached and new men report, an alert and careful check must be made at regular intervals (and always before getting underway) to see that the Watch, Quarter, and Station Bill is correct.

One factor of paramount importance in emergency drills is the manner in which they are conducted. Division officers must show the men why the drills are important. Aggressive and enthusiastic leadership is required to avoid the pitfalls of boring, lacka-daisical, and nonproductive drilling. Ideal drills are short, well planned, and chock full of purposeful activity.

Safety Instructions

> The Commanding Officer shall require that persons con-cerned are instructed and drilled in all applicable safety precau-tions and procedures, that these are complied with, and that applicable safety precautions, or extracts therefrom, are posted in appropriate places. In any instance where safety precautions have not been issued or are incomplete, he shall issue or aug-ment such safety precautions as he deems necessary, notifying, when appropriate, higher authorities concerned.—*U.S. Navy Regulations, 1973.*

Safety demands a special kind of training. The daily routine of handling ships, operating aircraft, and dealing with machinery and power tools all involve a certain amount of hazard. A divi-sion officer must shoulder a grave responsibility in this matter of safeguarding his men against accidental death and injury. It is not enough to know all the safety regulations and have them posted, or even to obey solely the letter of these rules. Safety must be taught and must be thought about; the division must be made safety conscious.

For example, it is not enough to see that men working over the side wear lifejackets. Each man should wear a kapok life-jacket, and the ties holding the collar up must be secured to sup-port the man's head above the water. Men have fallen into the water and been knocked unconscious. A kapok or fibrous glass-filled jacket with the collar tied will keep a man from drowning even when unconscious.

Ammunition, jet aircraft engines, aircraft propellers, fuel, chemical and atomic fission products—all these require special precautions which are listed in official publications.

Men must be kept alert at all times to the risks that surround them and their jobs. It is tough enough to lose your men in battle; it is worse to lose them in peacetime. The best way to avoid this is to keep pushing your safety training. The *Standard Organization and Regulations of the U.S. Navy,* Article 351, states, "A division officer will . . . carefully instruct his subordinates in all applicable safety precautions, and require their strict observance." For full details on shipboard safety see OpNavInst 5100.19, *Navy Safety Precautions Manual for Forces Afloat.*

Electric Shock

The use of privately owned electrical equipment on board naval ships creates a fire hazard as well as a hazard to the personal safety of the individual using such equipment. In addition, radios, phonographs, and other electronic equipment have emissive properties which may compromise the radio security of the ship. Therefore, no privately owned electrical equipment may be used on board naval ships except that specifically authorized by the ship's executive officer only after it has been inspected and approved by the engineer officer or his designated representative. The electronic material officer will make a similar inspection of all electronic equipment.

A steel ship is quite different from a house in its ability to conduct electricity. Most of us learn to handle electrical appliances at home, and may learn many habits that can be fatal aboard ship. Standing on a dry wooden floor at home is quite different from standing on a steel deck; the latter is usually an excellent conductor. The careless handling of ungrounded tools has led to considerable loss of life in the Navy. Even though grounded receptacles are now supposed to be standard equipment, there may be one that has been missed in your spaces. Or one of your men may bring aboard a small iron or coffee pot, and may electrocute himself before someone ensures that it is inspected and fitted with a grounded plug. Look up your ship's directive on this subject and impress on your men how much more dangerous an electrical accident can be aboard ship than ashore.

Safety Training

Because of the important nature of shipboard safety and safety training, the ship's commanding officer will have set up a safety program, under a safety officer, to implement Navy safety policies and procedures. The safety program will provide for dissemination of general shipboard safety precautions, instruction of personnel subject to special hazards, and for the supervision of personnel in matters of safety. It is your responsibility to implement this program within your division. Among other things, this requires that you appoint a senior petty officer, E-6 or above if available, to act as division safety petty officer, and that you ensure that your men receive accident prevention training. See Chapter 7 of the *Standard Organization and Regulations of the U.S. Navy* for a specific listing of your safety duties.

Your division training program must include a systematic approach to accident prevention, and should make use of such assistance as Navy training films, safety notes, and various publications issued by the Navy Safety Center. Your instruction should be tailored to the ship's schedule, to cover items of interest at appropriate times. For example, a shipyard overhaul, getting underway after a long inport period, and seasonal or unusual weather changes are a few things that should prompt a particular training session. As a minimum, your training program must include the following subjects, from Chapter 7 of the *Standard Organization and Regulations of the U.S. Navy*:

Electrical Safety
Damage Control/Firefighting
Industrial/Job Related Safety
Protective Devices/Equipment
Explosive Ordnance Safety/Ammunition Handling
Hazardous Materials
Fuels
Boat Handling/Deck Seamanship/Cargo Handling
Small Arms Training
Personal Hygiene/First Aid
Food Service
Toxic Gas/Oxygen Deficiency
Motor Vehicle Safety
Recreational Safety
Aviation Safety

Under the heading of safety may also be listed "Survival Training." World War II taught us that many lives can be saved if men are taught how to bail out of an airplane, how to abandon ship, how to act in a plane which makes a crash landing, how to keep themselves afloat, how to live in the jungle or on a small island, how to avoid flash burn, etc. Much of this training is given in schools but it should be reviewed on board ship. The *Bureau of Naval Personnel Manual* includes a pertinent section on survival. A more elaborate treatment of the subject is contained in *How to Survive on Land and Sea*.

Personnel Qualification Standards (PQS)

The Navy has developed a new tool for shipboard training, the Personnel Qualification Standards. These standards are written to describe all of the skills and knowledge a sailor needs to do a particular job. They are somewhat similar to programmed texts in that they provide a detailed, step-by-step breakdown of the learning process; however, the Personnel Qualification Standards contain no answers. They are something like an exam; the standards tell a man what he needs to know and what he should study, and allow him to prove what he has learned.

The Personnel Qualification Standards were developed as the need to provide detailed training guidance became apparent. In the past, such guidance had been provided on a continuous basis by officers and petty officers. But as the Navy's ships and aircraft became increasingly sophisticated while the operating schedules remained rigorous, it became increasingly difficult for the officers and petty officers to provide detailed direction to their men. To assist in this task, PQS was developed.

The PQS program is designed to be an element of the ship's training program. It will not supersede the division training normally conducted, but it will act as a guide for much of the maintenance and watchstations training. The division officer will still have to schedule and conduct his own training program, but the Personnel Qualification Standard will be a part of it. The Personnel Qualification Standard is broken down into several sections:

Introduction
Glossary of Qualification Standard Terms
Table of Contents
100 Series - Theory
200 Series - Systems
300 Series - Watchstations
400 Series - Qualification Cards
Bibliography
Feedback Forms

The format and organization of the Personnel Qualification Standard is explained in the Introduction. Throughout the PQS system the terminology has been standardized, and the key terms and phrases are defined in the glossary. The Theory section specifies the background information that the man should become familiar with before proceeding. For example, the Division Officer PQS Planned Maintenance Subsystem Theory section asks the division officer to:

Explain the following terms and how the contents of each are used:
a) MRC (Maintenance Requirement Card)
b) EGL (Equipment Guide List)
c) . . .

The 200 series, Systems, then breaks the material down into sections which can be studied and tested separately. Continuing with the previous example of the division officer PQS, the division officer is asked to: "Explain the purpose and objectives of the PMS (Planned Maintenance Subsystem) as stated in the 3-M Manual (OpNavInst 4790.4, Volume I)."

The Watchstations section asks the man to work with the system, to operate or maintain it. For the Division Officer 3-M requirements, he is asked to: "Fill out the weekly schedule," "Record a completed maintenance requirement on the weekly schedule," and so on.

Finally the 400 series, Qualification Cards, are used as a record of achievement. The cards are packaged separately and are pocket-sized to encourage the man to carry them with him. Doing so will allow the student to take advantage of training opportunities as they arise.

PQS Implementation Status

Personnel Qualification Standards have been written and implemented for a large number of systems within the fleet. A full listing is contained in CNET NOTICE 3500; new additions are also noted in CAMPUS Magazine. Some examples of the Personnel Qualification Standards that are implemented are:

600 PSI Steam Propulsion Plant
1200 PSI Steam Propulsion Plant (for several major ship types)
Damage Control
Deck/Underway Replenishment
Navigation/Ship Control
Communication Receivers
Communication Transmitters
Electronics Countermeasures

Additional Personnel Qualifications Standards are slated for development through fiscal year 1978. The list of standards available is extensive and covers the majority of shipboard systems.

PQS Record Keeping

Under the PQS system, the Qualification Card, (carried by the man), and the Qualification Progress Record Chart form the necessary records. The progress record chart shows each man's progress toward qualification for each watch he is training for. As each man completes his entire qualification package and is certified by his commanding officer, a page 4 service record entry is made.

To avoid duplication in record keeping, the completion of training that is covered by PQS need not be recorded elsewhere. For the areas where PQS is implemented, the following records may be eliminated:

Division Drill Schedule
Off-Ship Training Record
Individual Record of Off-Ship School Training
Group Record of Practical Factors
Supplementary Record of Equipment Qualification
Record of Qualifications at Watch/Battle Stations
Individual Drill Record

This means that the division officer will be maintaining two sets of records; one for the PQS covered areas (the Qualification Progress Record Chart), and the other, standard records, for any additional shipboard training.

Newly Reported Personnel

Enlisted Sponsor Program

When a man is ordered from one duty station to another, he will fill out a sponsor program form, on which he indicates whether or not he desires his new command to appoint a sponsor for him. If he does, the new command will usually designate a petty officer of equal rank from his prospective division, who becomes the man's point of contact with his new station. A man may hesitate to write to the executive officer, but will feel quite at ease "getting the dope" from someone he will work with at the new ship or station. The sponsor is asked to write to the new man, usually at his leave address, and send him a standardized packet of information on the ship or station, housing, quarters information, the ship's schedule, etc., which is provided by the personnel office. The division officer is notified when a sponsor is being arranged, and he should help the sponsor; it is not difficult, and it makes a very good impression on a newly reporting man when the command takes the initiative in helping him out.

Orientation Training

The indoctrination of newly reported personnel into the division is an important and necessary task of the division officer. Frequently the new man will be assigned to I division upon reporting to the ship. I division functions administratively under the executive officer and is formed for the orientation of new men. Its purpose is to instruct these men in their individual responsibilities, duties, and opportunities, and to acquaint them with departmental and special office facilities and functions. The I division officer will coordinate training for the new personnel on such matters as the ship's mission, organization, regulations, schedule, and advancement and educational opportunities. However, since the number of new men fluctuates at any given time, I division may be discontinued from time to time. In any event, the continued indoctrination of newly reported personnel is a responsibility of the division officer.

Once the man has completed his indoctrination with I division, there still remains the task of orienting the man in the division to which he is assigned. It is very important to take your new men in hand as soon as they report aboard. This is especially true of recruits, who are more easily squared away if some of the polish of the recruit training center is still upon them. One way of introducing a new man is to assign him a selected "buddy" to show him the ropes. Needless to say, the "old hand" selected should be one whose appearance, conduct, performance, and attitude are worthy of imitation.

The new man should be shown around the ship, squadron, or station, and should be fitted out with a bunk, locker, and a place on the Watch, Quarter, and Station Bill as soon as practicable. Positive means, such as a checkoff list, should be used to ensure that the new man has passed over all his administrative hurdles, from having his identification card checked to getting his inoculations up to date.

The last and most important step in the orientation program for the man is a personal interview with his division officer. This interview may be postponed for some good reason, but should never be omitted. In a very large unit this task of personal interviewing could be shared with a responsible assistant such as a junior division officer. It is well to review each man's record and health record before you speak to him.

The interview has three major objectives: to establish your position of leadership and responsibility in the mind of the man; to find out any special characteristics or aptitudes that are not revealed in his record; and to show the man that you have a personal interest in him. The interview should be friendly, not too formal, but thorough. Notes should be taken which can be used in assigning the man to duty.

Starting a new man off with the right attitude is a tremendous advantage for you—not only insofar as training is concerned but in possible disciplinary troubles as well. New men, fresh from recruit training, are bound to fall in with some of the less-talented types in your unit, who will try to tell them that everything written down in *The Bluejackets' Manual* is not necessarily gospel truth. They may be tempted to believe that the smart way to get along is to avoid work and look for a soft job. This is why it is particularly important to get new men squared away on the proper track. By showing your new man that you are interested in him as a person and in his plans and ambitions and at the same time making it plain what you expect from him, you make it much more difficult for him to accept poor advice from some of his new shipmates.

Basic Skills

Usually, most newly enlisted men reporting aboard ship are designated strikers. They have gone straight from recruit training to a Class "A" school and possess the basic skills of this rate. (This is true for practically all technical ratings such as operations specialist, radioman, fire control technician, electrician, missile technician, and gunners mate.) This greatly simplifies training, since they will already know something about the equipment aboard your ship. What they will need more than anything else is on-the-job experience, training in military duties and watchstanding within their rate, and indoctrination aboard ship. They will be standing quarterdeck watches, have fire party assignments, replenishment and sea detail stations, and many other duties not covered in school. This kind of training is also your responsibility, whether or not you personally supervise it.

You control their time and their working day, and thus you will have to work with other division officers (such as the damage control assistant in the case of fire party training) to round out their training as seagoing sailors.

Many ships have a policy of sending all reporting seamen, whether designated or not, to the deck force for a few months of indoctrination. The gentle tutelage of the leading boatswain's mate will be quite a variation from the technical themes of the "A" schools, but men will learn their way around the ship and acquire some important basic skills useful, for instance, during an underway replenishment. One point here: if you are, for example, OI division officer, and there are OSSNs assigned temporarily to the deck division, see to it that the chief or leading petty officer contacts them to let them know that their ultimate division is interested in them. You can arrange for an after-hours, small-scale indoctrination program in their prospective rate without interfering with their deck division duties, or, at the very least, tours of their future divisional spaces and equipment.

General Military Training

General military training is another responsibility of the division officer. It is by nature nontechnical and applicable to all ratings. This training properly conducted can improve the sailor's appreciation of his role in the Navy, both as a member of a combat unit and as an individual citizen. OpNavInst 1500.22 series lays down these objectives of general military training:

1. An appreciation of the unique role of the U.S. Navy in American history, including its contributions to peace-keeping.
2. An awareness of the benefits, rewards, and responsibilities of a professional career in the Navy.
3. An appreciation of the fundamental principles of American government and the forces which threaten its security.
4. An appreciation of the rights and obligations of citizenship— at home and overseas.

5. An awareness of Navy policy, personal responsibility, and assistance available in the conduct of personal affairs.
6. An understanding of the principles, practices, and techniques of naval leadership.
7. An awareness of the medical, legal, and social aspects of drug, nicotine, and alcohol abuse, and physical inactivity.

The division officer can definitely contribute to this program by his personal interest and guidance. He should act as moderator or lecturer during these military training sessions. The OpNav Instruction 1500.22 in its enclosures, along with BuPers Notice 1560, provides many aids to the discussion leader by listing various topics, a topic outline, and reference materials available. Of all training conducted on board ship, these subjects, if properly organized, will prove to be the most interesting, informative, and challenging. The challenge is to the division officer since the material at first glance appears so fundamental that everyone should already be familiar with it. A second, deeper inspection will indicate how little we really do know about the origins of our government, the reasons for certain policies, and all those other things we take for granted. You, as division officer, will find at first a challenge and then satisfaction in being able to lead your men in down-to-earth discussions of what the Navy is all about. Each of them will gain, as he participates, a deeper understanding of why his job matters, what his ship is doing, and how the whole success depends upon the smooth functioning of each part. Don't slight this opportunity to learn why, and then pass this "big picture" on to your men. The last subject—drug and alcohol abuse— merits some additional emphasis here. Drug and alcohol misuse is increasingly prevalent in our society, and consequently finds its way into the Navy as well. The division officer can play an effective role in educating his personnel in the hazards involved, both to the man and to his ship. Hopefully, an increased awareness of the problem, and of the Navy's programs for dealing with it, will help reduce and eventually eliminate drug and alcohol abuse within the Navy. (See the Human Goals Program in Chapter 8 for guidance in these areas.)

A firm foundation in these fundamentals of general military

training makes everyday and each task take on new meaning. As each man gains understanding, his gripes become fewer. His unit pride grows as the role of his unit takes on new meaning.

Advancement in Rating

A major part of a division officer's training activities is concerned with the advancement of the men in their rating. Almost without exception, advancements are made on the job, that is, as a result of in-service education and training. This is one of the factors that makes division officers so important in the Navy. They are the key people in the whole system of growth in skill and education which is so vital to the efficiency of the fleet. The Navy has little use for men with no skills and will, in the future, have even less use for just "laborers."

First of all, officers and petty officers must encourage their men to prepare themselves for advancement. At times, men—particularly, young men—will be reluctant to work for promotion. They may feel that the increased pay is not enough incentive, and that the increased responsibilities and complications of a higher rate are not worthwhile. One obvious cure for this lack of a desire to be promoted is to increase the position and prestige of petty officers. Petty officers should be treated by the division officers as junior assistants; they should be allowed to pass the "word" to their own men, and should be given all practicable privilege in regard to leave and liberty, bunk and locker space, and so forth. Responsible petty officers should be asked for their recommendations for promotion of the men under them. They should be convinced that only those who have earned it should be recommended. The men should be fully aware that their leading petty officers make these recommendations on the basis of merit and that the standards for recommendations are high.

A generally reliable method of influencing men to advance themselves is to explain the long term benefits which will result. Remind them that men with superior education can usually advance themselves more quickly in all walks of life. A division officer must provide his men with exact information on all requirements for advancement. Every ship, squadron, and station ashore has copies of the Bureau of Naval Personnel publications and effective letters which give this information in detail. This material must be given to the men; they should not have to dig for it themselves.

The division officer follows definite, prescribed procedures which are set up by BuPers for advancement. A brief outline of eligibility requirements for advancement in rating is furnished for guidance.

Service Requirements are those which relate to required time in rate and rating before a man can be eligible for advancement. Current service requirements are as follows:

Pay Grade	Time in Grade	Time in Service
E-1 to E-2	4 months	4 months
E-2 to E-3	8 months	1 year
E-3 to E-4	6 months	2 years
E-4 to E-5	1 year	3 years
E-5 to E-6	2 years	6 years
E-6 to E-7	3 years	8 years
E-7 to E-8	3 years	11 years
E-8 to E-9	2 years	13 years

Completion of Practical Factors demonstrates a man's knowledge of the Navy and his proficiency in rating to the satisfaction of his superiors. In order to provide a uniform set of standards for all enlisted men, certain military requirements and professional qualifications have been established. The military requirements section contains requirements on such subjects as customs, international agreements, security regulations, or career information, and are applicable to all ratings. The professional qualifications section, *Manual of Qualifications for Advancement*, sets forth the practical and knowledge factors appropriate to each individual rating. The Record of Practical Factors (NavPers Form 760) has been devised to simplify record-keeping and affords a check-off list for the practical military requirements and professional qualifications for each rating. A copy of this record must be maintained for each man until he has completed all requirements and evidence of this is entered in his service record.

Completion of Navy Training Courses prepares enlisted men for advancement. These courses cover most of the ratings and also the military requirements. They are primarily designed to satisfy the knowledge-factor qualifications and are an invaluable aid in preparing for advancement. Completion of certain Navy training courses is mandatory except in cases wherein certain schools have been satisfactorily completed. Division officers should consult *Training Publications for Advancement*, NavPers 10052, to determine which courses are mandatory in order for their men to be eligible for advancement. This publication also lists study material and courses which are recommended for each rating. This information should be made available to your men.

Required Service Schools apply to certain ratings, i.e., hospital corpsmen, dental technicians, and musicians.

Recommendation of the Commanding Officer is the most important requirement for advancement in rating. If the man has completed all other requirements and is in the proper path of advancement, he must still be recommended for advancement by his commanding officer before he is eligible to compete in the service-wide advancement examinations. He must be considered by his senior petty officers as capable of performing the duties of the higher rate, and have an overall performance mark of not less than 3.0. The division officer must necessarily act as primary adviser to assist the commanding officer in making this decision. The division officer, in turn, should solicit the opinions of responsible petty officers to insure that each man gets fair consideration.

Career Counseling

The career counseling program is a definite asset to the training program, because it provides a single source of information on the wide variety of career programs. Each ship will have a BuPers assigned career counselor who will supervise and coordinate the program under the direction of the executive officer. Working for him in collateral duty billets are departmental and divisional career counselors, who become contact points for men in the various divisions. The career counselor has all the information on programs such as SCORE (Selected Conversion and Retention), GUARD (Guaranteed Assignment Retention Detailing), Nuclear Power Training, and NESEP (Navy Enlisted Scientific Education Program). The career counselor will periodically interview your men to determine career intentions, inform them of Navy programs, and so on.

When a man has less than six months of obligated service remaining, he will automatically be interviewed by the career counselor. The idea here is to have division officers identify the best prospects for retention in the Navy; such men are then given a comprehensive look at what the Navy has to offer them. The career counselor in a sense works for division officers in that he is familiar with all the programs, while the division officers know which of their men are best fitted for retention. Obviously, only the best men are wanted in career programs.

Training for Officer Status

Leading petty officers should be given some training that not only will assist them in improving their present performance, but will fit them for duties of greater importance—perhaps promotion to warrant or commissioned status. There are various programs outlined in BuPers Instruction 1000.7 that enable enlisted men to obtain such promotion. The division officer shares the responsibility for bringing these programs to the attention of eligible men and assisting them as necessary in submitting applications and meeting requirements.

A course in the duties of the division officer, using this guide as a text, might be appropriate. Emphasis should be placed on teaching petty officers how to train their men. Talks on leadership problems and topics of current interest are also recommended. Such subjects as the meaning of a commission, the role of the Navy, principles of the American way of life, and the Constitution would be helpful. The Department of Defense distributes pamphlets on such subjects, as well as the excellent *Armed Forces Officer*.

A pitfall to be particularly avoided in officer training is boring the students with material that is either already familiar to them or is badly presented.

Educational Services Program

A word or two concerning the Educational Services Program may be pertinent here. This program is set up on a ship or station basis, but can succeed only if it is actively supported and encouraged by the division officer. The purpose of the educational services program is to raise the educational level of all active duty Navy men. This will in turn increase their value both to the Navy and to the country. To this end the educational services officer assists personnel in obtaining high school, college, business, and military education credits. He will conduct high school equivalency tests, sponsored by the Defense Activities Non-Traditional Educational Support Office. He may organize off-duty classes in English, mathematics, and foreign languages as the men's interests dictate. He will work with the division officer in executing the program and in conducting the necessary counseling and interviews.

Educational benefits available through the Veterans Administration are now extended to active duty men, and offer them undergraduate or graduate courses at most colleges. Such benefits can be a great retention factor, as a man can obtain a college degree while on active duty rather than waiting until he is discharged. Consult the Educational Services officer in all matters relating to formal education for your men.

Training Directives

Training directives are originated by the Chief of Naval Operations, under whose direction training policies are made and responsibilities fixed for both shore and shipboard training. All training activities with the exception of medical training have been combined under the command of the Chief of Naval Education and Training. Fleet commanders, through their training commanders and type commanders, are responsible for the conduct of shipboard operational and team training ashore.

Training References

[Note: The following sources—apart from the periodicals—are under almost constant revision. Publications are also being reissued under Chief of Naval Education and Training [NavEd-Tra] numbers, as they are revised or rewritten. Try to obtain the latest copies.]

General

Bureau of Naval Personnel Manual (NavPers 15791), Section 66 (Education)
Educational Services Manual (NavPers 15229)
Fleet Training Command Publications and Directives
General Military Training (OpNavInst 1500.22)
Handbook on Personnel Qualification Standards (NavTra 43100)
Manual of Navy Enlisted Classifications (NavPers 15105)
Opportunities Available to Enlisted Personnel (NavPers 15124)
Fleet Exercise Publications (FXP 1, FXP 2, FXP 3)
Fleet and type training manuals and instructions
Naval Training Bulletin (NavPers 14900) (quarterly publication)
BuPers instructions and notices series 1100, 1400, and 1500
Career Counselling Guide (NavPers 15878)
Career Information Counselling Kit (NavPers 15959)
All Hands (monthly magazine)
Navy Times (weekly newspaper)

Advancement in Rating

Bureau of Naval Personnel Manual (NavPers 15791), Section 22 (Enlisted Personnel Advancement and Change of Rate or Rating)
Bibliography for Advancement Study (NavEdTra 10052)
List of Training Manuals and Correspondence Courses (NavEd-Tra 10061)
Manual of Advancement (BuPers Instruction 1430.16)
Manual of Qualifications for Advancement (NavPers 18068)
Training Publications for Advancement (NavPers 10052)

Schools

Catalog of Navy Training Courses (NavEdTra 10500)
United States Naval Postgraduate School Catalogue

Information and Education

Catalog of Programmed Instructional Material (NavPers 93826)
A Guide to the Evaluation of Educational Experiences in the Armed Services, American Council on Education (also their newsletter of the Commission on Accreditation of Service Experiences)
Educational Services Manual (NavPers 15229)

Instructor Training

Manual for Navy Instructors (NavPers 16103)
Military Requirements for Petty Officer 3 & 2 (NavPers 10056), Chapter 14
Military Requirements for Petty Officer 1 & C (NavPers 10057), Chapter 6

Training Aids

Catalogue of Navy Training Film for U.S. Navy and Marine Corps (NavWeps 10-1-777)
OpNav Instruction 1551.3 (Training Aids and Devices; information and procurement)
United States Navy Film Catalogs (NavAir 10-1-777)
Training Devices Guide (NavExos P-530-2)
Catalog of Information Materials, Armed Forces Information and Education, Department of Defense (NavPers 92140)
Leadership Support Manual (NavPers 15934)

Special Programs and Services

The men in your division will come to you with all kinds of problems and requests for information on a wide range of subjects. You are not expected to know all the answers, but you should be able to assure a man you can help him, and find the answer. A great number of publications and instructions are available on board ship, and will be useful in handling such cases. Following are some of the subjects on which men may question you, with an official source of information on each:

ADVANCEMENT	NAVPERS	15878
IN RATE	BUPERSINST	1430.16
General	BUPERSMAN	2230120
Requirements	BUPERSNOTE	1418
	BUPERSNOTE	1430
Recommendations for	BUPERSMAN	3410150
based on Navy wide examinations	BUPERSMAN	2230160
advancement after reduction in rate	BUPERSMAN	2230200
ALL HANDS RIGHTS & BENEFITS	NAVPERS	15885C
AVIATION OFFICER CANDIDATE (AOC) PROGRAM	BUPERSMAN	6610360
	BUPERSINST	1120.35
BOOST (Broadened Officer Selection	BUPERSMAN	1020360
and Training)	BUPERSNOTE	1500
CHANGE IN RATE OR RATING	BUPERSINST	1430.16
	BUPERSMAN	1060010
	BUPERSMAN	2230180
	BUPERSINST	1133.25
CHOICE OF DUTY REQUESTS	TRANSMAN	2, 27
	NAVPERS	15980
	BUPERSNOTE	1306
COLLEGE	NAVPERS	15878
Early Separation	BUPERSMAN	3850220
to attend	BUPERSMAN	3830100
GI Bill	NAVPERS	15229
PACE	*NAVPERS	15229
NESEP	BUPERSMAN	1020350
NENEP	BUPERSINST	1120.37
NEDEP	BUPERSINST	1120.38

Tuition Assistance	NAVPERS	15229
Scholarship Program	SECNAVINST	1500.4
NROTC Scholarship Program	OPNAVNOTE	1533
COLLEGE DEGREE PROGRAM (Officer)	OPNAVINST	1520.20
COMPARATIVE OCCUPATIONAL PAY BRIEFS	NAVPERS	15878
	NAVPERS	18436
EDUCATIONAL/CAREER OPPORTUNITIES FOR ENLISTED MEMBERS	NAVPERS	15124D
EDUCATIONAL SERVICES	NAVPERS	15229
EQUAL OPPORTUNITY	SECNAVINST	5350.6B
EXAMINATIONS		
Advancement in Rate	BUPERSINST	1430.16
Classification	BUPERSMAN	1440220
Retake Basic Battery	BUPERSMAN	1440260
GENERAL EDUCATION DEVELOPMENT	BUPERSMAN	5030280
GENERAL MILITARY TRAINING (GMT)	CNT NOTE	1560
	OPNAVINST	1500.22
GENEVA CONVENTION CARD	BUPERSMAN	4620100
GI BILL	NAVPERS	15229
	NAVPERS	15878
GUARD (Guaranteed Assignment Retention Detailing Program)	BUPERSNOTE	1133
	NAVPERS	15878
LIMITED DUTY OFFICER PROGRAM	BUPERSMAN	1020290
NAVAL ACADEMY PROGRAM	BUPERSMAN	1020220
	NAVPERS	15878
NAVAL FLIGHT OFFICER CANDIDATE (NFOC) PROGRAM	BUPERINST	1120.35
NAVAL RESERVE PROGRAM	NAVPERS	15878

NAVY EQUAL OPPORTUNITY MANUAL	OPNAVINST	5354.1
NAVY RACE RELATIONS EDUCATION	OPNAVINST	1500.42
NEDEP (Navy Enlisted Dietetic Education Program)	BUPERSINST	1120.38
NENEP (Navy Enlisted Nursing Education Program)	BUPERSINST	1120.37
NESEP (Navy Enlisted Scientific Education Program)	BUPERSMAN	1020350
NROTC PROGRAM	CNET	153313
	CNET	P153313
NUCLEAR PROGRAM	NAVPERS	15878
Nuclear Field Program	BUPERSINST	1306.64
Nuclear Power Training Program	TRANSMAN	11
Nuclear Propulsion Training	BUPERSMAN	1050300
	BUPERSMAN	6610300
Nuclear Weapons Personnel Reliability Program (PRP)	BUPERSINST	5510.11
Nuclear Petty Officer Continuation Pay	SECNAVINST	7220.72
Incentive Pay	BUPERSMAN	2620150
OCS PROGRAM	NAVPERS	15878
	BUPERSINST	1120.35
PACE (Program for Afloat College Education)	NAVPERS	15229
	NAVPERS	15878
PEP (Personnel Exchange Program)	NAVPERS	15878
	NAVOP	80
	OPNAVINST	5700.7
	NAVPERS	15980

POSTGRADUATE PROGRAM (Officer)	SECNAVINST	1520.4
	BUPERSNOTE	1520
PRACTICAL FACTORS	BUPERSMAN	2230120
	BUPERSMAN	5030280
	NAVPERS	18068
PREP (Predischarge Education Program)	OPNAVINST	1560.5
	NAVPERS	15878
PREPARATORY SCHOOLS		
NESEP	BUPERSMAN	1020350
Naval Academy	OPNAVINST	1531.3
BOOST	BUPERSMAN	1020360
Military/Air Force Academies	BUPERSMAN	6620120
QUALIFICATIONS		
Enlisted	NAVPERS	18068
Officer	NAVPERS	15839
RACE RELATIONS EDUCATION (RRE)	OPNAVNOTE	1500
RACE RELATIONS FOR ARMED FORCES PERSONNEL; DOD Education in	DODINST	1322.11
REDUCTION IN RATE	BUPERSMAN	2230100
	BUPERSMAN	3420140
REEMPLOYMENT RIGHTS	BUPERSINST	1571.16
	NAVPERS	15878
SCHOLARSHIPS		
Navy Scholarship Program	SECNAVINST	1500.4
Navy Medical Osteopathic Scholarship	BUPERSINST	1520.104
Navy Dental Scholarship	BUPERSINST	1520.105
Dependents	BUPERSMAN	6210110
	NAVPERS	15003
NROTC	OPNAVNOTE	1533
STAR (Selective Training & Reenlistment)	BUPERSMAN	1060020

SCORE (Selective Conversion & Reenlistment)	BUPERSMAN	1060010
	NAVPERS	15878
	NAVPERS	15980
SWAPS	TRANSMAN	16
	NAVPERS	15980
TUITION AID	NAVPERS	15229
	NAVPERS	15878
UNDERGRADUATE PROGRAM (Officer)	OPNAVINST	1520.21

You may have noticed that the BUPERSMAN (Bureau of Naval Personnel Manual) appears many times in the above list. Because the contents of this publication govern the administration of Navy personnel, many of the questions your men ask can be answered by reference to it. Normally the personnelmen aboard ship will be available to answer questions relating to the BUPERSMAN but the division officer who has a knowledge of its contents will be better able to advise his men.

A companion publication to the BUPERSMAN is the Enlisted Transfer Manual (TRANSMAN). It is the official manual on the distribution and assignment of enlisted personnel, subjects of vital concern to your men. A familiarity with the TRANSMAN will work to your advantage.

6/Discipline

A Division Officer will . . . be responsible, under the head of his department, for the proper performance of the duties assigned to his division and for the conduct of his subordinates, in accordance with regulations and the orders of the commanding officer and other superiors.
—*Standard Organization and Regulations of the U.S. Navy.*

High standards in performance and discipline are vital to battlefield success—high standards not just in military proficiency and physical fitness, but in military appearance, in military courtesy, and in the cleanliness and squared-away appearance of the area where we live, work, and train, all a reflection of individual and group discipline. The true professional is aware that these standards are not ends in themselves, that in fact, they are the means by which we breed pride, and that pride, in turn, builds the kind of discipline that is essential to victory.
—General L. F. Chapman, Jr., 24th Commandant, U.S. Marine Corps.

Discipline has many definitions, one of which is punishment, but the most important meaning is expressed by the term *attitude*. Good conduct, high morale, and smart appearance are always the results of good discipline, and a high state of discipline is the direct result of the right kind of attitude on the part of the men. You as a division officer are responsible for the conduct and appearance of your men. When your men shoot a high score during weapons practice or present a perfect appearance at captain's inspection, you take the credit, and quite rightly so. Similarly, when your men fail to look their best or when some of them get into trouble with the masters-at-arms or with the civil authorities ashore, you must accept the implication that you have not done your job properly. Either you have not informed or indoctrinated your men thoroughly or you have not succeeded in persuading them that it pays to look well or to behave properly.

Good Discipline Depends on the Right Attitude

The right attitude makes the men willing, eager, and determined to follow orders, to fight courageously, to behave in a military manner, and to take pride in their Navy, in their ship, and especially in their division. It is a fair assumption that most Navy men, by and large, have the right attitude. The fighting reputation of the Navy throughout its history is proof of this spirit. It is the small percentage that seems to be always out of step that causes the trouble. *Standard Organization and Regulations of the U.S. Navy* and the *Uniform Code of Military Justice* are written for this small group. On them we shall focus our attention. Remember the primary reason for having a Navy is also the reason for maintaining a well-disciplined ship: combat readiness.

Responsible Supervision by Petty Officers

For the relatively few men who never seem to get the word, who leave their gear adrift, who tend to go over leave, who can be counted on to appear at mast regularly—for these men there is only one answer: responsible supervision. If these few problem men are not concentrated, but are scattered throughout the division, and if the petty officers are on the job, they can usually be straightened out. It often takes hard work and ingenuity on the part of the petty officers to do it; but if a man deserves the rate of petty officer, he must be able, above all, to direct his men in productive work and maintain good order and discipline. This does not mean, of course, that the petty officer should be permitted to haze or mistreat his men, or to assign punishments such as extra duty. But by example, by reason and persuasion, by his influence in recommending promotions, and by his power of assigning duties and working details, the petty officer has ample means to convince a man that being a contributing member of the team is the best way to enhance his own position and increase his privileges.

Petty officers, being human, very often do not take the necessary positive action. One of their men may look seedy at inspection. Here is where that word "responsible" comes in again. The petty officer must be convinced that he is personally and directly responsible for the conduct and appearance of his men. If this conviction cannot be established, he should be removed from his position of responsibility and his ability to perform the duties of a petty officer should be seriously considered. It appears, then, that the first step in attaining a highly disciplined unit is to train the petty officers to accept their responsibilities.

One of these responsibilities in connection with discipline is keeping the men informed. The men must be kept informed of ship's orders and of all directives which might affect their conduct. For example, if the time of expiration of liberty is changed at the last minute because the ship is getting underway sooner than expected, it is important to inform every man going ashore about the change, and, if possible, the reasons therefor.

The second step is to increase the prestige and authority of the petty officers. One way to do this is to put out the word to your petty officers first. Any changes in the employment schedule, any special tasks, entertainment, or events, should first be revealed to the petty officers, who can pass it down the line.

Let the petty officers know that they have a share and a voice in the management of the division. This can be done in many small ways without interfering in the least with the military authority of the division officers. For example, your division may be allotted 15 tickets to an entertainment ashore. Divide the tickets among your petty officers for distribution. They will be gratified by your confidence in them, and the men will note that rewards, as well as working details, flow from petty officers. Another way to increase the prestige and authority of your petty officers is to grant them special consideration in locker and bunk space, leave and liberty, etc. Sometimes these matters are outside of the province of the division officer, but often there will be small marks of confidence and trust that an alert division officer can show his petty officers. Above all, the division officer must back his petty officers in all matters. Even if he does not completely approve of how some affair was handled, there is always time later to tell the responsible petty officer privately how the matter could have been handled better.

Punishment is Not Discipline

Punishment, the second term associated with discipline, is often incorrectly used as a synonym. The two words should not be confused. Punishment occurs as a result of a *failure of discipline*. A perfectly disciplined military unit would have no trials by court-martial, no captain's mast; in short, it would have no punishment. Punishment, especially the fear of punishment, is an important factor in the conduct, appearance, and performance of any military unit. With all proper emphasis on the right attitude to be developed in men, and on concern for their needs, their well-being, and their dignity as individuals, it must not be thought that the efficient administration of a division is an easy task which will always bring more rewards than frustrations. You must maintain a balance between understanding and permissiveness. Once that balance is lost it is a painful process to regain it.

People can, for many reasons, be careless, irresponsible, and sometimes downright nasty. Such offenses as gross disrespect for authority, wilful disobedience, and sleeping on watch must be punished swiftly, impartially, and sternly. These offenses are matters which require the attention of the commanding officer. In case of such offenses, it is particularly important in its effect on the other men that punishment be administered quickly. The division officer must make a thorough investigation of the circumstances and should be prepared at captain's mast to throw all possible light on the offense. The division officer may be asked there for an estimate of the man's reputation or for a recommendation regarding punishment. In the recommending or awarding of punishment in disciplinary action, the objective should always be to direct the offender towards improved performance. Avenging a wrong will never right it and will almost always work against your interests.

Investigation of Offenses

In any case of wrongdoing or culpable negligence, it is very important to make as thorough and painstaking an investigation as possible. Except for very serious offenses, which are required to be investigated by the Naval Investigative Service (see SecNav directives), it is a division officer's obligation to discover all the details and background relating to an offense committed by one of his men. No one so quickly wins the scorn and loses the trust and respect of his men as an officer who accepts all "reports" at face value and just passes them along to the commanding officer. Even when your men are completely and obviously in the wrong, it is necessary to learn all the facts of the case. A man who is reported for fighting after being slurred or insulted is not in the same class as a man who is logged for beating up a shipmate while in a drunken rage. Some of your men may have grown up in a part of society in which fighting is the means to solve most any difference of opinion or difficulty. Others may have learned to tell the truth only when it is to their benefit and expect the same of others. You should encourage these men to demand more of themselves and point out that the Navy will demand more if they intend to advance. While you cannot condone their conduct you can often help such men get squared away in Navy life. This means that you must learn to manage your men efficiently, with an understanding of their human strengths, weaknesses, and cultural differences.

American society has undergone many changes in the more than three decades since the end of World War II. It is not the purpose of this book to judge these changes. We must, however, consider their effect on our working environment. The United States is a more permissive, liberal, and affluent society than ever before. The young men who are now entering the Armed Forces will be facing demands for performance and personal qualities that they may not have needed or even did not have the opportunity to learn in the civilian society they grew up in. Their reaction to the demand for personal sacrifice which the military life requires must be viewed with consideration of their backgrounds. The nature of our existence as a fighting force does not allow us the same privileges as our civilian counterparts.

A division officer has a special relationship with his men. He knows them better and should understand them better than anyone else. When they get into trouble, he should make every possible effort to see that his men get a fair deal. This means more than a plea to the captain or executive officer for leniency; it means getting *all* the facts together and being prepared to make a specific recommendation as regards punishment.

Unofficial Punishment

Punishment in the Armed Services is a responsibility and duty of the commanding officer. It is not proper, nor is it legal, for the division officer to punish his men by assigning them extra duty or depriving them of liberty, for example. Whenever an officer is tempted to violate the spirit of this rule, he should remember that his men are usually well aware of the regulations. Any punishment that is not considered legal or justified will be quickly resented, and the damage to the morale of the division will far outweigh the good effect that the punishment might have on a few individuals. There is never any real justification for unofficial punishment. The necessity that punishment be awarded only by the commanding officer or by courts-martial is apparent. Imagine the confusion among the crew if every officer and petty officer could hand out extra duty or loss of liberty according to his own standards. The division officer has ample means at his disposal to control all but the most hardened cases of bad conduct. Delaying opportunity for advancement, assignment to unpleasant work details, and denying special requests, such as those for early liberty, exchange of duty, or special pay are some of these means. Extra instruction after working hours is perfectly legitimate if it is related to the offense committed. This extra instruction must serve a useful purpose and must not be a cloak for unofficial punishment. The major point here is that division officers must recognize their own means of maintaining discipline, and must use these means instead of bringing all their men's problems to mast. An officer who does resort unnecessarily to mast is quickly revealed as weak and lazy.

Division officers in aircraft squadrons embarked on a carrier have a special problem in that the carrier commanding officer, instead of the individual squadron commanders, holds mast. This arrangement, however, does not affect the principles discussed above.

New Men with Poor Records

There are several other aspects of discipline which may profitably be discussed here. One of them is the problem of new men who have poor conduct records. In looking over the records of a new man, the division officer may discover the man has a history of offenses or that there is a marked change in performance at some point. A proper course of action is to call in the man and tell him frankly that you have seen his record, but that his past will in no respect influence his future in the division. Make it plain that you expect nothing but the best from him and that he will start off with a clean slate. This reassurance will be important to help him make a new start. All of us know men who have "fouled up" at one time or another, but who have done very well since. It is difficult for a man to stay out of trouble if he feels that he is a marked man and has two strikes on him from the start. It is important to understand that a man with a poor record will usually want to talk about it and tell you his side of the story. Listen to him with sympathy; let him get it off his chest even though you may not believe it all. Above all, really listen to him, don't just go through the motions. Make a firm effort to see life for a few minutes through his eyes—see how his problems look to him, not just the way they seem to you. The rewards you will have for tuning in on his frequency for a short while may be astonishing.

Interviewing Disciplinary Cases

An important aspect of discipline is the private interview or talk with a man who is in trouble. It is obvious that the sooner you can spot a man who is not well adjusted, and find out what makes him tick, the better are your chances of straightening him out. Lads who are still in their 'teens, as well as men who are new to military life, often get off on the wrong foot and their minor difficulties may be brought to your attention by the petty officers. Men with good records of performance and conduct may also fall out of step with the division and develop into disciplinary problems. All these men have some cause for their unsatisfactory behavior, and most of the time you can do something about it. The important thing is to find out where their troubles lie. To do this a private, informal talk is a good method. There should be no suggestion of a lecture or a "bawling out," although at another time such a procedure might be useful. Try to make the man feel comfortable; he may have trouble relating his problems if he feels threatened by the interview or feels his actions and attitudes are being judged as foolish or inappropriate. Remember if *he* feels a matter is important it will have the effect of an important matter on his actions. Many seemingly insignificant problems can become important to another man. You should treat that matter with the importance the individual has placed in it and he will know that you respect him and are interested in his well-being. During the interview if he wanders from subject to subject let him ramble; sometimes a man will only hint indirectly at his real problem. Sometimes the very subject he avoids, the things he does not say, may be significant. Some offhand remark as he leaves may present the clue. Remember that you are trying to find out what the man *feels;* do not be too concerned with the accuracy of his statements. Above all be relaxed, sympathetic, and a good listener. You can do all these things without being overly familiar with the man. Just be natural, sincere, and dignified.

Personal Relations with Your Men

The question of whether or not the men may themselves become too familiar and informal often concerns young officers. There may, of course, be an occasional "character" who will presume upon your interest in him to be disrespectful. A firm yet calm reminder of his military manners will usually square him away. But this will be extremely unusual. Almost invariably an officer who is dignified and sensible in his manner and speech will have nothing to fear on this score. Most men shy away from any idea of disrespect or bad manners.

Relations with men ashore sometimes pose problems for junior officers. In general, social activities with enlisted men ashore should be avoided. It is very hard for a young officer to maintain his status as a leader of a group of men if he becomes too intimate with them ashore. Of course, this does not preclude participating in athletics with your men, or even a few beers after a softball game. Nor does it mean that men who are related by blood or marriage, or who were good friends before entering the Navy, must avoid each other because one is an officer and the other an enlisted man. But it does mean that an officer should habitually pursue his social life ashore quite apart from his men.

Self-Discipline

The commanding officer and his subordinates shall exercise leadership through personal example, moral responsibility, and judicious attention to the welfare of persons under their control or supervision. Such leadership shall be exercised in order to achieve a positive, dominant influence on the performance of persons in the Department of the Navy.—*Navy Regulations, 1973.*

A division officer cannot favorably influence his men in their attitudes on behavior and conduct unless he himself sets a good example. He must look the part of a professional officer and must act in a reasonably military manner. Sloppy and nonregulation junior officers often gain the affection of their men, but they cannot gain the high confidence and respect so necessary for real efficiency and discipline. It is a profound obligation on the part of each officer, assumed at the time he was sworn in, to wear his uniform correctly, with dignity and decorum, and to behave as his men expect an officer to behave.

This important principle of setting a good example goes to the very heart of effective leadership. Officers who "shack-up" in foreign countries or who come aboard drunk are hardly in a position to encourage their men to good conduct. Officers who behave immorally not only are failing to lead their men effectively but are in direct violation of Navy Regulations.

Self-discipline includes the moral courage to correct your subordinates. No one likes to be unpopular, but it is often necessary to point out to your subordinates their shortcomings. This is sometimes difficult when the subordinate is a close associate and even a companion, as in the case of a junior officer. But that is part of your job, and is a duty that requires self-discipline.

Another example of self-discipline is the officer who passes along an unpopular order to his men. There should never be a suggestion that "The captain says" or "The exec wants." The order must be passed along and backed up with more than lip service.

The test of self-discipline comes in times of unusual stress. Not only will a leader's demonstration of this quality under pressure gain him the confidence of the men he commands, it will also clearly reveal to his men the value of discipline to themselves. A prime example of the value of this quality is seen in the experiences of men who have been prisoners of war. The records and statements of repatriates from communist POW camps clearly show that men with appreciation of the value of discipline to themselves proved able to resist the so-called brainwashing and were far more apt to survive the ordeal.

The development of self-discipline is, after all, the ultimate objective of all externally applied disciplinary measures and practices. For the totally dependable man—who will fulfill his responsibilities under any and all circumstances in the absence of direct and immediate supervision—is the one who has achieved the ability to discipline himself. It is such men who carry on the battle, when their leaders and shipmates have fallen.

A Division Officer Must Be Accessible

It is particularly important that a division officer instill in his men the feeling that if anything is troubling them they can speak to him in private and "off the record." This does not mean that the division officer should bypass his petty officers and encourage the men to come to him for every petty gripe or grievance. It does mean that the men should feel that if they have a real personal problem, they can tell it to their division officer. Some division officers pass the word around through the petty officers that they are available upon request for a talk. Others have been known to set aside certain hours on certain days when any man is welcome to come up and talk things over. Avoid, if practicable, having your men come into wardroom country. Details will vary with individuals and with circumstances, but the principle of a division officer being accessible should always be observed.

In a survey made by the disciplinary officer of the First Naval District, it was found that approximately 80 percent of the young men who had been sent to the disciplinary barracks for comparatively serious offenses had started these offenses in a comparatively non-serious manner. When asked why they had not gone to their division officer for help, most of them stated that they had no idea that their division officer would be willing to help them. If you do not know the answers to all the questions or problems your men bring up, find the answers. Avoid any suggestion of "brushing off" your men.

Your job as chief human relations expert in your division goes further than merely being approachable. You should try to be aware of the troubles that men endure even when they have not revealed these troubles directly. This awareness, it may be noted, is a characteristic of all truly mature persons. It is a sort of preventive medicine; it is the earmark of a really capable leader who knows his men well enough and knows human nature well enough to be able to detect and help men who are in trouble before a crisis of some sort occurs. For example, you may observe or hear that one of your quiet, studious men is becoming very careless about his work and is also hitting the bottle pretty hard on liberty. This does not seem at all in keeping with his past habits of sobriety. You understood that he was saving money to marry his girl back home. A few questions may reveal that he has recently received a *"Dear John"* letter from his girl and this has hit him quite hard. You can ignore the matter (and sometimes this may actually be the best procedure) or you can take steps to try to help him through the situation; perhaps a friendly talk, a week's leave, or a new and more interesting job assignment will do the trick. This positive action on your part might forestall an addiction to alcohol or drugs and the inevitable incident involving the police or shore patrol. The point is that your young men often need help in hurdling life's obstacles; it is more than humanitarian to help them, it is efficient management that pays off in more productivity, better behavior, and greater satisfaction from your job than you can imagine.

Importance of Group Feeling

In the first part of this chapter discipline was defined as a certain kind of attitude. If any officer has built up such an attitude, such a state of mind, in his men that they trust him and want to support him, then the force of group opinion will be the power that runs his outfit. The men will not want to go against the feeling of their shipmates, and the fear of punishment will not be needed. This is the true kind of discipline that pays off, and is the only kind suited to the American fighting man. To encourage and build up this group feeling is an important duty of division officers. Athletic and social events enjoyed by the division together are real aids in this direction. Competition in training and inspections are also valuable. Your divisional PQS progress chart is an excellent tool for training competition since the responsibility for completion rests with the individual. When the progress chart is conspicuously posted and you and your petty officers make it clear that you are interested in each man's progress, the entire division will respond and profit from the training and attention. Most important of all is the attitude of the division officer and his assistants. In many small ways, in speech and in deed, they can show their enthusiasm for and pride in the division and their strong sense of identification with it. The importance of setting an example cannot be overemphasized. It is not only the key to proper discipline in peacetime, but is the most vital factor in leading men in battle. If the officers complain of hardship or seem to lack vigor and aggressive spirit, then their men will quickly exaggerate these weaknesses and will lose their effectiveness. Inexperienced young officers often relieve their feelings by complaining and griping in the presence of their men. You will be hard pressed to find loyalty, obedience, and trust for authority in your men if you do not present a good example in your own behavior. If you complain about the directives of your superiors or about the demanding schedule, your men will assume the same privilege. Nothing could be worse for discipline.

It must be remembered that men cannot be assessed and treated as individuals alone. They must be treated as members of a group. For it is a group of men, a division, that you are managing, not a collection of individuals. A man can be taken out of a group, but the influence of the group cannot be removed from the man. In talking to a man, you must remember that he is hearing you against the background of the voices of his group. His attitude toward what you are saying is determined, to a large extent, by the goals and attitudes of the division. This is why decisions about individuals must be made with consideration of how these decisions will affect the group.

A valuable aid in assessing group feeling is the responsible petty officer who will represent the true feelings of the men to his division officer. This is not, of course, the vindictive type, the one trying to curry favor by carrying tales, or constantly complaining about the others. It is the sincere and concerned man who will discuss such matters objectively and frankly with the division officer. The division officer must make certain such a petty officer feels free to speak with him frankly.

Informal Groups

Every military unit or command, and a ship in particular, is a complicated social structure, made up of interacting groups who have their own leaders and who respond to many stimuli within the framework of the formal, visible organization. These informal groups can have a profound effect upon discipline as well as efficiency and their existence should be known, and their behavior studied, by all division officers. Informal groups cut across the visible lines of authority and responsibility. Often they center about a coffee pot in a workshop or compartment, or on the bridge. They may result from friendships on liberty or between families, or because of common hobbies or technical skills. Whether they are a force for good or for bad discipline depends on many factors; usually they are beneficial in that they increase their members' feelings of belonging. By observing those groups, an officer can sometimes spot men who are potential leaders, and thus further his training program. If an occasional malcontent or "loudmouth" becomes dominant in such an informal group, he should be given special attention and perhaps transferred to another detail. The important point is that division officers must be aware of informal, undefined groups, and be quick to take advantage of their good features, as well as quick to take action when they become troublesome.

Regulations

The foundation of our system of discipline is the same as the very foundation of our system of government—the preservation of the dignity of the individual.—General J. Lawton Collins, U.S. Army.

Another point should be discussed in any chapter on discipline. Some young officers are prone to set up their own standards of conduct as being superior to those required by appropriate authorities. Nothing can lead more readily to poor discipline. Regulations were written by capable and experienced officers who condensed the accumulated wisdom of generations of good leaders, and they have the status of law as it pertains to the naval service.

There is only one way to run a division, and that is in a regulation manner. It may not seem irregular to wink at gambling, for example, as a harmless diversion, but an inevitable sequel and accompaniment to gambling is theft. Aside from the moral and legal issues involved, it is smart to prevent gambling in any outfit. Running a division in a regulation manner is a most important requirement for good discipline. This must apply to officers, of course, as well as men. The old saying that a taut ship is a happy ship is still true. One of the reasons is that, on a taut ship, the men and officers know where they stand and what is expected of them. Work, hardship, and recreation are shared alike. Men can depend on their shipmates, because slackness is not accepted. Officers and petty officers are on the job and require their men to be on the job as well.

Most important of all the results of administering a military unit in a regulation manner is the pride and job satisfaction engendered. Men have a profound sense of professional pride and integrity; they take great pleasure in belonging to a unit that is run well and by the book. They know that they are good at what they are doing when the rules do not have to be stretched for them to measure up.

Appearance and Deportment

While it is impossible in a short guide like this to cover every disciplinary problem facing division officers, it is considered worthwhile to discuss some of the more common ones. The first of these might be called *appearance and deportment*, for want of a better term. This includes the cleanliness and dress of the men, as well as details of their general behavior, such as leaning on the lifelines, throwing trash and cigarette butts on deck, etc.

These matters often harass a division officer unnecessarily, with the result that he sometimes harangues his men ineffectually at quarters, admonishing them in general and often vague terms. The correct action is simple and effective: use your chain of command. Get your section leaders together and tell them in detail exactly what you expect in the way of everyday appearance and conduct. Direct the section leaders to use their subordinate petty officers, down to the last petty officer, to enforce these standards. Make it clear that if a man steps out of line, you will hold his immediate petty officer and all petty officers up the line responsible. This will result in all your petty officers remaining reasonably alert to the appearance and conduct of their men; and if the division is properly organized, it will result in the attainment of your high standards.

A classic example of how not to handle matters can be seen in the *Caine Mutiny,* when Captain Queeg, cognizant of sagging morale in the *Caine,* calls his officers together in the wardroom and details one of them to be the morale officer with the job of raising the morale of the whole ship.

When faced with having to reprove a man for not doing his job to your satisfaction, be careful not to arouse his resentment unless the case is a flagrant one and you decide that frank or even caustic remarks are needed to arouse the man. The latter should very rarely be needed. For example, suppose you have the first division on a guided missile cruiser and you have noticed that the quarterdeck for which you are responsible could stand a little improvement. Your Boatswain's Mate 2/c Harris is in charge of the quarterdeck. A good approach to Harris (assuming that he has shown that he is a competent petty officer) would be: "Harris, this area is falling off a bit, let's bring the deck out a little brighter. I noticed an Irish pennant on the port-side awning this morning." Harris should be chagrined enough at your specific suggestions, which impugn his judgment or alertness, to take adequate action. Or you could say: "Harris, the quarterdeck has improved in appearance, but let's push along further. Here are a few ideas. . . ." If you wish to make it a bit stronger, you can say: "Harris, the quarterdeck is not up to standards of appearance for this ship. If you cannot keep it up properly with the men you have, let me know and we'll look into a shift of work details here." If this does not get results, you should consider either replacing Harris or assigning more men. Note in the above examples that no personal attack is made on Harris; he is in no danger of losing his self-respect. This may seem an obvious point, but it is most important. It is almost fatal to put a subordinate in a position where he loses his self-respect. If you do so, your future relations with him will probably be marked by resentment and only minimum cooperation on his part. As Mr. Ordway Tead, the author of *The Art of Administration*, expresses it: "Sullen indifference and passive, reluctant, acquiescence are the fruits of arbitrary command."

In learning to exercise his authority, a division officer should not cling to outmoded patterns and manners of behaviors that he may erroneously believe to be standard or proper usage. Poor management of men is often the result of a mistaken idea of how leaders should behave. Bad manners, arrogant and sarcastic words, or a tough, heedless, peremptory approach are *not* the normal tools of a "boss" or leader. The democratic, productive division officer exercises authority and power with dignity and moderation, with a profound consideration for the welfare and personal integrity of his subordinates, and in an atmosphere of optimism and approval.

Hostility and Anxiety

The fact that you, as a division officer, have been placed in a position of authority over your men will inevitably inspire in them a certain amount of both hostility and anxiety. This cannot be avoided, but it can be minimized by your comprehension of some of the very natural and fundamental human feelings involved. It is quite normal for any group to be both anxious about and somewhat hostile toward a new leader. This is particularly true when the new leader first takes over. The feelings of hostility diminish at a rate and to a degree that depend on how effectively the officer establishes his leadership over his men.

Hostility toward constituted authority is not only natural, but, for Americans, at least, seems to be traditional. The rugged individualist, the free man of the frontier, is a universally recognized American whose rebellion against authority is one of his strongest traits. Most boys grow up with a feeling that it is socially acceptable, within reasonable limits, to grumble at the power of the police, parents, and the school. This American heritage of rebelliousness has been a source of strength in the growth of our republic, but its expression may sometimes try the patience and understanding of division officers.

Hostility can take many forms, and not all of them are bad. Some men seem to work harder, as if to work out their dimly-recognized feelings of resentment or dislike of authority. Other men may persist in being out of uniform or may commit other relatively minor offenses. Still others may become accident-prone, and may express their hostility subconsciously by repeatedly injuring themselves, without suspecting, of course, that their misfortunes are not accidental. Complaining is often an expression of hostility and is usually a harmless way for men to blow off steam.

There are more common forms of hostility. Men may become indifferent and seem to resist training of any kind. These men may be usefully thought of as having purposely cut their lines of communication with their leaders. Other men may express their hostility by becoming excessively competitive, a more socially acceptable form of expression.

The above is a bare outline of some of the aspects of hostility. The important point here is that division officers must recognize hostility as a very common human failing that many people are not aware of within themselves. All of us in our daily living experience hostility in one form or another. A mature man, placed in a position of authority, learns to accept without undue rancor the hostility of some of his men. It can be dissipated surprisingly easily. The one great pitfall to be avoided on the part of any leader is to react to hostility with hostility. Suppose, for example, that one of your good petty officers comes up to you in some heat, complaining about the excessive work load thrust upon his men by some unexpected emergency, such as fuel oil sprayed topside while the ship was fueling. His righteous frustration may spill over into his words and manner towards you; he may even seem to be blaming you for his troubles. Hear him out; he will usually cool off quickly as he talks and will go on about getting the job done, as you respond with a few expressions of interest and sympathy. If, on the other hand, you become irritated at his complaints, you will only enrage and embitter him, and make it harder for him to settle down and do his job.

Anxiety is a feeling that often accompanies hostility. It is always present in some degree in men who must deal with other men who are in positions of authority. Think of your own feelings when working for someone, such as the executive officer, or your head of department. If this superior becomes excited or upset, you naturally become anxious, not only for your own welfare and sensibilities, but for the feelings of other men involved. Your men, especially at first, will have the same feelings of anxiety about you. One of your jobs in dealing with people is to allay this anxiety in the interests of better morale and more efficiency. Of course, a small degree of anxiety is not such a bad thing for subordinates to feel; it can be considered healthy if it merely encourages a sense of responsibility for doing things properly.

Hostility and anxiety are to some degree interrelated. Suffice it to say that an officer should recognize both reactions as powerful human emotions which should be minimized whenever practicable.

Profanity

A feature of men's behavior which is sometimes troublesome is profanity. Division officers can meet this problem by convincing their men—again through the petty officers—that profanity is a self-degrading form of childish behavior and is not the mark of an experienced seaman. The difference between a few, well-chosen salty expressions at appropriate times of stress or turmoil, and the casual, incessant stream of foul chatter that some men substitute for the English language should be clear to all officers. As soon as officers and petty officers set a good example and show their disapproval of profanity, it will cease to be a nuisance.

Unauthorized Absence (UA)

The most common disciplinary problem is that of unauthorized absence. Except for the few misfits who only stay in the service until they have earned a bad conduct discharge, a properly organized and administered unit should not have men UA except under the most unusual circumstances. Generally, if there are such cases, there has been a failure of some sort at the top. Men will sometimes respond to a personal emergency with an unreasoning urge to go to their homes. Unless they understand that requests for emergency leave will always be sympathetically considered and granted if at all possible, they will often just yield to their first impulse and depart. If, however, they know that everything will be done by their division officer to help them—including financial and travel arrangements, if required—they will be inclined to request emergency leave.

Other men "go over the hill" because they feel a grievance against the leave policy or the employment schedule. Often an effort by division officers to establish a sound leave policy, and, at the same time, to inform their men of the reasons for the inconvenient deployment of their ship or squadron, can reduce the cases of UA. Of course, there will always be stubborn individuals who prefer to have their own way, no matter what action their officers take. These men can only be dealt with at mast by their commanding officer.

The big point is that all cases of unauthorized absence should be examined critically to detect any evidence of misunderstandings or misinformation.

Theft

Another common disciplinary problem is theft. Its relation to gambling has been mentioned. Some practical steps a division officer can take to reduce theft is to make it as difficult and risky as possible. The men should be required to keep their lockers locked, and should not be permitted to stow clothes and other gear in their bedding. Peacoat lockers and bag stowage should only be left open when necessary—and then under supervision. The newer uniform styles have created problems on smaller ships since there is inadequate room for stowage. In this situation you will sometimes find that several men will share a locker large enough to hang the uniforms in so as not to wrinkle them. These lockers only serve to exacerbate the security problem. Compartments where thefts have occurred should be patrolled and reasonably well illuminated, even at night. On occasions when the men draw large sums of money on pay day, such as upon the return from a long cruise, special steps should be taken to prevent stealing. One of these steps is to discourage the men from carrying large sums of money on their persons. This is easier to do if arrangements are made for the safe stowage of the money until the men need it.

If a theft is reported, and you have reason to suspect that the stolen property is in the locker of one of your men, you should immediately report the facts to the commanding officer, or to such other officer delegated the authority to order searches, in order to obtain specific permission for a locker search. Unless there is probable cause and specific authority, the search is illegal, and the thief may escape punishment, and you are liable.

Homosexuality

Homosexuals are considered a security risk, since they are particularly susceptible to blackmail by agents of unfriendly powers.

Certain misconceptions regarding homosexuality are common. Some of these are:

1. That a homosexual is easily detected by his or her characteristics of speech, dress, manner, etc. This is just not true and many have characteristics which are the exact opposite.
2. That venereal disease cannot be contracted through homosexual acts. In a New York clinic one out of four persons treated for venereal disease admitted recent homosexual activity.
3. That homosexuals are born, not made. For men to rely on this false assumption to avoid entrapment is dangerous. There are many factors that enter into the final determination as to whether an individual turns to homosexualism or retains a dominant heterosexual identity. Experimenters can easily become homosexuals and are susceptible to the same blackmail dangers after the first event of experimentation.
4. That the Navy will "cure" its homosexual persons. The Navy has neither the facilities nor the personnel, nor is it part of the Navy's mission, to attempt this difficult and not always successful treatment. Even if successfully completed, the "cure" could not remove the danger of blackmail. It should be noted that the American Medical Association has determined that homosexuals are not mentally ill. This cannot be considered to be a medical disability. The A.M.A. has termed homosexuality a behavior disorder and it is thus clearly a matter of unsuitability to the service rather than a medical problem.

The law and the Navy Department do not attempt to determine or to label an offender as a confirmed homosexual. Rather, disciplinary or administrative action is taken for engaging in an act or in conduct which constitutes the commission of an offense. From this point of view, the commission of a homosexual act is considered a military, rather than a medical, problem. Early separation from the service of persons who commit one or more homosexual acts or who admit to uncontrollable homosexual tendencies is essential for the welfare and security of the Navy as a whole. Normally such persons are separated by administrative action by the Bureau of Naval Personnel.

It appears that many service personnel feel that a passive homosexual act is not as reprehensible as one in which the individual concerned takes an active role. It should be clearly understood that in the view of the Navy Department and of federal law, a so-called passive member in a homosexual act is in all respects as guilty of an offense as is the active partner.

In many homosexual cases the offender contends that he was under the influence of intoxicating liquor and, therefore, not in full control, if his acts are committed after the individuals concerned have consumed varying amounts of alcoholic beverages. However, drunkenness is not an acceptable excuse for the willing participation in a homosexual act in any greater degree than it would be for the commission of other offenses.

Persons who have committed, or have attempted to commit, a homosexual act while in the naval service, must be promptly separated from the service, either through court-martial process or administrative discharge. Where force was used by such a person, or where the victim was a minor under the age of 16, court-martial action is appropriate. In other cases disposition is normally accomplished by administrative separation, except that where the person resists such separation, the case must be referred to a flag officer having general court-martial powers to determine whether a court-martial is more suitable in the case. If tried by court-martial and found guilty, the person convicted may be awarded a long prison sentence and a dishonorable discharge. If the individual elects to be separated under conditions other than honorable, he loses substantially all rights and privileges as a veteran, and finds humiliation, degradation, and difficulty in obtaining suitable employment. In either case, the effects are lasting and unavoidable.

Drugs

It is the policy of the Navy to prevent and eliminate the use of marijuana, narcotics, and other controlled substances by preventing their sale; by publicity, counseling, and instruction relating to drug abuse, including information concerning possible administrative separation or criminal liability flowing therefrom; and by stressing the responsibility of commanders for initiating disciplinary or administrative proceedings in drug abuse cases. The division officer has a vital role to play in enforcing this policy, especially in counseling. To do this he needs to keep himself informed on the subject. As with homosexuality, there are certain general misconceptions regarding the improper use of drugs in the Navy. Some of these are:

1. That only narcotics, such as heroin or cocaine are dangerous. This is not true. Federal law includes in the term "controlled substances" all non-narcotic products which the Attorney General finds have a potential for abuse.

2. That the use or possession of only marijuana or narcotics is prohibited by the UCMJ. This is not so. Article 520.36, *Standard Organization and Regulations of the U.S. Navy*, which is a general order under Article 92, UCMJ, prohibits the unauthorized possession or use of all controlled substances. This prohibition applies to barbiturates.

3. That marijuana is harmless. Not so. The Bureau of Narcotics records and Navy administrative experience show the marijuana user in general to be an inadequate personality, seeking solace and relief. Further, the marijuana user is unreliable and frequently seeks stronger drugs or narcotics to supplement his ever-growing personality void.

4. That LSD is not only harmless, but improves personality and physical functioning. This is dead wrong. It is well-established that the LSD-user is very likely to suffer severe, recurring, adverse physiological and psychological effects that produce personality change and an inevitable general physical deterioration.

5. That the use or possession of illegal drugs or narcotics is a minor offense. This is not true. Under the UCMJ, the use or possession of marijuana or narcotics is a felony, punishable by dishonorable discharge, confinement at hard labor for five years, forfeiture of all pay and allowances, and reduction to the lowest pay grade. It is the duty of the division officer to instruct his men regularly on the dangers involved in drug abuse and the administrative action or criminal liability which can consequently result.

Article 520.17 of the *Standard Organization and Regulations of the U.S. Navy* outlines the responsibilities of command "drug exemption representatives." These representatives offer a most positive move toward rehabilitation of drug abusers in the Navy. Through them individuals may voluntarily apply for counseling and treatment without fear of prosecution for their admitted use of controlled substances. SecNavInst 6710 gives the details of this program.

Perhaps we should consider the reason for these programs. The widespread use of drugs in American society has led the Navy to establish far-reaching drug education and rehabilitation programs. This is not an indication of lowering of standards or lessening of legal restrictions. The Navy has these drug programs because the chances for Navy personnel to become exposed to and involved in drugs is greater than ever before. An individual who actively seeks assistance in overcoming a drug problem obviously has retained his potential value to the service. The Navy has always taken care of its own and the subject of drug abuse should be no exception. The criminal abuse, possession, or sale of controlled substances is clearly a legal matter. These programs are not designed to allow those caught in a criminal act to avoid prosecution. They are only for the individuals who want to ensure they have the assistance and support of the Navy in overcoming potential problems within themselves and keeping themselves capable of contributing to the Navy's mission.

Alcohol

Seventeen out of every hundred Navy men and women have serious drinking problems, and nearly two out of these seventeen appear to be chronic problem drinkers who need immediate help.—Rosemary Purcell, *Navy Times*, 14 May 1975.

Although use of alcohol is not illegal (except aboard ship) in the Navy, its abuse presents serious problems to the individuals involved and to those responsible for supervising their work. Your men are separated from home and their normal system of psychological supports much of the time. For some this may be their first experience on their own. This and other factors creating stress may lead to the abuse of alcohol. Dependence upon or continued abuse of alcohol is considered to be alcoholism. This can lead to great suffering for the abuser and is always detrimental to good discipline.

A man who is an excellent sailor aboard ship, but cannot handle his liquor ashore, needs and deserves your help. You will find that some men who perform poorly as a result of alcohol abuse will become valuable members of your organization if you can help them with their problem. Alcoholism is a complex failing that can sometimes be conquered, but it is not easy, either for the victim or for those who believe in him enough to help him.

The alcoholic will not be able to live up to the responsibilities of his job and others, therefore, will have to do his work. This inevitably leads to hard feelings and if allowed to continue will ruin discipline in your division.

The division officer should take action as soon as he suspects that alcohol abuse may be becoming a problem for any of his men. As noted in Chapter 2, "Capabilities and Needs," counseling should approach the matter from the standpoint of performance of duty. Let your men know that you will not tolerate poor performance as a result of alcohol abuse. This should not be presented as a condemnation of all drinking but as an instruction in the hazards of alcohol abuse. The aspect of its effects both on the individual and the group are your concern as division officer.

SecNav Instruction 5300.20 (series) promulgates the policies of the Department of the Navy relative to alcoholism and alcohol abuse among Department of the Navy personnel, and establishes responsibility for implementation of those policies. Subordinate echelons of command have issued instructions to provide specific guidance in procedures for administering local programs for alcohol abusers.

Navy Department policy admits the personal responsibility of all Navy personnel to avoid dependence on alcohol. Each individual is equally responsible for seeking assistance should he or she become an alcoholic. The Navy, however, attempts to identify and treat alcoholics whether they seek treatment or not. Alcoholism is not of itself reason for discharge for reasons of unsuitability since it can be cured. If an individual does not cooperate with rehabilitation efforts he may be separated.

Uniform Code of Military Justice (UCMJ)

This is not the place for a full exposition of the *UCMJ*. The code is something a division officer uses every day when handling men, and its understanding, insofar as it relates to disciplinary problems, is important. There are a few aspects, however, which may not be covered in a course in military law.

Bringing a man to Mast (making out a misconduct report) must be considered as a last resort. It cannot be the easy solution to a division officer's problem; it should be used only when all other disciplinary means have failed. There will be times, however, when the gravity or frequency of occurrence of an offense leaves you no choice.

It is sound practice to have officers and petty officers under you obtain your concurrence, as their division officer, before placing one of their men on report. Make it a practice to settle your problems yourself within the division if at all possible. In the case of a man from another division, it is also wise to consult with his division officer before you place him on report for a serious offense; there may be some aspects of the incident of which you are unaware. It is at the least a mark of courtesy to your fellow division officers to consult them before taking action.

Apprehension and Restraint

An officer of the deck must know the difference between *apprehension* and the three degrees of *restraint*.

The officer of the deck will have occasion to receive custody of men charged with misconduct. The men may be delivered by the Shore Patrol or by an officer or petty officer aboard ship. They may even deliver themselves for minor offenses, such as being out of uniform. It is important that the officer of the deck know the legal meanings of the terms involved, and also know what action to take.

All officers, petty officers, and noncommissioned officers of any service have authority to apprehend offenders, subject to the *Uniform Code of Military Justice.* Other enlisted men may do so when assigned shore patrol, military police, and similar duties. *Apprehension* is accomplished by clearly informing the person that he is being taken into custody. He should be told at the same time what he is accused of. It should be noted here that *apprehension*, in the armed services, has the same meaning as *arrest* has in civilian life. Just as a police officer informs a citizen that he is under *arrest*, so does a naval officer tell a man that he is being apprehended or is being taken into *custody*. *Custody* is temporary control over the person apprehended until he is delivered to the proper authority (on board ship, the officer of the deck). In general, persons who have authority to apprehend may exercise only such force as is actually necessary. Petty officers should apprehend officers only under very unusual circumstances, such as to avoid disgrace to the service or to prevent the escape of a criminal.

Restraint as a general term involves some degree of deprivation of free movement of the person restrained. There are three degrees of restraint: *confinement, arrest,* and *restriction in lieu of arrest.* The degree of restraint used should be no more severe than that necessary to ensure the presence of the offender at further proceedings in his case. Thus, even though a man has committed an offense or is suspected of such, he need not be restrained to any degree if his presence is assured at future proceedings.

Only the commanding officer may impose any degree of restraint on a commissioned officer or a warrant officer. If it is desired to restrain an officer, the commanding officer must be notified.

Only officers may ordinarily impose any degree of restraint on an enlisted man. However, the commanding officer may delegate this authority to warrant officers and enlisted men.

Confinement is an actual physical restraint imposed in serious offenses to ensure the presence of the person.

Arrest is the moral restraint of a person, by an order, oral or written, to certain specified limits pending disposition of charges against him. It is not imposed as punishment. It is imposed only for probable cause, based on known or reported facts concerning an alleged offense. *Arrest* relieves a man of all military duties other than normal cleaning and policing. *Arrest* is imposed by telling a man (or officer) of the limits of his arrest.

One of the disadvantages of placing an accused in arrest is that he may no longer be required to perform his military duties, and if the authority ordering this type of restraint requires the accused to perform his military duties, the arrest is automatically terminated. Consequently, a lesser form of restraint is allowed. This is called: "Restriction in lieu of arrest."

Restriction is a restraint of the same nature as arrest, imposed under similar circumstances and by the same authorities, but it does not involve the suspension of military duties.

Persons apprehended aboard ship are delivered to the custody of the officer of the deck, together with a misconduct report. The officer of the deck informs the executive officer (or command duty officer) and receives instructions as to the nature of restraint to be imposed on the man. This, of course, normally depends on the gravity of the offense. Assuming that formal restraint, such as arrest, is ordered, the officer of the deck notifies the offender, insuring that he, the offender, understands the nature of his restraint and the penalties for violation of restraint. The officer of the deck secures the offender's written acknowledgment of his notification by his signature upon the misconduct report slip, and then turns the offender over to the master-at-arms. The whole matter is logged, of course, with full details.

Restraint does not have to be imposed on an accused. According to the *Navy Corrections Manual*, " . . . restriction may be imposed because the man's continued presence is necessary pending investigation or because the officer considers it a wise precaution to restrict him to remove him from the temptation of misconduct similar to that for which he is already charged. . . ." Thus, if the offense is relatively minor, and it can be assumed that the accused will not attempt to leave the area to avoid trial, no restraint is necessary. "Confinement prior to trial," continues the same manual, "should only be employed if it is considered necessary to ensure the presence of the accused at trial or because of the seriousness of the offenses charged, or because other factors indicate that the man's release would present a distinct threat to the safety of life, limb, or property." The lesser forms of restraint impose a burden on the accused, because it is a punishable offense to violate the limits of the restraint. Restraint once imposed may not be removed except in the following circumstances: Arrest and restriction in lieu of arrest may be lifted by the authority ordering the restraint, or a superior in his chain of command. Once a person is confined, he passes from the jurisdiction of the person ordering confinement, and can only be released by order of the commanding officer of the activity where the confinement takes place. On board ship, this poses no special problem because, generally, the authority ordering the confinement is also the commanding officer of the confining activity.

When discussing an offense, or a suspected offense, with a man, be meticulous in informing him of his rights under the Code. The suspected offender should be warned that he need not testify or even say anything at all, and that whatever he does say may be used against him. He should further be told that he has the right to the presence of an attorney during the interrogation and that, if he desires, an attorney will be appointed for him by the Navy at no cost to him. He should also be told that, if he consents to questioning without the presence of counsel, he may terminate the questioning at any time. Failure to observe this requirement may well result in the acquittal of a man charged with a serious offense, even though the evidence indicates that he is guilty.

Remember that Article 137 of the Code requires that each commanding officer explain certain parts of the Code to every enlisted man at the time of his entrance on active duty, after 6 months' active duty, and again upon his reenlistment. A copy of the Code should be posted in your division living spaces or working spaces. This will be checked during an administrative inspection.

All your men should understand the gravity of offenses involving absence without leave and missing ship. The extent and limitations of non-judicial punishment should also be understood. The standard manual for the three Services is the *Manual for Courts-Martial, United States,* 1969 (Rev.). There is also a *Manual of the Judge Advocate General,* issued by the Secretary of the Navy, Chapter I of which implements in the naval service various sections of the *Code* and the *Manual.* Especially useful for officers with limited legal experience is *Military Law,* published by the U. S. Naval Institute, which offers a concise, thorough review of the *Manual.*

Your major disciplinary problem will probably be concentrated in the persons of the few immature young men who are characterized as malcontents. This small percentage of men is evident in almost every command and causes a seemingly constant source of unrest within the command. These men can often be reformed and persuaded to become useful sailors, but there will always be a few with attitudes too warped and corrupted to ever become useful members of the naval service. These hopeless cases are eventually separated from the service by some sort of discharge, either by sentence of court-martial or awarded administratively in accordance with the *Bureau of Naval Personnel Manual.* In either case, it is important for the division officer to make up his mind about these men and, if they are beyond redemption, to recommend them for separation by the commanding officer. There is nothing to be gained by avoiding the issue; if no useful work can be obtained from a man, the sooner he leaves the Navy, the sooner another, and more useful, man can be enlisted. Remember that only conviction by a court-martial is legally considered a previous conviction. Repeated nonjudicial punishment, therefore, is not enough to build a legal case for a bad conduct discharge. Nonjudicial punishment does count, however, in evaluating a repeated petty offender for one of the adverse types of administrative discharges specified in the BuPers Manual.

In handling the few really incorrigible men who cannot stay out of serious trouble, you may run into a few men who appear to welcome a bad-conduct discharge. It often sobers these lads to learn how serious a bad-conduct discharge really is in terms of loss of veteran's rights and privileges. The impact a bad conduct discharge carries into civilian life—upon getting a job, upon parents and friends at home, and even upon the children he may hope to raise some day, is worth mentioning to the youngster who claims that he doesn't care how he gets out of the Navy.

The Effects of a BCD

The real meaning of a sentence of bad-conduct discharge and the consequences which may result from such a sentence are often not clearly understood by enlisted men.

This is probably because of the fact that there may be a distinction between a bad-conduct discharge awarded by a general court-martial and one awarded by a special court-martial with respect to entitlement to certain federal benefits. A bad-conduct discharge awarded by a general court-martial always results in loss of benefits under federal laws.

A bad-conduct discharge awarded by a special court-martial may be determined by the Veterans Administration to be a discharge "under dishonorable conditions," and this may also result in loss of most benefits under federal laws.

The following benefits are always denied members of the naval service who are separated with a bad-conduct discharge awarded by a special court-martial:

Travel allowance
Right to retain and wear uniform
Honorable service lapel button or pin
Honorable discharge button
Certificate of satisfactory service
Shipment of household goods or trailer
Reemployment rights
Civil service preference
Burial in a national cemetery

The following benefits may also be denied in a case of bad-conduct discharge awarded by a special court-martial upon determination by the Veterans Administration that the discharge was under dishonorable conditions:

Federal vocational rehabilitation
Educational rights (such as assistance in going to school, G. I. Bill)

Loan guaranty (which includes G. I. Loan for home or business)
Employment assistance (aid in getting federal or private employ-
    ment)
Service-connected disability compensation
Pension for disability not service-connected
Hospital care in Veterans Administration facility
Medical care and prosthetic appliances (such as false teeth, limbs,
    etc.)
Compensation for death due to naval service
Pension for death not due to naval service
Burial allowance
Burial flags
Right to join Veterans organizations requiring honorable dis-
    charge.

There are other serious consequences which stem from a bad-
conduct discharge in addition to the loss of benefits under federal
or state laws. Many employers, particularly large corporations,
base the hiring of former members of the naval service upon the
type of discharge which the man has obtained from the Navy. The
bad-conduct discharge affects the whole future life of the individual concerned.

A division officer should be familiar in general terms with the
procedure for separating men from the Navy administratively.
Men whose conduct has been poor and whose performance of
duty and value to the Navy are low can be discharged under
honorable conditions by the Chief of Naval Personnel. Division
officers should nominate for administrative discharge men whose
contributions are negative and whose reform and improvement
seem unlikely.

Regard your soldiers as your children and they will follow you
into the deepest valley; look on them as your own beloved sons
and they will stand by you even unto death. If, however, you are
indulgent, but unable to make your authority felt; kindhearted,
but unable to enforce your commands; and incapable,
moreover, of quelling disorder, then your soldiers must be
likened to spoilt children; they are useless for any practical
purpose.—Sun Tsu on *The Art of War,* about 500 B.C.

7/Inspections

The division officer shall by personnel supervision and frequent inspections insure that the spaces, equipment, and supplies assigned to his division are maintained in a satisfactory state of cleanliness and preservation.
—*Standard Organization and Regulations of the U.S. Navy.*

General

Inspections are an important, fundamental part of the Navy. They are not merely a traditional or ceremonial drill but fulfill a most vital function—a means of evaluating the efficiency, morale, and quality of discipline of a military unit.

Knowing when and how to inspect is a skill that all officers take pride in developing. It is one of the important skills that you cannot learn from a book. You must learn by doing and by evaluating your efforts. This chapter will help you get started, however, and will explain the principles and procedures that relate to efficient inspecting as well as to the successful preparation for being inspected.

Note in the quotation above that division officers are required to make "frequent inspections." This directive should be taken literally; there can be no substitute for periodic visits to all the spaces for which you are responsible. These visits not only ensure that work and training is progressing satisfactorily, but, equally important, they indicate your interest in your men's activities. They give the men a chance to see you and talk to you. Frequent inspections should not simply imply frequent criticism or attitudes of carping complaint; your approach should be friendly, with praise for work well done unless deficiencies are noted. Remember that an atmosphere of approval, whenever possible, results in maximum cooperation from your men.

Anyone can go through the motions of inspecting without really seeing anything, and with no result at all except the time wasted by the men who stand by. This is not really an inspection, because an inspection means a careful and critical examination. To examine carefully and critically requires a considerable amount of knowledge, hard work, and judgment. You may have to develop your knowledge as you go along in a new job, so do not hesitate to ask questions. Your men will appreciate your interest and your honesty if you do. As you learn all about your machinery and ordinance, your compartments, and spaces, or the personnel for whom you are responsible, your increase in knowledge will help develop judgment. "Do my men present as smart an appearance as they should? Is my gear as well maintained as that in the other ships in the squadron? Are my compartments in a satisfactory state of cleanliness and preservation? Should I paint the living compartment or touch it up again?" There is no simple answer to those questions. Many factors have to be taken into consideration. The most important one is the policy of your superior officers. Find out what they want and then give it to them. The reasons may not be clear to you, but their long experience has taught them many things that may not be apparent immediately to junior officers.

There are other considerations that may influence your judgment—such as funds available for paint, the past and future employment of the unit, and the demands of drills, leave periods, and similar necessary interruptions to your maintenance schedule. Following the policies of your superiors should not, of course, stifle your own initiative.

Types of Inspections

There are many types of inspections that will involve you in one way or another. You will conduct some inspections yourself; some will be held by men in your division. Some inspections will be formal and extensive; others will be informal and rather cursory.

Division officers commonly hold personnel inspection, daily material inspection, and locker and seabag inspection in their divisions, and they sample rations in the general mess. There are no special procedures for holding such inspections, but this should not imply any lessening of their importance. In addition, your division will have to make preparations for several graded, formal inspections by senior officers, as follows:

Executive Officer's Messing and Berthing Inspection—The executive officer will inspect all messing areas, galleys, and berthing compartments daily—usually about 1000, after the messmen and compartment cleaners have them in order. The chief master-at-arms, and possibly a medical corpsman, will accompany him. His main concern is to discover any major hazards to health and safety in the messing and berthing spaces, but he also inspects the appearance and condition of stowage and preservation in such spaces.

When the executive officer inspects a berthing compartment, the regular compartment cleaner should be standing by to present the compartment and accompany him through it. You may not be required to be present during such inspections, but it is a good idea to show up for some of them so you can get an idea of what the executive officer's standards are, and see how your spaces compare. It is also recommended that you check the compartment before he arrives so as to take care of any last-minute items.

In addition to the executive officer's messing and berthing inspection, on larger ships which have an assigned medical officer, he will conduct routine inspections of the unit's messing, food service, living, berthing, and working spaces to ascertain the sanitary conditions of these spaces. The medical officer is required to prepare and submit a weekly written report to the commanding officer setting forth the discrepancies noted during his inspection.

Commanding Officer's Zone Inspection—Frequent periodic zone inspections are necessary to ensure that proper measures are being taken to maintain machinery, spaces, and equipment in a satisfactory state of operation, preservation, and cleanliness. As most ships are too large for one officer to inspect completely in a short period, they will be divided into zones and the captain will assign other officers to inspect the zones he cannot cover. The captain will be looking for a general impression of the ship, but he will also check some specific items that he suspects could become problems.

It will generally be required that you have a man standing by in each of your spaces, to present the space and accompany the inspection party through it. After the inspection, a list of discrepancies will be published so that you can remedy them.

Formal Personnel Inspection—This will be made by the commanding officer or another senior officer. Unless otherwise specified, men will wear their best uniforms and shoes. You will be required to muster them in military formation and formally present them to the inspecting officer, as described hereinafter. As in other formal inspections, a discrepancy list will be published after the inspection for your action.

InSurv Inspection—The Board of Inspection and Survey is the closest thing to a group of "professional inspectors" that you will see in the Navy. Under the cognizance of the Inspector General of the Navy, this group consists of senior officers and petty officers well-experienced in their respective fields. Collectively they are able to authoritatively conduct comprehensive inspections on every item of ship's equipment and material. This inspection is normally held shortly before a ship is scheduled for shipyard overhaul or at least once every three years. The findings of the InSurv Board are used to determine overhaul requirements. Additionally, InSurv information is used by higher authorities to gain an overall idea of the condition and capabilities of a ship.

You want your spaces and equipment to make a favorable impression during an InSurv inspection, but don't try to cover up problems. Besides the fact that they will probably be discovered anyway, problems that are missed will fail to receive outside assistance at the shipyard level and will continue to be problems. You must be willing to admit the existence of defects and document them correctly prior to the board's inspection.

Administrative and Material Inspections—The type commander will have his representatives conduct annual inspections of the material condition and administrative status of your ship. The inspectors will look for proper maintenance of required records, and examine the condition of the ship itself. The ship's maintenance program will probably receive the most attention. Major PMS or MDCS discrepancies (see Chapter 9) will greatly reduce your ship's final grade.

Surprise Inspections—In addition to the inspections just described, your ship is always subject to inspection on a nonscheduled, short-notice basis. The best preparation for the surprise inspection is obviously day-to-day excellence in material upkeep and administrative procedures. If this is not the case, the inspection will probably reveal it, which is the principal reason for such an inspection.

Preparing for Inspection

Preparing for inspection can be discussed under five headings:
ORE, Personnel, Material, Zone, and Administrative.

ORE

As a division officer, you play a key part in preparing men for
battle. ORE (Operational Readiness Evaluation) will test your
success. NBC, first aid, and damage control knowledge are all
stressed. Men are selected at random by the visiting inspectors and
are asked questions. Your men must also wear their battle dress
faithfully and correctly. All of this requires careful indoctrination
and is properly done on the division level. The battle problem,
which is the heart of an ORE, is by necessity largely an exercise of
the imagination. Your job here will be to persuade your men that
this is something worth doing, and that only by contributing a
little enthusiasm and imagination can all hands learn something
and at the same time get a good mark for the division and the
ship.

Personnel Inspection

To bring the men up to a high standard of appearance at formal
inspections, the division officer should inspect his men regularly
and frequently. Men must be required to maintain daily a reasonably neat and regulation appearance. The sooner this habit is
instilled in a division, the better. A division officer should take a
few minutes in the morning to check his men for haircuts, cleanliness of face and hands, frayed and soiled clothing, and dilapi-
dated and nonregulation shoes.

In working to improve the appearance of your men, you
should first of all deal with them through their petty officers. If
these petty officers are made to feel responsible for their men, they
will take appropriate action. Only if a petty officer reveals his
failure to straighten out one of his men, should the division
officer step in.

Personnel inspections are sometimes a source of difficulty for division officers. Men often work long hours and stand many watches, and then, with very little time to prepare, are expected to fall in and look smart, clean, and regulation. An inexperienced officer might be inclined to sympathize with the men in this case and feel that it is unfair to expect them always to look their best. This attitude on the part of the officer is never justified. If his men are properly organized they should be able to present a regulation appearance with an hour's notice.

The secret here is to ensure that every man not only maintains a regulation full bag, but that he has in his possession at all times a complete inspection outfit. This means fairly new, clean, pressed suits of blues, whites, and dungarees, a good pair of shoes capable of taking a high gloss, and a new hat or cap, white shirt, and tie. All items must, without exception, be regulation issue and marked properly in accordance with *Uniform Regulations.* The suit of blues or whites must, of course, be complete with rating badges, hash marks, ribbons, etc. Once a man gets in the habit of keeping one good complete outfit of each uniform on hand, he never has to scramble before an inspection, and his division officer's problems are greatly simplified. Also, the requests to be excused from quarters will sharply decline. Haircuts may need emphasis for a special occasion, but here, again, if the men acquire the habit of having their hair cut regularly the division will never look shabby for a surprise inspection.

It goes without saying, of course, that all officers and petty officers should present an immaculate appearance at all inspections to serve as a model for the men. This is a military and moral obligation that not all young officers and petty officers perhaps fully appreciate. Young enlisted men are very impressionable and tend to imitate in dress, action, and speech the leaders whom they respect.

In making an inspection it is always well to take a positive, confident attitude, rather than a negative, complaining one. Commend those who look particularly smart. Teach your subordinates to take a positive attitude as well. For example, a petty officer notices a pair of shabby shoes flanked by two pairs of well-polished ones. He could sharply reprimand the owner of the

shabby shoes and might get results. But a more certain and dignified way to handle the offender is to tell him that he is known to
be as capable of shining his shoes as any of his shipmates, and
will be expected in the future to do so. Appealing to a man's pride
is usually more effective than criticizing him. Of course, there
will be times when sterner methods are required. The point is that
the positive approach should be tried first.

Here are a few points that experienced officers note when
inspecting personnel:

Combination cap square on the head with brim clean.

Hair cut in accordance with current policy.

Matching trousers and blouses, blues and whites.

Shoes shined along soles, heels.

Good posture, no exaggerated brace.

Ribbons in proper order, no plastic covers on ribbons.

No cigarettes, comb, etc. showing in pockets.

Men should look straight ahead while being inspected.

Material Inspections

Preparing for an inspection of the machinery or spaces for which
you are responsible involves the same principles of meticulous
supervision described above in preparation for personnel inspection. The first step in preparing for a material inspection is to
obtain copies of the check-off sheets to be used by the inspecting
party. There is nothing secret about these lists and they should be
consulted on a daily basis as they provide an excellent guideline
in ensuring that your material readiness is constantly being maintained. The second most important aspect of preparing for material inspection is to learn how to inspect. This is needed in establishing the correct standards for your men to follow.

Material inspections can be divided into two major parts. The
first, of course, is the inspection of decks, compartments, and
voids or spaces. The second is the inspection of machinery,
ordnance equipment, electronic gear, etc. A typical compartment
on board ship will be discussed first. Unless the division officer
makes a more thorough and exacting inspection of his spaces

than any of his seniors is likely to make, he cannot expect to be successful. The first thing to look at in entering the compartment is its overall appearance. Then go over all details, methodically and carefully. Look into, under, over, and behind everything. It is in the corners, over and under lockers, and behind pipes and fittings that you are likely to find dirt. You can be sure that if you do not find it, someone senior to you will. Have all lockers, drawers, and switch and control boxes opened up. Take nothing for granted; wear a working uniform and get down on your knees if you have to.

Nothing is so likely to infuriate a senior inspecting officer as finding dirt, cigarette butts, and other trash under a locker or other piece of furniture. His immediate and logical reaction is that the young officer responsible for the cleanliness of this space either is too lazy to bend over or is ineffectual.

In addition, the neatness and condition of the paint must be noted, as well as the absence of paint from gaskets, brightwork, pipe threads, name plates, electric leads, knife edges, etc. It is important to check all movable fittings such as fans, ventilation gear, valves, fire-fighting equipment, etc., for freedom of operation. Inspect electric wiring for frayed insulation. Test all standing and emergency lights and lanterns. Check electric plugs and receptacles for proper grounding connections. Inspect all damage control fittings such as gaskets and dogs; these must not only be clean and free of corrosion, but, most important of all, must be in condition to perform properly their damage control function.

This is only a very brief mention of a few of the important points in checking a compartment. Living compartments, as well as other division spaces, should be inspected daily. There is no shortcut to look for in making a good inspection. It takes knowledge, hard work, and judgment.

Another major kind of inspection is one that concerns machinery, ordnance equipment, electronic gear, etc. Again, the key to success will be personal attention to detail. The emphasis here must be on the material condition of the machinery, as well as on the overall appearance of the compartment or battery. If the ship's employment has kept your gear operating, with little time to scrub and polish, it is obvious that appearance must suffer. But nothing should interfere with upkeep and maintenance that is within the capacity of the ship's force. All current directives in regard to alterations, repairs, maintenance, safety precautions, and operating instructions should be meticulously observed. Allowances can sometimes be made for cracked paint or dull brightwork, but it is inexcusable for an inspecting party to find evidence of faulty lubrication or the omission of required maintenance checks.

In preparing for a material inspection the division officer may often overlook checking to see that calibration data is on gauges, test equipment, and thermometers. Such equipment must, of course, be in good operating condition. Labeling must be correct and complete, and include flow-direction markers, remote controlled equipment, and all handwheels.

A list of all out-of-commission equipment must be available with all pertinent information such as the CasRep (Casualty Report), if applicable, and the proposed plan to correct the deficiency. All PMS records must be available so that machinery clearances, etc., can be verified.

Before formal material inspections by higher authority, the division officer should make a detailed last-minute check, noting particularly that all lockers, files, drawers, etc., are open. The difference between a mark of "Good" and a mark of "Excellent" often depends on the last-minute efforts of the men who are standing by, waiting for the inspecting officers.

Zone Inspections

As previously discussed in this chapter, the commanding officer will hold periodic zone inspections of the ship. These inspections may be either formal, with your men presenting the spaces, or they may be of an informal nature with your men working in the spaces. Regardless of the type chosen, the importance of this inspection remains unchanged.

As division officer you will either stand by your spaces or

accompany the inspecting officer through them. You must also ensure that all lockers, stowage cabinets, drawers, and so forth are all unlocked and open for inspection. Remember that during a zone inspection is not the time to be looking for the keys to unlock something which the inspecting officer wishes to see.

Prior to reporting to your department head that all assigned spaces are ready for the inspection, you must assign personnel to stand by. In preparing for a zone inspection the procedures set forth for the executive officer's messing and berthing inspection and the material inspection should be followed, as the zone inspection will closely resemble the significant parts of each.

After the zone inspection, a discrepancy list will be promulgated for your corrective action. You will be required to prepare and submit to your department head a report on the status of all discrepancies.

Administrative Inspections

As in the material inspection, the first step to take in preparing for an administrative inspection is to obtain copies of the check-off sheets used by the inspecting party. All ships have them on hand to use when directed to assist in the inspection of another ship of the same type. They provide an excellent check-off list for your own preparations. The check-off sheets are particularly useful in checking your organization and paperwork and in keeping prepared for a surprise inspection. They also apply to the inspection of machinery, ordnance, compartments and spaces, and personnel.

In addition, the division records must be in good order for an administrative inspection, but this should be a normal day-to-day characteristic of your records and no lengthy preparation should be needed. It is a good practice to pencil in the date, together with your initials, when you periodically correct the Watch, Quarter, and Station Bill. This will reveal to a casual inspection that you are keeping that important bill up to date.

Locker and Bag Inspections

> Commanding officers shall require the clothing of all
> nonrated personnel to be inspected by division officers at regular
> intervals to ensure that each person possesses his prescribed out-
> fit. Clothing of petty officers may be inspected on an individual
> basis if appropriate—*U.S. Navy Uniform Regulations.*

There are two other inspections that deserve brief mention:
locker and bag inspections. No special methods are recommended; the important point is that these inspections must be
regularly scheduled. The men must learn to stow their lockers
neatly and keep them that way. The reason for this policy is that
only by learning to keep in their possession a minimum amount
of gear, neatly stowed, can men adapt themselves comfortably to
the crowded living conditions aboard ship or in barracks. Many
of the younger men have never learned to keep their personal
effects in order either at home or in school. If they are permitted to
live aboard ship in the same confused manner, they will always
have gear adrift, will look sloppy at inspection, and will be disor-
ganized in general.

The importance of requiring men to maintain a regulation
full bag cannot be stressed too heavily. Inexperienced young officers are inclined to be indulgent and to overlook some deficiencies.
This indulgence is not justified; the men get a clothing allowance
and must be required to maintain a full bag. Ships can and do
receive sudden orders which may involve radical changes in cli-
mate. See *U.S. Navy Uniform Regulations* for a list of items in a
full bag.

All the men's clothing that is a part of their uniform must be
regulation. Officers are sometimes tempted to overlook an
occasional suit of "tailor mades" or a pair of nonregulation
shoes. For the men's own interest, nonregulation items should
not be permitted. Regulation issue clothing is far better in quality
and usually less expensive than articles purchased ashore. The
men should be thoroughly informed on this score and should also
be given frequent and regular opportunities to buy small stores.

Small stores to fill the men's bags should be drawn shortly after payday, while the men still have funds. Men on watch and stragglers should be checked as soon as possible after the division bag inspection.

An important point is to ensure that all clothing is clearly and properly marked. Marking instructions from *U.S. Navy Uniform Regulations* should be given to each man, and this standard marking should be insisted upon. This uniformity will add greatly to the appearance of your division at inspection. Second-hand clothing must be DC'd; that is, stencilled with the letters DC (which stands for deserter's clothing) by the master-at-arms. This indicates that the clothing has changed hands legally and will discourage the illegal "borrowing" of clothing. The practice of marking dungarees with mottos, slogans, nicknames, names of hometowns, etc., should be discouraged. Unless dungarees are marked in a regulation manner, your men will present a very poor appearance at an inspection in which dungarees are specified as the uniform.

Follow-Through

Making a careful and critical examination is only the first step in conducting a successful inspection. To get results, you must record all discrepancies, fix the responsibility for their correction on the right person, and then follow up to ensure that corrections have been made. This requires a little planning. Unless you have a yeoman who can record your notes, it is advisable to write them yourself in a pocket notebook. The best method to fix the responsibility for the correction of deficiencies is a conference of responsible petty officers and officers. With a detailed record of the inspection before them, these leaders can work out their tasks. They should leave the conference with a clear understanding of the corrective action you expect. The final and important step is the follow-up, and this is the payoff. Make sure that every item on the inspection notes is accounted for. There are various ways to do this. In the case of a personnel inspection, you can require informal memoranda from the responsible petty officers stating that certain action has been taken. For material inspections, it is advisable to make the follow-up check yourself.

In correcting deficiencies noted during zone inspection or during captain's inspection, remember that your department head expects you to look carefully through the list of deficiencies distributed a day or so later and *take positive corrective action.* Nothing is more discouraging to your superiors than for them to find the same deficiency again. If it is a material deficiency that cannot be corrected within a normal working day, you will have to submit the necessary 3-M forms (see Chapter 9).

How to Present Your Division

There is much that a division officer himself can do to make his personnel inspection a success. He may not realize it, but he is the first person to be inspected as he salutes the inspecting officer and presents the division. First impressions are always important. The division officer should have a good uniform with bright gold for special occasions such as inspections. In addition to looking very smart, a division officer should present himself and his division in a snappy, alert, and military manner. The exact method of presentation varies a little throughout the Navy. The presentation should be uniform for each division in a ship. An accepted shipboard procedure is as follows:

When "Officer's Call" is sounded, all hands not on watch or specifically excused will fall in at their division parades. On completion of the muster, division officers will prepare their divisions for inspections. Men will be formed in either two or four ranks, according to height, with the tallest men in each rank at that end of the division which the inspecting party will first approach. Junior division officers and chief petty officers will form a rank or file in the rear of the division, with the junior division officer at the same end of the division as the tallest men.

The division should be given the command to open ranks, which means that the ranks face each other about two paces apart, deck space permitting. The men can then stand at parade rest while waiting for the inspecting party to arrive. This is a fine opportunity to conduct training, either by appropriate reading or by group discussion.

The division officer will fall in so that the inspecting officer will approach from his right side. When the inspecting party approaches, the division will be called to attention. When the inspecting officer is within six paces, the division officer will order "Hand . . . SALUTE!" He will then greet the inspecting officer with, "Good morning, Captain (Commodore, Admiral)." After the inspecting officer returns the salute, the division officer will give his division the command "Two."

The division officer then will address the inspecting officer as follows: "_____ division, ready for your inspection, Sir, _____ men, no unauthorized absentees (or the number of absentees)." The division officer shall be prepared to provide the inspecting officer with an exact breakdown of his personnel, stating the number of men and their disposition, if requested.

As the inspecting officer and his party inspect, the division officer will fall in just behind the inspecting officer, on the side away from the rank under inspection.

At the request of the inspecting officer, the division officer will give his division the command to about face and uncover.

Upon completion of the inspection, he shall give his division the command to cover, about, face the rear rank (or first and third ranks), and order "Close ranks."

The division will stand at "parade rest" until the inspecting party is clear of the next division being inspected, when the division may be allowed to stand at ease.

Divisions will remain at "division parades" until the entire personnel inspection has been completed, unless otherwise directed by the executive officer.

How to Present a Compartment

There is also a method of presenting a compartment to an inspecting officer which will provide a good first impression. The man in charge of the compartment, space, or particular item of equipment being inspected should salute the inspecting officer and give his name, rate, and station. "Good afternoon, sir. Doe (rate). Compartment (name) ready for inspection, sir." He should be prepared to demonstrate a thorough knowledge of his responsibilities. All lockers and drawers should be open, if practicable, or at least should be unlocked. It is advisable for the division officer to require the above procedure as he makes his own inspections, so that no special rehearsals will be necessary for the more formal inspections.

The group pride and satisfaction that the men of the division as a team derive from a good performance at inspection is your major objective. It is a very rewarding one. To increase it, you should immediately pass on to your men any complimentary remarks you receive during the inspection.

8/Counseling, Human Goals, and Welfare

A Division Officer shall take such action as may be necessary for the efficiency of his division and the welfare and morale of his subordinates.—*U.S. Navy Regulations, 1948.*

In Chapter 2, "Capabilities and Needs," the overriding importance of people was stressed. The point was made that your men are your major means to achieve combat efficiency. In this chapter the concept will be expanded and some practical means described that should assist you in managing this, your greatest resource, the human person.

Of major importance are attitudes—yours as a division officer and theirs. We have already briefly discussed feelings and an atmosphere of approval. Here we will emphasize again the complexities of personal relationships with some specific steps you can take (counseling) to meet the inevitable human problems that arise.

There is another field of action which can be of immense help to you in solving some of your personnel problems. This is the Navy's Human Goals program described in this chapter. You already know about this program, no doubt, but perhaps have not thought about it as a leadership tool.

The Individual

Perhaps the easiest way to recognize the importance of each man as an individual is first to consider yourself. You are the individual you know the most about. You react to each new situation in your own way. This is probably a way which is very similar to most others around you but at the same time has certain aspects which make it very clearly your own. For instance, if you are from Florida you may look forward to an at-sea training period which includes a port visit at Mayport over a holiday weekend. The married men on board might have preferred to be in homeport during that time and so won't share your enthusiasm over the port visit. However, some of these men may be looking forward to the at-sea period because they will be involved in a missile shoot or a competitive gunnery exercise for which they've been training for some time. Each man will see each situation in his own way based on his background, experience, expectations, and personal prejudices and desires. You may be the type of individual who will do anything he is asked but reacts negatively to being ordered around with little apparent consideration. If this is the case (as it is with many people) you will probably be happier and more effective working for a man who uses the approach of saying, "Would you help me out by . . ." or "We need to dress up the bridge wings, could you see that it gets taken care of for me?" Someone who simply told you, "Get the bridge wings painted out before liberty call" would probably rub you the wrong way.

What we're talking about here are the differences in personality that can result in harmony on the job or a morale problem that would affect the quality of work. You can easily see how the actions of others can cause you to react with enthusiasm or animosity. It should be obvious to you that you will affect others in much the same way. Which way you affect the men who work for you will be determined by how well you know them and by how considerate you are in your approach. Obviously you should never apologize because a job is too demanding. You might well take the time, however, to let your men know you realize that doing their job requires a sacrifice from time to time. Tell them that this particular job requires an extra effort and although it may be difficult or inconvenient it must be done and done well. Whenever the situation makes it possible, take the time to explain why a job has to be done. A good time for this is at quarters when your men are together. They will appreciate knowing more about the reason for their work. Remember that someday you may have to ask them to risk their lives, and those situations don't usually allow time for explanations. If your men know that you have asked them to do jobs always with good reason they will not hesitate to follow you when the going gets rough.

Each man wants to feel that he is important. He wants to know that he is making some kind of worthwhile contribution. Unfortunately, all of his duties may not leave him with this impression of himself. This is especially true of the more junior men. You know that you feel better about yourself when you feel a degree of personal worth, when events leave you with the feeling that you have value as a person. This feeling of worth can best be described as a good self-image and is extremely important to an individual's happiness. A person who feels that he has nothing of worth to contribute will probably not be capable of doing a good job at anything since he won't be interested in his work.

We get our self-image mostly from the information provided by those around us. If our supervisors treat us as if we are important to them or to the accomplishment of vital functions we feel better about ourselves. However, if they don't ever acknowledge the fact that we are needed, we could easily start to believe that we were unnecessary. As a division officer it is your responsibility to keep each of your men working to the best of his ability towards the successful completion of your mission. If one or more of your men are down on themselves you won't be able to get all they are capable of from them. Fortunately for you, your position as their leader will make your input to their self-image very important to them. If you treat each man with respect and dignity he will more easily accept the fact that he is a valuable part of your division. Be sure that your watchstanders not only know the technical information required to tune a radar scope, but that they realize the importance of that equipment being in top operational status at all times. Once a man realizes he is charged with the responsibility to perform critical functions even though his job may be routine, it is less likely to be boring and he will perform those duties conscientiously.

The way the men of your division feel about the workload they are assigned, themselves as individuals, and the division as a working group is termed morale. You are responsible for the quality of work, discipline, and morale of your division. These responsibilities are interrelated and you cannot work towards fulfilling one without consideration of the need to fulfill the others. If you approach each one of these facets of leadership properly you will be working on all three each time you work on one. At the same time you should realize the neglect of any of them will cause an eventual degradation of the others.

Personal Problems

When men feel they are not important or that their importance is not recognized by those around them they may, perhaps unconsciously, take action to change that situation. They may become braggarts, liars, bullies, or just loud mouths. In some cases they may become loners or even antisocial. This could lead to serious problems for the men and indirectly, their shipmates. Your men could become involved in drugs or dependent on alcohol. All of this may be simply an attempt to get attention or deal with the personal disappointment associated with a lack of a satisfactory self-image. As a division officer you should know your men well enough to recognize these problems while they are developing so that they don't cause personal disasters for the men involved or affect the quality of your division's work.

Men who have special difficulties of any sort need advice and assistance, and they should be encouraged to turn to their division officers. If they do not come to you voluntarily you may have to reach out to them. Perhaps a man is not getting along with a shipmate or feels that a particular petty officer is picking on him. His difficulty may be an alcoholic parent or an unfaithful wife or a child stricken with disease. Whatever their personal problems, our men must know that, whether trivial or serious, their problems may be taken to their division officer. One of your most demanding duties is that of being a counselor to your men.

An attitude survey covering 10,000 enlisted men revealed that two-thirds of the men felt that their officers were *not* interested in their welfare. Whether the officers concerned actually were interested in their men is not relevant; the important fact is that most of their men *felt* that they were not. See that the men you are responsible for do not acquire this attitude.

Counseling

There are no hard and fast rules that can be offered to assist you in counseling your men. You will be more effective, however, if you can realize the subjectivity of each situation. Remembering that each man is a unique individual will start you off right. What works in one counseling session may be exactly the wrong thing to do in the next. Only experience can prepare you for the myriad possibilities you will face when a man approaches you for help or you call a man aside to show your concern over some change in his behavior. Understanding men and knowing their backgrounds, sympathy for the unfortunate, and ingenuity in finding a solution are all parts of the wisdom an officer acquires. Above all, he must listen patiently; that in itself may be enough to help a man in trouble. For the man to talk it out, get it off his chest, is often the best medicine.

The skill of active listening to help someone must be cultivated and tried again and again if it is to be effective. There are many techniques and training courses you could take to develop listening skills, but the most essential one and also the easiest to master is the skill of letting the speaker know that you understand both his problem and his feelings. This can be done by the simple paraphrasing of the content of his words, adding statements about how you perceive his feelings. Most people are quite capable of solving their own problems, if only they can find an attentive ear to listen to the problem.

Second in importance to being a sympathetic listener is having the perception to recognize a problem that exceeds your limitations. The best thing to do in this case is to help the individual to get an appointment with someone with professional training, such as a lawyer or psychiatrist. It is most important that the man doesn't get the impression that you are sending him on to someone else because you don't want to waste your time with him. Follow up on the appointment both with your man and the professional you referred him to. Ensure that he knows he has your support and concern while he is working out his problems. This may seem insignificant but it may provide him with the motivation to return to his former position as a contributing member of the team more rapidly.

Men in combat or under pressure of hard work and demanding conditions, or sometimes for no apparent reason at all, may slip a cog and lose their ability to get along with people and do their work. They may complain of headaches or other pains, or declare that they cannot sleep, or become extremely irritable or depressed, to mention a few of many symptoms. If a man is really sick there is nothing to do but send him to the doctor.

Giving him a pep talk or trying to shame him are both useless methods. There will be men, of course, who do not need a doctor, but who do need man-to-man advice or perhaps just an old-fashioned "bracing up." Sometimes your instincts or prejudices will tell you a man is truly a malingerer. Before acting on this instinct you should think twice. A mistake in the case of a sincerely troubled man would be traumatic for him and could prove disastrous. If in doubt, have the man see a doctor.

The important point is that all possible steps should be taken to salvage your human casualties and return them to useful duty. Sick men are a military liability, whether they have pneumonia or a disordered mind.

If you find that it is necessary to call a man in because he has for some reason fallen down on his responsibilities you should consider the situation closely before taking any action. Perhaps the man will be less threatened and, therefore, more receptive to counseling if you approach him less formally while speaking with him in your spaces. When you first broach the subject, whether on his territory (the working spaces) or yours (your stateroom), it may be helpful to tell him first how you feel about his performance to date and express your disappointment or annoyance, if appropriate, at the present turn of events. Let him know that his contribution is important and that you will not and cannot accept any degradation in his performance. He may at this point open up to you and tell you what is bothering him. Don't accept excuses; if he can give you a reason for his poor performance then you can work together to correct the situation. If he merely tells you that his work is good enough or he feels he is giving the same effort, don't accept it. Be firm, let him know you care. If you back down he'll feel you only care about productivity. If you pursue the point of *his* performance he'll know that it is he, personally, that you have noticed and care about. Nothing can substitute for sincerely caring for your men and nothing can convince them you do if that is not the case.

There are also men who may need the services of a chaplain. A man may be grieved by the loss of a wife or a child. Another may have trouble with his wife or relatives. Chaplains are exceedingly useful experts in human problems. They have had special training, have developed special skills, and should be used freely as counselors, particularly in matters concerning death and grief. This is not to say that the division officer does not have an obligation to take whatever action appropriate to assist a man in a stressful situation. Reassignment to more active working details or perhaps a brief leave or special liberty could help, depending on the personality of the individual.

At any rate, it is you, as a division officer who are responsible for the well-being of your men. Regardless of the demands made upon you by your other duties or by your personal matters, you should not slight the responsibility of ensuring that your men are well cared for.

As Admiral Arleigh Burke once pointed out:

> The average division officer, under these conditions (multiple duties), directs most of his attention and efforts to those tasks whose results are most immediately apparent to his seniors, or in other words, to those tasks which, if omitted or neglected, would cause immediate repercussions. In this process the supervision, guidance, knowledge, and understanding of the men of his division are often neglected.
>
> It is important to emphasize that only by knowing subordinates is it possible to evaluate their talents and limitations. Only by knowing men can they be properly placed. There must be continuous concern about men, and not concern just when they get into trouble or are about to ship over or go out.

The continuous concern that is the basis of a division officer's relationship with his men is rooted in a moral charge to be responsible in the leadership of men.

Navy Human Goals Program

The purpose of the Navy's Human Goals Program is to ensure the development of the full potential of its human resources and application of that potential toward maximum effectiveness in the performance of the Navy's primary mission. The Navy recognizes that to fulfill this purpose its Human Goals Program must promote sound leadership, good order and discipline,

responsibility, authority and accountability, pride and profession-
alism, morale and esprit, and individual dignity and worth.—
OpNavInst 5300.6 (series)

The Navy Human Goals Program is aimed at increasing
awareness and sensitivity to the problems of contemporary society
as they exist in the Navy. The program is really a series of projects
to assist the Navy to best deal with pressing issues of interpersonal
and intercultural relations. The various projects are two-pronged,
usually including both a training phase to prevent problems from
spreading and a remedial phase intended to help solve problems
associated with drugs, alcohol, race relations, and career development. Many facilities and assistance groups have been established to provide support to fleet units and shore stations. Previously they would have had to deal with these problems whether
they had personnel assigned with the expertise required to effectively handle the situation or not. The division officer should
know that almost any problem arising within his division may be
handled by his becoming involved with and using the resources
made available by the Navy Human Goals Program or one of the
organizations which have helped the Navy traditionally with the
more long-standing problems. Educational programs can increase the division officer's personal ability to recognize and act on
trouble areas with which he may have previously had no first-hand
experience. The following summary of instructions should give a
basic understanding of the scope of the Navy Human Goals
Program:

DOD Directive	Subject
1010.2	Alcohol abuse by personnel of the Department of Defense

SecNavInst	
5300.20	Alcohol abuse and alcoholism among military and civilian personnel of the Department of the Navy
6710.1 (series)	Illegal or improper use of drugs
6710.2	Drug exemption program, voluntary disclosures

OpNavInst
    5300.6 (series)   Navy Human Goals Plan
    6330.1   Alcohol abuse and alcoholism among Navy personnel
    6710.2 (series)   Department of Defense drug abuse testing program

BuPersInst
    6710.1 (series)   Drug and alcohol education and action program and personnel resources

BuPersNote 6710
    21 Aug. 1972   Administrative procedures for disposition of enlisted members identified as drug abusers

Race Relations

One of the major areas of concern in the Navy Human Goals Program is race relations. This is so critical an area of sensitivity that it merits special mention.

This subject is covered in detail in OpNavInst 5300.6 (series), which is quite broad in concept. The policy of equal opportunity practiced by the Navy has its roots in the U.S. Constitution, which all U.S. Navy personnel are sworn "to support and defend," and in the moral concept of human dignity. It is the policy of the Department of the Navy that each man be fully informed of the intent of this OpNav instruction and of the "Human Goals Credo" contained therein (Figure 8-1) and be aware of the consequences of willfully disregarding its direction. Individual commands are to instruct all those under their supervision of the concept of equal opportunity through the Command Action Program and Affirmative Action Program, which were designed to insure that any form of discrimination be identified and eliminated. The force of this instruction is sufficient to justify the separation of any member who disregards its precepts and fails to respond to counseling.

The problem of race relations is an offshoot of intercultural

DEPARTMENT OF DEFENSE
HUMAN GOALS

Our nation was founded on the principle that the individual has infinite dignity and worth. The Department of Defense, which exists to keep the Nation secure and at peace, must always be guided by this principle. In all that we do, we must show respect for the serviceman, the servicewoman and the civilian employee, recognizing their individual needs, aspirations and capabilities.

The defense of the Nation requires a well-trained force, military and civilian, regular and reserve. To provide such a force we must increase the attractiveness of a career in Defense so that the service member and the civilian employee will feel the highest pride in themselves and their work, in the uniform and the military profession.

THE ATTAINMENT OF THESE GOALS REQUIRES THAT WE STRIVE ...

To attract to the defense service people with ability, dedication, and capacity for growth;

To provide opportunity for every one, military and civilian, to rise to as high a level of responsibility as possible, dependent only on individual talent and diligence;

To make military and civilian service in the Department of Defense a model of equal opportunity for all regardless of race, sex, creed or national origin, and to hold those who do

business with the Department to full compliance with the policy of equal employment opportunity;

To help each service member in leaving the service to readjust to civilian life; and

To contribute to the improvement of our society, including its disadvantaged members, by greater utilization of our human and physical resources while maintaining full effectiveness in the performance of our primary mission.

ORIGINAL ISSUE DATE
August 18, 1969

Figure 8-1. Department of Defense Human Goals.

prejudices, stemming from widespread misconceptions regarding the capabilities, dignity, and worth of individuals of another race, creed, or national origin. These prejudices have pervaded our society at one level or another since 1776. The most notable abuses have been in black-white relationships; however, yellow-white and red-white clashes have been present throughout U.S. history. It is indeed difficult to overcome the false beliefs of different segments of U.S. culture. But if we fail to ensure the equality of all men both morally and under the law we make a farce of the Constitution and so our very profession.

As a division officer you are an integral part in the implementation of the program. This is a responsibility of the highest order because the dignity of man and the justification of your profession hang in the balance. The practical aspects of the Human Goals Program are very real and should be used as a tool in solving some of your personnel problems.

Other Supports

The division officer may find that his men will require quite a broad system of supports to feel truly secure and to have the necessary resources in time of personal need. The Navy has over the years developed an extensive system of supports and agencies for emergency assistance which operate both in official and semiofficial capacities. These services range from counseling, to financial assistance in time of personal crisis, to recreation designed to increase and maintain morale during times of separation and to increase group pride and identity. Some of these services are considered here in more detail.

Chaplains

Referral to a chaplain is particularly important in matters that relate to a man's religious requirements. Cruisers, tenders, repair ships, and major support ships usually have chaplains. Carriers usually have both Catholic and Protestant chaplains. At major shore activities there may be representatives of several religious denominations. Jewish chaplains are usually available where fleet forces are concentrated. Many chaplains "circuit-ride" within organizations such as flotillas and squadrons. In any case, chaplains stand ready to counsel men referred to them, regardless of organizational relationships, or see that they are directed to the appropriate chaplain.

Whether a chaplain is available or not, it is the duty of the division officer to offer what immediate help he can. This may only take the form of reassurance of your continued interest in assisting a man, of aiding in finding a new approach toward resolutions of the problem, or of ensuring that he will be given opportunity to see a chaplain as soon as possible. Whatever can be done to assist a man who is in personal difficulty will help to return him to his job.

Navy Relief and Red Cross

There are two semiofficial welfare agencies with which every officer should be familiar. These agencies are the Navy Relief Society and the American Red Cross. Both will, when circumstances warrant, assist financially and perform other services to Navy men and their dependents. In addition, the Red Cross, with its many field representatives scattered throughout the country, is very useful in providing information for service personnel or their families when it is believed that an emergency exists.

Detailed information on these two organizations is available in current directives and from the chaplain, welfare and recreation officer, or executive officer.

With respect to the Navy Relief Society, complete information is contained in current BuPers Instructions of the 7040 series.

The Navy Relief Society is maintained and operated by Navy men and women for naval personnel. Its sole mission is to help naval personnel and their dependents by providing them grants or loans.

This organization has achieved an outstanding reputation for its long record of assistance on behalf of Navy men, women, and children. In order to be ready to advise their men and to assure them of the real value of Navy Relief, division officers should familiarize themselves with the society's purpose, functions, and operations.

The American Red Cross is authorized to conduct a program of social welfare which includes financial assistance for naval personnel, medical and psychiatric casework, and recreational services for the hospitalized. The Red Cross is an authorized medium of communication between families of naval personnel and the Navy. In furnishing information the primary interest of the Red Cross is to develop the facts concerning matters referred to it.

Another source of emergency financial aid is the ship's recreation fund, which can advance money to a man in need. This source is usually immediately available in an emergency, and it is the division officer's responsibility to know the ship's policy in this regard.

It must be emphasized that any personal financial dealings with your men, even for the best of reasons, should be scrupulously avoided by officers and petty officers.

Recreation

Recreation is, of course, an important part of the lives of young Americans. The division officer's job is to help his men take advantage of recreational facilities and, if those facilities are limited or do not exist, to help his men improvise. The creative use of leisure time is to be encouraged. Money and elaborate facilities are not as important as imaginative leadership.

Recreation does not mean only parties and social events, it means healthy and interesting activities. Some men on liberty in a foreign port will look for the nearest bar. You can be assured that many men will do so if nothing else occurs to them. This is where a little planning and initiative pays off. Sight-seeing tours, trips to resorts, hunting and fishing parties are all activities that can be arranged, and most men will prefer something of this nature.

A major point concerning recreational activities is their enjoyment. Simply directing your men to go ashore and play ball is not enough. To be classed as recreation, an activity must be well planned and organized, and free of restrictions and formality. Any sort of a project, from a steak fry to a fishing trip, can turn out to be a hardship if no one organizes it. It is all very well to announce a softball game at 1600, providing the day's work is finished; but unless someone gathers the gear, arranges for a field, and requests a boat in time, the whole idea will have caused more confusion and hard feelings than recreation.

A second major principle is that recreational activities must never be used as substitutes for good leadership. This means that a beer party may be an appropriate reward for good performance or may just be a good idea in itself. It should not serve to make up for poor organization and sloppy administration.

A third principle is not to over-organize your men's activities. Do not attempt to schedule *all* their free time.

Recreational activities are too many and varied to be described in this chapter. Depending on the size and location of your outfit, and the time available, you can organize anything from a spear-fishing party in a tropical lagoon to a bear-hunt at Kodiak. But here are a few points about the major recreational activities that might help division officers to evaluate them.

Division parties are recommended as excellent opportunities for the men to enjoy themselves. They also add to the *esprit* of a division; the men get to know each other better, and new men more quickly identify themselves with the division. This division spirit is immensely important, and the right sort of party will add to it. Wine, women, and song are all appropriate in reasonable proportions and within the bounds of reason. Do not let any of the more ribald elements in your division talk you into approving anything that you would be ashamed to take your wife or best girl to. While division parties are not official in any sense of the word, they are, in fact, an activity of a group for whom you, as division officer, are responsible. If a division party gets out of hand, the division officer will be held responsible by the commanding officer, who may himself be embarrassed if the affair becomes widely known. In addition, therefore, to the basic moral principles involved, it is just not smart for an officer to permit a division party to be open to criticism. A wise division officer will discourage parties that involve heavy drinking. Many of the younger men are not accustomed to hard liquor, and it certainly is not sensible to further their education along these lines. Heavy drinking invariably leads to trouble—why stack the deck against yourself?

Information Contributes to Welfare

There are many aspects of naval life that, while not directly related to the activities of your division, are of intimate concern to your men. Among these are pay, allowances, travel of dependents, dependents' housing, the transportation of household effects, Navy Exchange activities, and medical care for dependents. If you are not married most of these subjects will not interest you, but they are of interest to your married men. While Supply Corps officers are the recognized authorities in supply matters, and the ship's doctor should have the latest word on dependents' medical care, it is still necessary for you as a division officer to be reasonably familiar with all naval matters that are of real importance to your men.

Recreation Fund

Each ship and station maintains a unit recreation fund, the income of which is derived from Ship's Store or Navy Exchange profits. These funds support the unit's recreation program covering, among others, such matters as athletics, dances, all-hands parties, games and associated equipment, hobby craft, and sightseeing tours.

Expenditures are usually made as a result of recommendations of the unit's Recreation Committee—composed of enlisted personnel. The division officer can see that the needs and desires of his men can be recognized by ensuring not only that his division's representative on the recreation committee fully understands his duties but that the men of the division are aware of his appointment. The *Special Services Manual* requires that the recreation committee be kept fully informed about the condition of the fund and, when disapprovals are necessary, the reasons therefor.

Athletics

Athletics are, of course, the most popular and beneficial of leisure-time activities. Within reasonable limits the utmost encouragement should be given to all types of active sports, particularly intramural games and competition. But there is one yardstick that should be applied to athletics: Do a large part of your men participate in and enjoy the game? There is little percentage in having a few stars in a division who are excused from most of their work in order to attend practice on a "varsity" team. Their shipmates have to do their work, and the stars are a loss to their unit when it comes to military training and combat. The simpler team sports which all men can play, such as softball or touch football, usually pay off best because more men can take part at the same time.

The principle of maximum participation should be applied, however, with some judgment. If enough men enjoy watching the games or rooting for the team, then there is good reason to emphasize ship or squadron teams. Nothing is finer for the spirit of any unit than supporting a team of some sort. But the support must be voluntary and spontaneous; elaborate athletic programs set in motion by directives from above never accomplish anything unless they reflect the desires and capabilities of the men. Of course, most of this is beyond the control of the division officer. You can only inform your immediate superior if you consider that certain athletic requirements are interfering with the work or training of your men. Within the division, you should encourage athletics with vigor and ingenuity upon all occasions when your primary objective, training for combat, permits.

Other Recreation

In addition to athletics, other forms of outdoor activities such as hunting, fishing, and camping deserve support. Local sportsmen are usually glad to cooperate, and a small outlay in time and energy on the part of an officer will often pay large dividends. It is wise to supervise the preparations and to designate a competent officer or petty officer to be in charge of hunting, fishing, and camping trips. You should feel responsible for your men at all times.

Other important leisure-time activities are movies and books and magazines. Little can be said about movies except that most men enjoy them and that you should do all you can within reason to obtain good pictures and show them comfortably. One thing *not* to do is to request the showing of training films just before the regular evening movie. There are times, of course, when it may be justified, but in general it is considered an encroachment on the men's well-earned free time.

Books and magazines are recreation items that require constant attention. They are of no value if they cannot be conveniently used. This requires a personal interest on the part of the division officer, and appropriate action if so indicated. The ship's recreation committee is a means of voicing the men's desires in selecting the magazines the men want to read, since magazine subscriptions are paid for out of the ship's recreation fund.

It is important to look into the facilities available to men for reading, studying, and writing letters. A large ship should have a crew's lounge that is adequate. Every ship should have some space for these activities, with adequate lighting in each compartment, and such space can nearly always be found. If you see your men writing letters and reading in dim corners, you know that some action is called for.

Like all other activities, those connected with recreation involve paperwork and planning. Officers who are detailed as custodians of recreational funds and equipment are well advised to consult the effective and pertinent directives. The *Special Services Manual,* a Bureau of Naval Personnel publication, is a basic directive.

9/Maintenance, Material, and Damage Control

A Division Officer shall supervise the administration and performance of the work centers within his division in carrying out the shipboard maintenance and material management system.—*Standard Organization and Regulations of the U.S. Navy.*

Most of this book has dealt primarily with people and their supervision; this should come as no surprise, since people are the most valuable resource of any efficient organization. Without a good crew, properly motivated and directed towards proper maintenance techniques, a ship would be little more than a floating mass of steel, integrated with sophisticated engineering, electronic and weaponry systems, unable to defend herself even against the passage of time. As the division officer, you play a fundamental role in ensuring that the upkeep, preservation and maintenance of machinery, ordnance, compartments and deck spaces for which you are responsible are kept in perfect order, with every piece of gear performing to its designed capability. Maintenance, material, and sound management go hand in hand, and will always make the difference between a good ship and a great ship.

This chapter will focus primarily upon the Navy's 3-M System: Maintenance, Material and Management. However, closely related subjects such as damage control and supply matters will also be discussed.

The two subjects, people and material, are not, of course, separate and distinct. Men, properly motivated and managed, are needed to perform the upkeep and maintenance for which a division is responsible. The division officer and his assistants must learn how to achieve this.

Although it is not within the scope of this book to cover everything that a division officer must know concerning the Navy's Maintenance, Material and Management System, you will be able to learn how the 3-M System works and hopefully gain new insights toward the complex everyday problems that you will face. The sources from which this knowledge can be obtained are outlined in this chapter.

Attention is again invited to the importance of a ship, squadron, or station organization. Efficient material maintenance depends on the form and the effectiveness of this organization. Responsibility for the care of material is clearly defined in the *3-M Manual*.

A distinction must be made between highly technical knowledge of each piece of ordnance or machinery and the "know how" to see that this gear is maintained properly. It would be ideal to know more about the radars and turbines than your highly trained petty officers do. But, normally, this is not possible. You should strive, instead, to be familiar enough with the gear to ensure that it is kept in excellent working condition. This involves extensive knowledge of maintenance procedures, particularly the check-off lists. It also means that you are able to judge when the machinery is operating at maximum efficiency—as in an air search radar, for example, which must be kept finely tuned for maximum detection of aircraft. It is also your job to see that the technicians have an opportunity to read and study the various technical bulletins, notices, and instructions which are promulgated by the technical commands. Finally, you must ensure that your men continue to increase their technical knowledge by attending Navy schools, by completing correspondence courses, or by furthering their education through the numerous educational programs available to them.

Responsibility for Maintenance

As a division officer, you will always be responsible for the maintenance of certain spaces and machinery. If you have a deck division, the emphasis will be on spaces, although the assigned machinery must be maintained. You will then probably have large deck areas, much of the exterior of the hull, as well as numerous passageways, storerooms, etc. below decks. If you have the boiler division, for example, you will have more machinery to take care of than spaces. In the OI or CIC division, you will have few spaces, but large quantities of complicated electronic equipment. In all cases, you will have two major responsibilities for material: its maintenance to ensure that it will operate reliably and effectively, and its appearance to assure its conformity with current military standards of cleanliness and preservation. These two requirements should be considered as complementary and not conflicting. If, in a rare instance, a choice must be made, the former—operating efficiency—will always take precedence. If you must make a choice between preparing your fireroom for inspection and cleaning the firesides of your boilers, for example, there is no question but that the firesides come first. If this be the case, your division will, no doubt, be excused from inspection.

In the interests of conserving manpower and in order to maintain properly the increasingly complex machinery of our Navy, it is mandatory that a systematic approach to maintenance and upkeep be employed. The key to success here is careful and thorough assignment of each space and piece of equipment to one of your men. He must know that he alone is *responsible* for that space or that machine; others may assist him in his work, but *he* is responsible. This is done by proper assignment on the weekly and quarterly maintenance schedule, which sounds obvious and may seem hardly worth emphasizing, but the violation of this principle is the single largest cause of material failures and of ships that are below standard in appearance.

The Navy will always be short of skilled technicians and mechanics. This is why it is so important to organize and assist the many unskilled men who must be trained to maintain the machinery. They can do this job efficiently if they know their responsibilities and are provided with maintenance schedules and check-off lists. The few highly skilled men can then be used as troubleshooters and as supervisors.

The same philosophy applies to the upkeep of spaces in which cleanliness and appearance are major considerations. Each passageway, compartment, or deck area must be assigned, in writing, to a man who will be held responsible for it.

The upkeep of passageways, deck areas, and spaces in general is largely a matter of attention to detail. Men will sweep down spaces and keep bulkheads reasonably clean without much supervision, but ladders, doors, scuttles, and hatches are details that are difficult to take care of and thus are prone to be ignored. These details are, of course, the very items that inspecting officers look at, and their cleanliness and smartness are an immediate indication that the space is in good shape.

As a division officer, it is your responsibility to maintain all of your spaces and compartments in top material condition. Experienced division officers have found that a thorough weekly inspection of all compartments (this includes passageways and deck areas) is invaluable in determining if the cleanliness, preservation, and watertight integrity of each space has been maintained in top condition.

Cleanliness, or the lack of it, is not difficult to judge. See the procedure recommended in the chapter on inspections. Touch the horizontal surfaces of overhead beams in search of dust; check the covers, and behind and under furniture and machinery. Dirt, trash and dust have no place anywhere in the Navy; and their presence in some locations, such as in the back of electrical switchboards and in ventilation ducts, is downright dangerous. Costly and damaging electrical fires result from an accumulation of dirt in places where short circuits are possible.

Preservation, as used herein, means primarily the absence of or freedom from corrosion. It also means the absence of any indication of extreme wear, such as frayed or worn electric cable insulation or loose pipe lagging. *Lagging* is a naval term for the canvas or sheet metal covering for the insulation used around piping aboard ship. The technical term for this insulation is *clothing.* Worn threads, missing ladder pin chains, frayed lifelines or lifeline leathers are all included under the general term "preservation." The most important aspect, however, is the one first mentioned, freedom from corrosion. Sometimes this corrosion is not apparent and can reach alarming stages of advanced decay under an apparently normal surface. The installation of fire-resistant linoleum tile over steel decks to improve habitability reintroduces an old problem of corrosion that can be well concealed.

Watertight integrity, in addition to cleanliness and preservation of a space, is another responsibility of the division officer. At first glance, you may be inclined to brush this off with the thought that you really cannot determine watertightness without making an air test. Consequently, any visual inspection is of little value. Nothing could be farther from the truth. Weekly visual inspections are vital to preserve watertight integrity between the periodic air tests. During an air test the compartment is closed completely and air is pumped in through a special air test fitting in a door, hatch, or scuttle. The maintenance of a certain air pressure for a specified length of time is a measure of the watertightness of the compartment. Between these tests it is important to determine by regular and frequent visual inspection whether anything has occurred which might imperil watertight integrity. Holes drilled in bulkheads are a too common example; these highly illegal perforations can be seen more readily if adjoining compartments are kept well lighted and the lights are momentarily turned off on your side of the bulkhead. Another important aspect of watertightness is the condition of knife edges and gaskets on doors, hatches, and scuttles. Grease on the knife edges to prevent corrosion promotes the deterioration of the gasket material. That is why grease must not be used, and frequent touching up with very fine emery cloth is the recommended treatment for knife edges.

Work-Study Principles

The Navy has learned from its extensive work-study program that six steps are fundamental to work and management improvement. These are: to select, to examine, to develop, to record, to install, and to maintain. Each step must be completed before the following step can be taken. In the case of material management, the first four steps define the equipment involved and delineate what should be done. The last two concern themselves with actual performance.

Standard Navy Maintenance and Material Management System

The 3-M System (for Maintenance, Material and Management) was developed in accordance with the above management and work-study philosophies. It is broken into two basic subsystems: The *Planned Maintenance Subsystem* which assigns responsibility and designates the method to be used to maintain equipment; and the *Maintenance Data Collection Subsystem* which assigns responsibility and designates the method to be used to evaluate and to improve this maintenance and to ensure a return or feedback of information from the fleet to the various cognizant material commands.

When the Planned Maintenance System was introduced as part of the Standard Navy Maintenance and Material Management System (3-M System) by CNO Instruction 4700.16, it was pointed out CNO was developing and implementing these procedures so that (1) a fleetwide standard of maintenance planning and control would be provided for the uniform accomplishment of planned maintenance and (2) a fleetwide uniform system for collecting, processing, analyzing, and distributing feedback information would be provided to facilitate line and other appropriate commands in their management functions.

Today, the primary objective of the Ship's 3-M System is to ensure maximum equipment readiness. To this end, the intermediate objectives of the 3-M System are as follows:

1. Achievement of uniform maintenance standards and criteria.
2. Effective use of available manpower and material.
3. Documenting information relating to maintenance.
4. Improvement of maintainability and reliability of systems and equipment through analysis of documented maintenance information.
5. Provision for reporting ship configuration changes.
6. Identification and reduction of the cost of maintenance and maintenance support.

Planned Maintenance Subsystem (PMS)

The PMS has been developed to provide each ship, department, and supervisor with the tools to plan, schedule, and control planned maintenance effectively. It specifically provides for the following:

1. Comprehensive procedures for planned maintenance.
2. Minimum requirements for preventive maintenance.
3. Scheduling and control of the performance of tasks.
4. Description of the methods, materials, tools, and personnel needed for maintenance.
5. Prevention or detection of impending malfunctions.

The PMS supercedes all previous planned or preventive maintenance systems or programs. Where there is a difference between PMS and other technical publications or systems, PMS requirements will prevail. Equipment not supported by PMS will continue to be maintained in accordance with existing procedures (manufacturer's and SYSCOM's technical manuals) until PMS is developed and installed.

The Planned Maintenance Subsystem includes a *Planned Maintenance System Manual, Planned Maintenance System Schedules* (cycle, quarterly, and weekly), and *Maintenance Requirement Cards* (MRCs).

A *Planned Maintenance System (PMS) Manual* contains: a list of all equipment covered by a particular ship's system; *Maintenance Manual Index Pages* that summarize all the planned maintenance prescribed for each system, subsystem, or component along with the rates and times required; and a man-hour summary for the class of equipment (radar, sonar, etc.) that must be maintained (Figure 9-1). There is also a list of equipment for which no maintenance is required. The manual is primarily used by the various department heads in planning and scheduling maintenance, and for documentation control. (Obtain a copy of the *PMS Manual* and study it until you are familiar with the instructions and forms involved. Some of the forms are reproduced in this chapter, but others, particularly the cycle, quarterly, and weekly schedules are too large for a book of this size.)

Actual scheduling is accomplished by using the three interrelated Planned Maintenance Systems Schedules—cycle, quarterly, and weekly. The cycle schedule, based on a ship overhaul cycle, lists the system and subsystem components in each maintenance group. Their annual, semiannual, and overhaul cycle maintenance requirements are fitted into a quarters-after-overhaul time frame. The cycle schedule is used by the department head in making out the quarterly schedule. Although this is the department head's responsibility, he depends upon the division officers to supply him with the information and proposed schedules for each division. The division officer must maintain and keep each schedule current.

SYSTEM, SUBSYSTEM, OR COMPONENT	REFERENCE PUBLICATIONS	DATE September 1974			
Main Circulating Pump					

SYSCOM MRC CONTROL NO.	MAINTENANCE REQUIREMENT	PERIO-DICITY CODE	SKILL LEVEL	MAN HOURS	RELATED MAINTE-NANCE
94 E87Z N	1. Inspect lube oil. 2. Lubricate speed limiting governor. 3. Turn pump several revolutions by hand; if steam is available, turn by steam.	W-1	MM3	0.6	None
94 E86M N	1. Test speed limiting governor.	M-1	MM3 FN	0.2 0.2	None
94 E87F N	1. Back flush lube oil cooler.	M-2	MM2 FN	1.0 1.0	None
83 D18A N	1. Inspect packing gland adjustment.	M-8	MM3	0.1	None
94 E86Z N	1. Renew lube oil. 2. Clean lubricating oil filter. 3. Inspect reduction gears.	Q-1	MM3 FN	2.0 2.0	None
94 E86P N	1. Test combination exhaust-relief valve.	Q-2	MM2 FN	0.2 0.2	None
94 E87G N	1. Clean and inspect turbine steam strainer.	A-1	MM3	1.0	None
52 1FZZ A	1. Inspect foundation bolts for tightness.	A-9	FN	0.4	None
94 E86Q N	1. Inspect internal parts.	C-1	MM1 2FN	12.0 24.0	R-8
83 D18G N	1. Inspect carbon packing. 2. Inspect turbine exterior.	C-3	MM2 FN	3.0 3.0	None
94 E87J N	1. Clean lube oil cooler chemically; test cooler hydrostatically.	C-5	MM2 FN	2.5 2.5	None
94 E87K N	1. Renew packing. NOTE: Accomplish when packing gland has been tightened to within 1/4" of pump housing.	R-8	MM/EN3	1.0	None

SYSCOM MIP CONTROL NUMBER E-5/86-94

Figure 9-1. Maintenance Index Page.

The quarterly schedule displays present and future quarter maintenance requirements to be performed, and is blended with the ship's operating schedule. Each quarter is divided into 13 weekly columns. Maintenance requirements are written into the specific weekly column in which the work is expected to be done. The cycle and quarterly schedules combined give the overall planned maintenance program for the ship.

The weekly schedule, located in the work space, assigns specific personnel to perform specific tasks on specific components involved in the maintenance group area in which the schedule is posted; and is used by the working area supervisor to assign work and record its completion.

Maintenance Requirement Cards (MRC) are written for components, subsystems, and system interfaces. These cards (Figure 9-2) explicitly describe to the maintenance personnel: what is to be done; the tools, parts, computer programs, and materials required to accomplish the task; unique safety precautions to be observed; and a step-by-step procedure for performing the task. A deck of appropriate MRCs in a metal container is installed in each maintenance group working area where they *will be readily accessible* to those performing the maintenance tasks. The division officer must ensure that a complete and current deck of MRCs is installed. This can only be accomplished by continuous review. A master deck of all departmental MRCs and *Maintenance Index Pages* is assembled into master *PMS Manuals* containing material related to each working space and maintained at the working group level.

The division officer must ensure that the assigned maintenance is being accomplished, and further, being accomplished by the designated method. One way to provide this assurance is to watch every job from start to finish, but a more practical method is to use a statistical method of random sampling.

1. Select a MRC for a task that has recently been scheduled and X'ed through as being completed.
2. Read the task and procedure on the MRC to become familiar with what should have been accomplished.
3. Point out the assignment to the man who accomplished it, and

SYSTEM	COMPONENT	MRC CODE	
	Main Circulating Pump	E-5	C-1

SUBSYSTEM	RELATED MAINTENANCE	RATES	M/H
	R-8		12.0
		2FN	24.0

MAINTENANCE REQUIREMENT DESCRIPTION	TOTAL M/H
1. Inspect internal parts.	36.0

SAFETY PRECAUTIONS	ELAPSED TIME:
1. Comply with Navy Safety Precautions for Forces Afloat, OPNAVINST 5100 Series.	12.0

TOOLS, PARTS, MATERIALS, TEST EQUIPMENT

1. Scissors
2. Wood block
3. Wire brush
4. MRC R-8
5. Safety tags
6. Feeler gauge
7. 24 Gauge wire
8. Lifting strap
9. Lint-free rags
10. Flange scraper
11. Gasket punch set
12. Pencil and paper
13. 1/16" Gasket material, Symbol 2150
14. _____ Combination wrenches
15. Gasket sealer, MIL-S-45180A Type 3
16. 1/2-ton Chain hoist
17. 6" Slip-joint pliers
18. Oil, Symbol 2190 TEP
19. Inside micrometer set
20. 1-lb Ball peen hammer
21. 3/4" drive Socket set
22. Outside micrometer set
23. Circle and hole cutter
24. Portable extension light
25. 8" Normal duty screwdriver
26. 10' of 21-thread Manila line

PROCEDURE

Preliminary
   a. Wire applicable isolation valve(s) shut and tag "Do Not Open."

1. Inspect Internal Parts.
   a. Open drain valve and drain main condenser; shut drain valve.
   b. Open bilge suction valve and drain pump; shut bilge suction valve.
   c. Remove piping or tubing interference, as applicable.
   d. Remove packing gland nuts and gland halves.
   e. Remove case cover nuts; remove taper pins from parting flanges.
   f. Remove case cover and gaskets.
   g. Remove packing.
   h. Clean case, cover, suction head, propeller, case liner, and throat bushing.

LOCATION	DATE
	September 1974

PAGE 1 OF 3

94 E860 N

Figure 9-2. Maintenance Requirement Card.

question him as to what the task was and how he performed it (do not allow him the benefit of reading the MRC until after the questions have been answered). The man should be able to identify the task and quite accurately describe the steps of the procedure.

4. If disassembly was a part of the procedure, inspect the equipment for evidence of disassembly (the quality of reinstallation could be examined at this time also).

This type of sampling must be unannounced. The interval between samples must vary, and the MRC must be selected at random to assure that each of the work center codes are sampled at some time. Select a different man each time.

PMS Feedback Report Procedures

The *PMS Feedback Report* (Figure 9-3) is a form used by Fleet personnel to notify the Systems Command or the Type Command as applicable, on matters related to PMS. The report is a five-part form composed of an original and four copies. Instructions for preparation and submission of the form are printed on the back of the last copy. These forms are obtainable through the Navy Supply System.

The Feedback Reports, submitted by shipboard personnel, point out apparent discrepancies, errors, or voids in some aspect of PMS; they can also be used to request new or replacement PMS software or hardware. The PMS Feedback Report assists in timely and effective management and in improved PMS.

Repair Categories

As a result of *Planned Maintenance System* (PMS), necessary repairs are discovered, some of them before they become serious. These repairs fall into three basic categories: organizational maintenance (ship's force), intermediate maintenance (tender), and depot maintenance (shipyard).

Organization maintenance items are those that will be accomplished by the ship's force. They are blended with the PMS.

REPORT SYMBOL OPNAV 4790-4

SEE INSTRUCTIONS ON BACK OF GREEN PAGE

FROM (SHIP NAME AND HULL NUMBER)	SERIAL #
	DATE

TO

☐ NAVY MAINTENANCE MANAGEMENT FIELD OFFICE (Category A)

☐ TYPE COMMANDER (Category B)

SUBJECT: PLANNED MAINTENANCE SUB-SYSTEM FEEDBACK REPORT

SYSTEM, SUB-SYSTEM, OR COMPONENT	APL/CID/AN NO./MK. MOD.
SYSTEM MIP CONTROL NUMBER	SYSTEM MRC CONTROL NUMBER

DESCRIPTION OF PROBLEM

CATEGORY A	CATEGORY B
☐ MIP/MRC/EGL REPLACEMENT	☐ TECHNICAL
☐ EQUIPMENT ADDITION	☐ TYCOM ASSISTANCE
☐ EQUIPMENT DELETION	☐ OTHER (Specify)
☐ CHANGE TO EQUIPMENT	

REMARKS

ORIGINATOR	WORK CENTER CODE
DEPARTMENT HEAD	3-M COORDINATOR

TYCOM	☐ CONCUR	☐ DO NOT CONCUR	☐ TAKES ACTION	☐ PASSES FOR ACTION

SIGNATURE	DATE

OPNAV 4790/7B(6-73)   **ACTION COPY**   PAGE _____ OF _____
S N 0107 − 770 − 3147

Figure 9-3. PMS Feedback Report.

Items in this category include system troubleshooting, isolation of specific deficiencies, and repair or replacement of defective components. MRCs are developed for specific corrective maintenance actions which are frequently found to be necessary as a result of preventive maintenance actions. These cards are identified by the designator *R*.

Intermediate maintenance items are also generally discovered while performing the maintenance required of the PMS and are kept in a separate file. These will be accomplished by a repair facility, repair ship, or tender. Items in this category are generally confined to the repair of unserviceable assemblies on a return-to-user basis.

Depot maintenance items are those requiring extensive work by a completely tooled activity capable of repairing, rebuilding, or overhauling equipment components and assemblies. As these requirements are uncovered during the course of utilizing PMS, they are documented and filed. These items make up the major portion of the shipyard work requests. They are compiled and submitted to the type commander prior to being approved at the Arrival Conference, which defines total work that will be accomplished during a shipyard overhaul or availability.

Division Officer Responsibilities During Depot Maintenance

The inspection of work being accomplished by a repair activity for a ship is the responsibility of the commanding officer of both the repair activity and the ship. The ship's commanding officer relies heavily upon his officers in determining if the work is progressing satisfactorily. As a division officer, you are responsible for checking and inspecting the work of repair activities concerning your division and reporting the status to your department head. Those who operate and fight a ship must be those who ensure that the repairs and alterations are made properly, and that all gear and machinery is working when the ship goes to sea. *No secondary considerations of recreation or leave periods can be allowed to interfere with this primary responsibility.*

In addition to following the progress of repairs and alterations, it is important to make exhaustive tests, where practicable, before accepting a job as being finished. Repair facilities have heavy workloads and difficult commitments to meet, and will often exert understandable pressure to get a job accepted. Ship's officers must, at times, resist this pressure and be certain, within reasonable limits, that everything is in order. In the rare instance that a serious difference of opinion arises, the division officer should submit his views in writing to his department head.

In addition to inspecting work done by the repair facilities, a division officer has other special problems during a shipyard overhaul. One of these is the health and comfort of his men. Living spaces on board ship are apt to become noisy, overcrowded, dirty, and either too cold or too hot. Washroom facilities are usually reduced. If the men are moved to a barracks temporarily, many man-hours are lost in travel between ship and barracks, and a great deal of administrative work and effort is necessary to maintain the barracks. It is best, if possible, to keep the men aboard ship and to maintain the ship in as clean and orderly a manner as practicable. Trash accumulates quickly during an overhaul, and this presents two problems: fire hazard, and the cost of removal. If the shipyard laborers remove the trash, the ship will be charged for it, and money that could have been spent for needed repairs and improvements is drained off. This is why a smart division officer keeps his spaces swept down and free of trash at all times. Workmen usually do better work in clean spaces and are, at the same time, sometimes encouraged to reduce dirt and disorder.

A ship under overhaul will require special precautions against fire, theft, and sabotage. The shipyard will assist, of course, but the ship has full responsibility for security.

The greatest continuous hazard during overhaul is fire. Ship's fire-fighting facilities are often disrupted, and burning and welding are usually going on every day. The ship must provide fire watches, and it is the division officer's job to ensure that his assigned fire watches are instructed in fire-fighting techniques, the location of the nearest shipyard fire alarm boxes, etc.

In addition to the responsibilities mentioned above, during shipyard periods you will also be concerned with maintaining those pieces of equipment not scheduled for the overhaul period. Planned Maintenance During Overhaul (PMDO) supplements the Planned Maintenance System (PMS) for use during regular overhauls and other long periods when a ship is not operational. PMDO MIPs (Maintenance Index Pages) and MRCs (Maintenance Requirement Cards) are used in lieu of PMS documentation for inactive systems and equipment which is the responsibility of the ship's force.

PMDO is installed at a time specified by the TYCOM, normally two months prior to the start of the ship's regular overhaul. PMDO is, in most respects, scheduled like PMS except that MIPs cover systems, equipments, or functional groups. PMDO operations do not alter the shipyard's or ship's responsibilities during overhauls. They merely provide a schedule for the upkeep of equipment which is not under shipyard cognizance for overhaul or modification. After a shipyard job has been completed and accepted by the ship it becomes the responsibility of the ship to schedule and perform the required maintenance on the equipment.

Division officers play a vital role during normal shipyard overhauls. In addition to ensuring that PMS has been scheduled, completed, or deferred, and documented prior to an overhaul, you must schedule PMDO and ensure that your personnel continue to keep up those systems which are not being affected during the overhaul. As has been previously mentioned, you must frequently check the status of all shipyard work and ensure that all problems that you cannot handle are immediately brought to the attention of your department head.

Material History

The material history is compiled by a computer ashore as a result of the reporting of PMS actions taken, and is sent to the ship periodically. This includes depot repair actions. However, this does not replace a thorough up-to-date running record of important work that has been accomplished on the equipment under the cognizance of the division officer. Some form of division workbook is recommended.

Maintenance Data Collection Subsystem (MDCS)

The Maintenance Data Collection Subsystem, the second major subdivision of the 3-M system, alerts the systems commands to basic problems concerning performance of equipment in the fleet and the reliability and maintainability of such equipment. Improvements, if needed, can be made. Furthermore, CNO and type commands can determine the readiness of the fleet units, the overhaul and availability requirements, and personnel manning level requirements. MDCS is currently being used to provide for:

1. Producing automated Current Ships Maintenance Project (CSMP) reports which categorize and sequence deferred maintenance actions, as required by fleet managers.
2. Producing automated work requests from deferred maintenance actions for submission to activities external to the ship (i.e., tenders, shipyards, ship repair facilities, etc.).
3. Producing automated deficiency documents for use by the Board of Inspection and Survey (InSurv).
4. Effective management and control of Intermediate Maintenance Activity (IMA) workloads.
5. The fleet to report configuration changes and subsequent changes in PMS and Coordinated Shipboard Allowance List (COSAL) due to these changes.
6. Depot level maintenance activities to inform Navy managers of estimated and actual resource expenditures.
7. Producing an automated input into the Ship's Force Overhaul Management System (SFOMS) for coordination and management of ship's force work during a shipyard overhaul.
8. Fleet units to supply activities responsible for supporting the fleet with information necessary to improve reliability and maintainability.
9. Gathering information and reproducing automatically, on demand, a history of maintenance information.

The purpose of MDCS is to provide information about certain fleet maintenance and maintenance support actions for use by various levels and areas of management throughout the

Navy, with particular emphasis on providing information at the shipboard level. Standard data elements are used to record most of the information to allow the use of automatic data processing equipment (ADPE).

The basic flow pattern of the MDCS reporting is as follows:

1. Maintenance personnel
   a. Prepare documents for own work
   b. Initiate work request
   c. Initiate supplemental data report

2. Supervisors
   a. Screen for accuracy and completeness
   b. Sign
   c. Add comments: work request or supplemental data report

3. 3-M coordinator
   a. Screens for accuracy and completeness
   b. Assigns maintenance control numbers
   c. Forwards for processing center via type commander

4. Processing center
   a. Key punches data
   b. Prepares type commander's *Current Ship's Maintenance Project* (CSMP)

5. Maintenance support office
   a. Processes data and serves as central data bank
   b. Prepares reports to systems commands and CNO, and all levels of Navy management.

As a division officer you must understand all aspects of the Navy's 3-M System, especially PMS scheduling and MDCS reporting procedures. It is strongly recommended that you acquaint yourself with the four volumes of the 3-M OpNavInst series in order to utilize the system to its full potential. In addition, computer printouts are available to all commands from the Maintenance Support Office (MSO) on a variety of topics which are contained in the 3-M Manuals.

Alterations and Equipment Changes

The division officer is often requested to, or desires to, submit an alteration request. Before doing so, he should study the *Fleet Modernization Instruction*. *No* alterations may be made without proper authority.

Fleet modernization is that form of ship maintenance which provides for the enhancement of the military and operational characteristics of ships by the accomplishment of improvements or alterations. Directives promulgated by OpNav, by the material commands, and by fleet commanders are the basis for approval, authorization, and accomplishment of ship alterations (Ship-Alts), ordnance alterations (OrdAlts), and equipment changes.

The Fleet Modernization Program (FMP) is intended for the accomplishment of alterations in active and reserve fleet ships, and encompasses the budget year and four additional years. The FMP consists of two basic administrative plans; the Military Improvement Plan (MIP) and the Technical Improvement Plan (TIP). Planning procedures for the FMP are described in OpNav Instruction 4720.20 series.

ShipAlts

Approval by cognizant authorities of a proposed ship alteration is evidenced by the issue of *Alteration Approval Record (NavSea Form 99)*, more commonly known as a ShipAlt. ShipAlts are issued to cover all approved ship alterations under the technical cognizance of NavSea whether or not military characteristics are affected. ShipAlts are planning documents only and do not in themselves constitute authorization to accomplish an alteration on an individual ship. Policies and procedures regarding Ship-Alts are contained in NavSea Instruction 4720.27.

ShipAlts are classified as:

Title A—Authorized and funded by NavSea with construction or conversion funds within the funding obligation period. Not included in FMP.

Title K—Authorized and funded by NavSea. Usually requires procurement of special program material by cognizant material commands. Accomplished by shipyards requiring NavSea approval. On a case basis a Title K can be redesignated as a Title D for accomplishment by forces afloat. Included in the FMP.

Title D—Alteration-Equivalent-to-a-Repair. Approved by Nav-Sea, authorized and funded by type commander. May require special program material by cognizant material command. Accomplished by forces afloat or by shipyards as designated.

Title F—Approved by NavSea, authorized and funded by type commander. Does not require special material. Accomplished by forces afloat only.

Alterations Requests

Commanding officers are responsible for initiating alteration requests when the proposed change satisfies one or more of the following criteria:

1. Increases the offensive power of the ship.
2. Increases the power of survival of the ship under the various forms of attack or other hazards to which it might be exposed.
3. Increases the radius of action under war conditions.
4. Significantly simplifies or increases the reliability of an equipment installation.
5. Reduces personnel manning requirements.
6. Is significantly beneficial to personnel safety, health, and morale.
7. Is necessary to the safety of the ship or its equipment.
8. Increases the military effectiveness of the ship.
9. Significantly improves maintainability.

Because of the long lead time required from initiation of an alteration request to approval and final authorization for accomplishment during a specific availability, it is essential that action be taken as soon as possible after the need becomes apparent.

Each alteration request shall be made by letter. For alterations affecting military characteristics, the letter shall be addressed to CNO via type commander, fleet commander, and the cognizant systems command. For alterations not affecting military characteristics, the letter shall be addressed to the cognizant systems command via type commander.

The description of the requested alteration should cover all facets of the problem.

Alteration Equivalent to a Repair (AER)

An alteration shall be considered equivalent to a repair when such alteration involves:

1. The use of different materials which have been approved for like or similar use, and such materials are available from standard stock.
2. The replacement of worn-out or damaged parts, assemblies, or equipment requiring renewal of later and more efficient design previously approved by the systems commands concerned.
3. The strengthening of parts which require repair or replacement, in order to improve reliability of the parts and of the unit, provided no other change in design is involved.
4. Minor modifications involving no significant changes in design or functioning of equipment, but considered essential to prevent recurrence of unsatisfactory conditions.

AERs are approved and issued by NavSea as Title D ShipAlts.

Ordnance Alterations (OrdAlts)

Ordnance Alterations are issued to cover nonexpendable ordnance equipment under the technical cognizance of NavSea. Policies and procedures regarding OrdAlts are contained in NavSea Instruction 4720.27.

2. OrdAlts designated for forces-afloat accomplishment are automatically authorized as specified by the NavSea Instruction. OrdAlt material should be obtained through normal supply channels unless otherwise directed. Commanding officers are encouraged to schedule the accomplishment of forces-afloat OrdAlts as the availability of time, material, and manpower permit.

Electronics Field Changes

Electronic Field Changes are issued to cover electronic equipments under the technical cognizance of NavShips. Policies and procedures regarding electronic field changes are contained in *NavSea Technical Manual,* and amplified in applicable Electronics Installation and Maintenance books.

Electronic field changes are furnished in kit-form and are identified by change number and parent-equipment nomenclature. They are further identified by type and class designations which indicate funding responsibility and accomplishing activity, and the information and material included in the kit.

Class A changes are automatically authorized for accomplishment by forces afloat and shall be accomplished at the earliest opportunity.

Class B changes are authorized and funded by type commanders for accomplishment by industrial activities. Shipyard work requests shall be submitted to type commanders when accomplishment of a Class B change is desired.

Class C changes are authorized and funded by NavSea as parts of the Fleet Modernization Program and are usually issued as ShipAlts.

Electronic field change completion should be reported within three days of actual completion of installation work.

Ship's Equipment Configuration
Accounting System
(SECAS)

SECAS is a program for equipment validation and configuration change reporting which replaces the old equipment accounting systems such as Ship's Electronic Installation Record and Preliminary Equipment Component Index (PECI). Currently, SECAS is performing pre-overhaul and post-overhaul electronics validation and is designed to add hull, mechanical, electrical, and ordnance-related equipment in the near future. SECAS maintains ship configuration files based on SECAS validation and updating through fleet reports. The type commander is responsible for monitoring the progress of this validation to ensure that all equipment is COSAL supported and is able to be maintained in accordance with existing 3-M procedures.

Allowance Lists

Allowance lists are developed and maintained by various systems commands, and record all equipment and repair parts required aboard your ship. For example, the Naval Sea Systems Command Allowance List contains all machinery required in the main plant, equipment needed in various spaces such as binoculars, fans, desks and safes, and repair parts needed for machinery and equipment. The Ordnance Equipment Allowance contains a listing of all gunnery equipment and repair parts. Officers should review applicable allowance lists. While equipment is the responsibility of various departments, the receipt, storage, and issue of repair parts is a responsibility of the Supply Department.

Supply Matters

In order to properly direct the work of his division, the division officer must be assured of the ready availability of the materials essential to the work performed by his division. While most functions of procurement, stowage, and issuing of materials are performed by officers of the Supply Corps, certain responsibilities necessarily fall upon the division officer. For example, a supply officer can only obtain the item desired if it is properly identified and described, and the only reliable identification is a stock number. Any other type of description lends itself to misinterpretation.

Most materials used in the Navy are identifiable as an 11-digit Federal Stock Number and the Supply Department personnel will assist in locating this number through the many catalogs provided the ship. With the new equipment being introduced into the fleet each day, however, it is virtually impossible for the cataloging and publication programs to keep abreast. There will be occasions, therefore, when the only acceptable identifying media are the technical publications, drawings, and instruction books in the hands of the division officer.

Since the division officer will be required to order parts and assure that spare parts for his equipment are on board, he should be acquainted with the supply lists and abbreviations which follow:

Allowance Appendix Page (AAP) Appendix to the COSAL.

Allowance Equipage List (AEL) Documents which are used to specify requirements for shipboard equipage. AELs also are used to list miscellaneous material requirements for mechanical, electrical, ordnance, or electronics systems. Normally, items on AELs will be carried in operating spaces aboard ship rather than in the storeroom, although in certain instances storeroom requirements will be shown. AELs will be coded to indicate operating-space items and distinguished from storeroom items.

Allowance Parts List (APL) Document prepared for each individual equipment or component that provides a part's breakdown, circuit symbol, or part number to FSN (Federal Stock Number) cross-reference and other useful supply and maintenance information.

Coordinated Shipboard Allowance List (COSAL) Document prepared for an individual ship which lists the equipment or components required for the ship to perform its operational assignment. It includes the repair parts and special tools required for the operation and the overhaul, the repair parts required for such equipment, and the miscellaneous portable items necessary for the care and upkeep of the ship itself. The COSAL is both a technical and a supply document: technical in that the nomenclature, operating characteristics, technical manuals, numbers, etc., are included; supply in that the COSAL will provide a complete list of all parts required to operate and maintain the ship and the equipment installed therein.

DD Form 1348M Requisition System Document (Mechanical). Other suffix letters indicate other equipment areas.

Fitting Out Activity (FOA) The FOA is that activity designated by CNO to assist the ship's force in loading the ship's allowance material.

Inventory Control Point (ICP) Single supply-demand control point assigned the responsibility of assuring that the repair parts, irrespective of cognizance, required for the operation and maintenance of equipment assigned to it, are furnished to the ship.

NavSup Form 1114-C Stock Record Card, Afloat.

Naval Supervising Activity (NSA) The NSA is a naval activity responsible for administering Navy and other Department of Defense shipbuilding, design, conversion, repair facility, equipment, repair-part contracts and purchase orders. The NSA may be a supervisor of shipbuilding, resident supervisor of shipbuilding, or commander of a U.S. naval shipyard.

Outfit Supply Activity The naval activity designated by NavShips to order government-responsible material identified as OM. The OM Symbol is used to indicate the government-furnished material that will be ordered by the outfit supply activity.

Stock Number Sequence List (SNSL) List of parts by stock number in numerical sequence.

The Supply Department will be constantly reviewing its outstanding requisitions to ensure prompt delivery; however, it has no way of knowing the relative urgency of the many documents it is required to process. It will then become necessary for the division officer to inquire as to the progress being made on the higher priority items. To assure that his inquiries are meaningful, the division officer should be acquainted with the procedures whereby each line item is identified, marked, stowed, located, and accounted for. The procedures will include the controls necessary to ensure that:

1. The ship's supply officer has NavSup Form 1114 (Stock Record Card, Afloat) for every allowed item in the defined allowances.
2. Only allowed items, or substitutes therefor, in the allowed quantities are stowed in the ship's stowage devices.
3. All items stowed in the ship are identified exactly as they appear in the ship's defined allowances.
4. All shortages relate to a due-in document number.
5. All due-in document numbers relate to meaningful status.

Hence, in making inquiries it is essential that the supply personnel be provided the number of the requisition used by the Supply Department in forwarding the requirement. The requisition will contain all necessary information. The requisition number will normally be provided at the time the demand is first made known, and it should be maintained on record until the material is finally delivered.

Control of Material

Whether or not a strict departmental budget is in effect, there will be constant emphasis on the economical use of funds available for expenditure. There is a natural tendency to stockpile certain materials when the opportunity presents itself. The excess material redistribution program, in particular, frequently makes this type of material available, but there is good reason for resisting the urge to accumulate such a hoard. If the material is needed on a continuing basis, the Supply Department should make it available from its stocks so that usage data may be accumulated and a continuing supply assured. If material is used from the unofficial stocks held by the division, the actual ship's usage will not be recorded; and when demand is finally placed on Supply Department stocks, there is insufficient lead time to prevent a gap in the supply cycle.

The foregoing points up the necessity for the closest liaison between supply personnel and the division officer. It is only through an easy flow of information between the two that the changing requirements of the technicians can be met.

It can be very beneficial for a division officer to learn all he can about the intricacies of supply documentation. All too often, the parts center receives incomprehensible or illegible paperwork from the divisional work centers, mostly due to ignorance or carelessness on the part of the people who fill them out. The division officer whose work centers turn in consistently correct requisition forms will inevitably get better supply service than one whose supervisors leave it to the supply personnel to untangle their documentation errors.

Conservation of Material and Man-Hours

The tremendous size and expense of the armed forces has resulted in a great deal of pressure upon the services by the taxpayers for economy and the conservation of material. This is a most natural expression of concern by those who pay for our military strength. We in the Navy are more than the custodians of military strength; we are the trustees of a huge investment. It must be remembered that we all pay the taxes that pay for the Navy. The income taxes alone paid by a ship's company are about equivalent to the ship's annual allotment for upkeep. Looking at it this way, it can be said that the crew of a ship is paying for its own ship's upkeep. This is a good point to get across to the men.

Conservation is not the hoarding of materials nor the refusal to use them in the quantities needed; it is the means by which the least is made to do the most at the lowest cost possible. It can just as well be called maximum utilization. Conservation is really the maintenance of combat readiness and effectiveness by the most economical expenditure of manpower, material, and time.

A piece of equipment should be carefully used and conscientiously maintained to insure a maximum life span of performance in the duty for which it was intended. Even then, before being scrapped, it should be overhauled, repaired, or cannibalized for its parts, if this is functionally possible or economically feasible. When deemed no longer of service, it can then be disposed of as scrap to be reduced to its basic material content and placed into the production cycle in the form of a new piece of equipment.

Scrap is an important source of metal, but not so important as to cut the life span of products fabricated from metals. Before a piece of equipment is relegated to the scrap pile, uses other than that for which it was originally intended should be considered. In this manner the drain upon procurement of new equipment is lessened if discarded pieces can serve in a useful capacity. Too often equipment is relegated to the scrap pile when it could still serve a useful purpose. Good maintenance and conservation go along hand-in-hand. For example, the intake duct of an exhaust blower in your living compartment needs cleaning. Be certain that the blower is secured before the screen is removed. Careless men will sometimes be too lazy or thoughtless to do so, with the result that a cleaning rag is sucked into the fan. This can jam the blades and burn out the fan motor, costing thousands of dollars to repair.

Conservation goes beyond saving money and material; it involves man-hours too. This is more difficult to appreciate because Navy men are not paid by the hour. That is why wasted man-hours are too commonly observed in the Navy. Work must be organized and supervised, and that is where the division officer comes in. If, despite careful planning, something has gone wrong, be alert for opportunities to avoid wasting man-hours by fruitless standing around and waiting. Conduct training of some sort or give your men some time off.

If your division work never seems to get done, make a survey of actual man-hours on the job. Perhaps you have enough men, but they are not properly supervised. If a large proportion of your men are off waiting to get a haircut or a gedunk or some cigarettes, or are in sick bay or at the post office, you cannot expect to get much useful work from them. Be money conscious, material conscious, and man-hour conscious.

Damage Control

The control of damage, either due to enemy action or accident, is an all-hands job. This means that all division officers who are responsible for any spaces at all have damage control duties. This section is presented on the assumption that you do not have access to the damage control technical manuals and could profitably use a short review of the subject.

Shipboard damage control has three basic objectives:

1. To take preventive measures before damage occurs, principally by the preservation of watertight integrity, removal of fire hazards, and the upkeep and distribution of emergency equipment.

2. To combat damage as it occurs, by means of fire fighting, the control of flooding, the preservation of stability and buoyance, and the first-aid treatment of personnel.
3. To make emergency repairs to restore maximum fighting effectiveness.

The second and third objectives are somewhat beyond the scope of this text, since they are carried on mostly by specialists (damage control personnel) and do not always involve the division officer. The first objective will be discussed as being more intimately and directly related to the duties of a division officer.

The preservation of watertight integrity is assisted by a damage control check-off list in each compartment. These compartment check-off lists are permanently posted in the compartment or area concerned, and provide an itemized list (indicating the location of all classified fittings and other facilities useful in damage control) for the quick use of personnel responsible for setting material conditions. *Classified* means that it is a lettered fitting which is kept open or shut in accordance with the material condition prescribed for the ship as a whole. Examples of the items listed in compartment check-off lists are:

1. Doors, hatches, scuttles, manholes, shutters, skylights, air ports, airtight windows, and hoist covers.
2. Ventilation blowers and closures.
3. Valves of the firemain, oil, sprinklers, compressed air, and drainage systems.
4. Air test fitting caps, sounding tube outlets, etc.

At this point you, as a division officer, are perhaps wondering how all of this affects you. The check-off lists in your spaces are your responsibility. Not only must they be absolutely accurate with no omissions or other errors, but in many cases opening and closing of the listed fittings will be the responsibility of your men. The importance of these check-off lists can hardly be exaggerated; they provide the basis for effective damage control. During operational readiness inspections, a single error will cause a compartment to be unsatisfactory in damage control. Two or more compartments that do not pass are enough to give the ship a mark of unsatisfactory.

Material conditions referred to above should be defined. A ship is normally in a certain material condition, depending on her activities at the time and her location. This means that certain fittings are either open or closed. If all are closed, which, of course, is the ideal condition insofar as watertight integrity is concerned, then maximum watertight integrity is achieved. Since this is most inconvenient for the crew, this condition, known as Condition Z, is assumed only when the ship is entering or leaving port during wartime or when the ship is at General Quarters (ready for action). In contrast, Condition Y is set for normal, peacetime cruising. This condition permits a maximum amount of access about the ship for the convenience of the crew, while at the same time it preserves a reasonable degree of watertight integrity. There are a few special designations; for example, the capital letter D enclosing a letter, such as Z, means that this particular Z fitting is closed during darken ship. You must remember that all items in your compartment check-off lists are classified and marked either W, X, Y, Z, Circle W, Red Circle Z, Black Circle X and Y, and Z surrounded by a black D. Unless someone else is specifically assigned to open and close the fittings in your spaces (sometimes, on large ships, the repair parties make certain closures), it is your responsibility to see that your men take proper action when the word is passed directing a certain material condition to be set. It should be apparent now how important compartment check-off lists are. A single error, a single vent left open, for example, could result in progressive flooding in the event of damage.

Division Damage Control and Damage Control Inspections

A division officer shall ensure that all damage control equipment, fittings, and checkoff lists in his assigned spaces are maintained in proper working condition and are properly labeled.—*Standard Organization and Regulations of the U.S. Navy.*

Each division officer is responsible for the damage control equipment located within his spaces and compartments. According to the *Standard Organization and Regulations of the U.S. Navy*, each division officer assigns a divisional damage control petty officer for damage control functions of the division and related matters. It will be your responsibility to acquaint him with all phases of the ship's damage control organization and procedures. You may want him to assist you in the instruction of division personnel in damage control, fire fighting, and NBC defense procedures. In assigning a divisional DCPO, remember that you are not assigning responsibility; that rests with you as the division officer. It is highly recommended that either a second or first class petty officer be assigned as the DCPO.

In addition to keeping your divisional DC equipment in good operating condition, you must ensure that the preparation and maintenance of damage control check-off lists for all spaces under the cognizance of the division are kept current, posted, and are easily readable. The proper posting of safety precautions and danger signs within the division is highly important. Additionally, all compartments, piping systems, cables, and damage control and firefighting equipment must be properly stenciled or identified by color codes.

Your divisional DCPO will set the specified material condition within your divisional spaces and make the proper reports as required. However, it is highly recommended that you as the division officer occasionally check the setting of the material condition to ensure that your DCPO is faithfully carrying out his assigned duties. In addition to performing all damage control related PMS, he will weigh all portable CO_2 bottles, inspect and test damage control and fire-fighting equipment, and ensure that all battle lanterns, dog wrenches, and spanners are in place and in usable condition in all divisional spaces.

As you recall, the division officer is responsible "through frequent inspections to ensure that the spaces, equipment, and supplies assigned to (your) division are maintained in a satisfactory state of cleanliness and preservation." Each division officer is responsible for conducting damage control, safety device and watertight inspections in the spaces assigned. You must inspect the assigned spaces for cleanliness, state of preservation, watertight integrity, and proper operation of safety devices.

Effective use of these routine inspections for discovering deficiencies in the ship's material condition requires that the following principles be observed:

1. A systematic approach must be adopted to ensure thorough inspection of all spaces.
2. Inspection of assigned spaces must be thorough, noting more than the general appearance of the assigned compartment. For example, inspection for the state of preservation must include examination for hidden corrosion underneath, behind, and at foundation joints or welds of fixed equipment. Inspection for watertight integrity must include thorough inspection of all piping, cable stuffing tubes, ventilation ducts, and associated gaskets and fittings.

Watertight Integrity

Piping, wiring, and air-conditioning systems, shafting, and access openings installed in ships are most important in their function and operation for the attainment of the objectives of damage control. For them to perform their functions, they must pierce watertight bulkheads or decks, and thereby they create great hazard to the maintenance of the ship's essential watertight integrity. Unless the necessary action is taken to counteract and minimize this danger, an otherwise sound damage control program may not be able to save the ship when severe damage is experienced. Part 1(a) of all Damage Control books of large ships contains the following statement:

> The most highly trained gunnery and engineering personnel
> and the most highly perfected gunnery and engineering material
> are of no avail if the hulls on which they are carried into action
> sink, . . .

Every naval vessel is subdivided by decks and bulkheads, both above and below the waterline, into as many watertight compartments as is compatible with the ship's mission. In general, the more minute this subdivision, the greater is the ship's resistance to sinking from damage. A modern aircraft carrier has well over a thousand watertight compartments. The condition of this subdivision (the watertight integrity) is of the greatest importance and must be maintained in the highest degree of perfection.

The watertight integrity of boundaries to watertight compartments shall be rigidly maintained. The Naval Sea Systems Command stresses the importance of maintaining watertight integrity at the highest possible standard, and has instituted methods of inspection and test to demonstrate periodically the degree of watertightness which is being maintained. It is realized that this procedure has imposed a heavy burden on the forces afloat. All activities are warned that this vigilance must not cease, even though it imposes increasing duties and responsibilities on operating personnel. On the contrary, maximum effort should be extended to consolidate the gains already made.

Of the several degrees of tightness, watertightness claims the closest attention for the control of damage. Loss of watertightness may result from:

1. Corrosion
2. Holes in, or improper fit of joints of, structural members
3. Loosening of boundaries or joints
4. Defective closures or fittings at bulkheads or decks
5. Defective piping, tubing, ventilation ducts, and similar installations
6. Carelessness in making alterations.

Corrosion or rusting is oxidation of metal caused by the combined action of air or electrolysis. Corrosion is accelerated by the presence of salt, and has a tendency to be increased when one metal is placed in contact with a dissimilar one. Corrosion weakens structures, boundaries, joints, piping, and ventilation ducts. It hampers the operation of, and causes defects in, fittings. Because it reduces structural strength and attacks watertight integrity, corrosion must be kept under control.

The quantities of fuel, water (including required ballast),

provisions, stores, and ammunition carried must not exceed the amounts permitted by directives from the Systems Commands of the Navy Department, except as may be ordered for a specific operation by an operational commander. Division officers are responsible for reporting their loading requirements and must ensure that they are satisfactory in all respects.

Material deficiencies which are discovered during inspections and are within the capability and capacity of the ship's force, should be corrected. They should be incorporated in the *PMS Schedule*. Deficiencies which are deferred for any reason shall be reported and made part of the deferred-action PMS file.

Weight and Stability Control

There is a marked tendency for naval ships to gain weight and lose stability, with corresponding loss of reserve buoyancy, generally the result of taking aboard a large number of relatively small items. The tendency toward loss of stability is explained by the fact that such weights are usually located high in the ship. Drastic measures have sometimes been necessary to avoid compromising survival power by the accumulation of these small unauthorized weight additions. Division officers must check their spaces for these types of items.

The following measures will help to prevent overloading:

1. Prohibit unauthorized alterations.
2. Identify unnecessary equipment, structures, fittings, and stores and recommend removal or reductions of quantities.
3. Make recommendations on items which can be made lighter.

The ability of a ship to survive damage is closely related to its loading. If the liquid loading prescribed for torpedo protection and ballast is maintained, the power of survival generally increases as the displacement decreases. Limiting displacements have been established for all ship types, and limiting draft marks should now be installed on all ships.

10/Correspondence

The ability to communicate clearly in writing is a decided asset to the division officer, and distinguishes him from his peers. Its importance is illustrated by the following true incident.

As is the custom, a newly commissioned ensign, orders to his first ship in hand, wrote an introductory letter to his first commanding officer. He had a form letter commonly used for this purpose, but, exercising his initiative, he elaborated somewhat on his background and preferences for initial assignment. His letter was not overly long but it did reveal a person with a genuine point of view and an ability to communicate. When the ensign reported aboard, the executive officer greeted him with the words, "So you're the new ensign who knows how to write a letter."

Until he left the ship two years later, the ensign in the illustration enjoyed a close working relationship with his XO. His writing ability enhanced his overall professional performance and development.

Some of you who read a good deal and who have done well in English and in literature in school probably write with reasonable ease. A letter is no great chore to you and you may even enjoy writing. Others, whose major interests may be science or math, have not read widely and find concrete facts and figures more appealing than some of the abstractions of literature. For you in this second group writing is something of a task.

All of you as officers, however, face certain obligations whether pleasant or not, and writing memos, official letters, and reports is one of the duties that becomes increasingly frequent and important as you advance in rank. The ability to write easily and clearly is a distinct professional advantage and one that is highly prized by your superiors. A young officer who writes well is usually spotted at once and, all else being about equal, stands a better chance to get choice assignments.

References

Innumerable writing guides and textbooks have been published, and there is a good chance you already have one of these from college. Two of the most reliable and complete handbooks available are the *Prentice-Hall Handbook for Writers* and the *Harbrace College Handbook*. Both of these texts deal with broad and specific areas of writing. A recent book, John R. Trimble's *Writing with Style: Conversations on the Art of Writing* (Prentice-Hall, 1975), is an excellent and readable guide to effective writing.

The best short guide for the nonprofessional writer is the classic, *The Art of Readable Writing*, by Rudolph Flesch. Its companion, *The Art of Plain Talk*, is also useful. Dr. Flesch has long been an advocate of simple and understandable language. His target is obscurity in any form, especially that professional jargon beloved of medical doctors, lawyers, economists, and other professional men.

Some Basic Rules

Before describing the common forms of naval correspondence, it may be of value to outline the basic rules of good writing. Writing, as an important means of communicating, is essentially the transfer of facts and ideas from an author to his readers; the objective is to do this in the simplest, shortest, clearest, and most effective way. Thus, good writing is a tool as well as a communications system.

Brevity, simplicity, clarity—these are the marks of good writing, from a naval letter to a novel by Hemingway. The unusual words listed each month in the *Reader's Digest* are enjoyed by millions and provide an interesting and educational exercise, but they should rarely be used in daily writing. Never say "effect the unloading" when you mean "unload." Avoid adjectives unless they are vital to the meaning of a sentence. When you can say "flood" avoid "inundate," when you mean "unusual" why use "esoteric," and when you mean "plain" avoid "mundane." Use short sentences as a rule instead of linking a series of clauses together.

The basic building block of all writing is the sentence. The sentence should be effective as a unit in itself and as a contributing part to the paragraph. You must have a firm grasp of the concept of a complete sentence. Incomplete sentences and run-on sentences indicate a lack of maturity as a writer. To be an effective writer you must frame your thoughts within correct sentence structure.

Paragraphs are recognized as divisions of your overall idea. The paragraph should clearly reflect the central thought, which is usually stated in the topic sentence. All sentences in the paragraph should contribute something to that central point. Inexperienced writers commonly underestimate the importance of this relationship of the parts to the whole as well as the problem of transition. You do not want to insult your reader's intelligence by overstating yourself, but you do want to ensure that you provide the necessary conveyance from one idea to another. The texts referred to above can help you in this all-important area.

The yeoman who types your letter or report should know how to punctuate and spell but since your name is on it you should be sure it is right. If you use a technical or nautical term be sure you are using it accurately. The Naval Institute Press, the publishers of this volume, also publish *Naval Terms Dictionary*. There should be a copy in your ship or station library.

Nothing longer than a message or a simple notice should be written without first writing an outline. This helps you organize your thoughts, ideas, and facts, and enables you to present them in a logical manner. Start your outline early so you have a framework on which you can hang your ideas. It may sound strange but it often happens that your subconscious mind works on while you sleep or work and may develop ideas and crystalize thoughts without a conscious effort on your part. So if you have something important to write it pays to let it simmer on the back burner, as it were.

Getting started on any writing project is probably the most difficult task for many writers. Even the outline becomes difficult to put to paper. Instead of staring at a blank piece of paper and getting discouraged by your inability to get in the groove, let your mind run freely. Jot down your ideas in sentence form or as an outline without regard to order, grammar, punctuation, or syntax. Keep writing as long as the ideas keep coming. This method may seem ineffective and contrary to good writing practices, but you have overcome a big hurdle and have gotten your ideas on paper. Once you have done that you can reread, review, and reorganize your thoughts into a clear, concise, and readable form. When you come back to it at a later time you have a base from which to work.

Every letter or report should have an introduction. Sometimes only a sentence or two is needed but it is vital to give the reader an idea of what follows. Many busy people may pick up your letter or report. You should capture their interest and get their attention on track. Start off with a clear statement such as "the purpose of this letter (report, etc.) is to describe a series of casualties the USS *Nonesuch* has suffered with the Mark X Thingamajig, analyze the probable causes, and submit relevant recommendations." This sort of a start ensures that your paper is routed to the right people immediately and does not get hung up on the desk of someone who has no real interest in, or responsibility for, the subject.

After the introductory paragraph comes the body of the letter or report, followed by conclusions and/or recommendations.

Naval Correspondence

There is little difference between naval correspondence and any other written correspondence, with the exception of certain format and procedural considerations. These exceptions improve naval correspondence through standardization. This facilitates preparation, reading and comprehension, filing, research, retrieval, job orientation, and performance, particularly beneficial in a situation where personnel are rotated frequently.

It is not within the scope of this chapter to present all of the types of naval correspondence that you as a division officer are likely to encounter. In addition, space limitations prevent the inclusion of many examples. Guidelines for naval correspondence are found in the *Correspondence Manual of the U.S. Navy* (SecNavInst 5216 series). All naval correspondence, whether a letter, memorandum, message, or report, follows the same basic principles of brevity, simplicity, and clarity emphasized earlier.

In addition, this correspondence contains certain important similarities regardless of the subject or type of correspondence. A short summary of the most important ones follow:

1. State the purpose—*introduction*
2. Discuss and prove the findings—*body*
3. Present conclusions or recommendations—*findings*
4. Include the pertinent details—*appendix/enclosures*.

If your correspondence includes the material covered above you should be well on your way to providing your reader with the information that he desires. The main differences between one form of correspondence and another concern format and procedures. If you are able to write a good clear letter, chances are that you will be able to duplicate your success in a well-written report.

Special Types of Naval Correspondence

Standard Naval Letter

One of the simplest forms of naval correspondence is the standard naval letter. The usual purpose of a naval letter is to provide your reader with concisely stated information about a single subject. Standard formats and stereotyped styles can expedite reading as well as writing because your reader knows where to look for what he needs.

The idea of one letter for one subject should be emphasized. You do not save time or paper by accumulating a bagful of problems, comments, and requests and then unloading them in one long, confusing, and rambling letter. Visualize who must answer each item and how long such answers will take. When in doubt, divide a letter into two or more letters.

The organization of a naval letter is essentially simple. The first paragraph should tell your reader what the letter is about; the next paragraph(s) should explain circumstances and state the action—that is, give orders, make requests, give consent, refuse permission, etc.

The remainder of the letter should closely follow the important concepts presented earlier concerning the body, the findings, etc. A word concerning enclosures and references is in order since these will generally provide pertinent details to the reader, as in the enclosure; or inform the reader where he will find other information not included in the letter, as in a reference.

Some writers become so accustomed to a list of references at the top of a Navy letter that they are uneasy unless they can list such references. References should be given only if they are useful—not to be impressive. As a rough working rule, unless you direct attention to a reference in your letter, don't use it. Conversely, if you list a reference, then say something about it in your letter so that people who read your letter can know, without searching, what the reference is about.

For example:

1. Reference (a) requested information about the allowance lists for the next 3 fiscal years. Reference (b) pointed out that such information is available for only 2 years in advance and that figures for those 2 years were not yet ready. The figures are now available for fiscal 1977 and 1978 and they are as follows.

Enclosures, as with references, should not be included in a letter just to make the correspondence look "official." If an enclosure would provide necessary information or assist the reader, then by all means include it with your letter.

After you write a letter or report, sit back and try to read it with another's eyes. Is it clear and to the point? Is it complete? Is it exactly what you really mean to say?

Now is the time to shorten, cut, and simplify. Cross out every adjective and modifying clause and phrase that is not needed. Excess wordage is a waste; never a decoration. Substitute simple, short words for long ones wherever you can unless the longer word is useful for precision and clarity.

Check your letter for coherence—do thoughts, ideas, conclusions, and recommendations follow in a logical manner? They will if you have made a good outline. Have any important addressees been omitted? Are references and enclosures complete but not redundant? Do all your addressees have copies of the references? If not, add the reference as an enclosure. Are your references up to date? Again, put yourself in the reader's position—would you be content to receive this letter?

The Department of the Navy uses two basic formats for all of its correspondence. The business letter, which is used by commercial and private institutions and the public, generally is used in writing officially to addressees outside the Department of Defense. It may be used for informal correspondence (even though concerning official subjects) instead of a memorandum, between individuals of the Department. The naval letter is normally used in writing officially to addressees within the Department of Defense, and may be used when writing to addressees outside the Department who are known to have adopted, or to be accustomed to receiving, similar letters.

The standard naval letter is from one person or organization to one addressee. With very slight variations, the format of a naval letter serves as the format for the memorandum, and, to a lesser extent, for such other special types of naval correspondence as the speedletter and the telecommunication message. Finally, there is considerable similarity between the naval letter and the Department of the Navy's formal Directives System (instructions and notices), which will be discussed later in this chapter.

Since the style of the naval letter sets the pattern for all types of correspondence, it is most important and logical that you start with it. Throughout the discussion of the naval letter you may wish to refer to Figure 10-1, which shows both the form and style of an unclassified naval letter.

The first page of a naval letter is written on the letterhead stationery of the activity of the chief official under whose title it is written. Second and succeeding pages are typed on plain bond paper, similar to the letterhead in size, color, and quality.

You will note that no salutation or complimentary close appears on a naval letter. The letter is prepared in block style; that is, without indenting, except for the first lines of subparagraphs or for extensive quotations. Each paragraph is numbered flush at the left margin with an arabic numeral. All paragraphs are single spaced, with double spacing between paragraphs. The date, which is typed or stamped, refers to the date the correspondence

DEPARTMENT OF THE NAVY
HEADQUARTERS NAVAL MATERIAL COMMAND
WASHINGTON, D. C. 20360

IN REPLY REFER TO:
PBX:ABC:PLM
5 Jan 1975

From: Chief of Naval Material
to: Commander, Portsmouth Naval Shipyard
Via: Commander, Naval Ships System Command

Subj: Correspondence practices; recommendations of NAVMAT
       team concerning

Ref: (a) NAVMAT ltr PBX:ABC:PLM of 1 Jan 1975 to COMONE
       (b) FONECON between Mr. Dial, NAVMAT, and Mr. Davis,
           Portsmouth, 3 Jan 1975

Encl: (1) NAVMAT survey team report of Portsmouth Naval
           Shipyard
       (2) (SC) Department of the Navy Correspondence
           Manual (2 copies)

1. In response to reference (a), the findings of the
Headquarters, Naval Material Command survey team are
provided in detail in enclosure (1). The information on
correspondence practices in this letter and in . . .

        (2) Between all other heading entries, and between
the last heading entry and the body of the letter, there
is a blank line.

4. The month may be abbreviated or spelled in full. The date
may be either typed or stamped.

                         PETER L. MURPHY
                         By direction

Copy to:
CNO
COMONE

Figure 10-1. Format of an Unclassified Naval Letter.

was signed. Finally, the correct classification for the naval letter—Top Secret, Secret, Confidential, or Unclassified—must be assigned by you as the originator.

Memorandum

Another form of naval correspondence is the memorandum or memo. As a division officer you will become quite familiar with this form of naval correspondence. It is one of the quickest and simplest means available to you for communication within your division and the ship. It is generally used for informal communication between subordinates, usually within the same activity. The "From-To" memorandum, as it is sometimes referred to, may be typed on plain bond paper, on the Department of the Navy Memorandum (OpNav 5216/144), or, when addressed outside the ship, on letterhead paper. Informal communications within your division may be written on the OpNav form by hand. Copies of a memorandum dealing with a short-lived or inconsequential subject are not required. A complimentary close is not desired or required. It may be well to mention the fact that a junior officer such as yourself will sign correspondence "very respectfully" when submitting to a senior officer, and "respectfully" if you are sending your correspondence to subordinates. All other guidelines and format considerations are identical to those previously discussed for a naval letter. Figure 10-2 shows a typical example of a "From-To" memorandum.

Speedletter

A speedletter is a form of naval correspondence used for urgent communication which does not require electrical transmission. Its primary purpose is to call attention to the communication, so that it will be given priority handling by your recipient. In addition, speedletters are generally opened prior to the opening of routine mail and are delivered promptly to the addressees. Figure 10-3 shows the standard naval form to be used when writing a speedletter. A speedletter may be written in an informal, abbreviated style, or in the very brief style of a naval message, provided the meaning will be complete and clear to your recipient. If the

19 May 1975

MEMORANDUM

From: Engineer Officer
To: Executive Officer
Via: (1) Senior Watch Officer

Subj: Full Power Trial; requirements of

Ref: (a) CRUDESLANT Letter of 9 May 75
        (b) PHONECON between Lieutenant VILLAROSA and
            Lieutenant PETRIE of 14 May 75
        (c) CRUDESLANT Inst. 9520 of 10 April 74

1. Reference (a) delineates the requirements for a full
power trial. Reference (b) establishes the commencement
date of the exercise as 1 June 1975. Reference (c)
recommends that engineering department officers remain
exempt from standing OOD watches during engineering trials.
Therefore, it is requested that engineering department
officers be exempted from standing OOD watches from 25 May
1975 to the completion of the trial.

                              JOHN P. VILLAROSA
                              LT   USN

Copy to:
DCA
MPA

Figure 10-2. Format of a Typical "From-To" Memorandum.

text is brief, and if the time required for reply is unusually short,
handwritten speedletters may be used. If so, special care should be
taken to ensure that they are clearly legible. The remaining format and guidelines of the naval speedletter are identical to that of
a naval letter.

Naval Message

A naval message is used only when information is of an urgent
nature and must be transmitted rapidly, or when communication
by any other means is infeasible due to underway operations. A

OPNAV 5216/145 (Rev. 3-71)
SN-0107-770-8110
USE FOR URGENT
LETTERS, ONLY

Naval Speedletter

DO NOT CLEAR THROUGH
COMMUNICATIONS OFFICE

CHECK TYPE OF MAIL	CLASSIFICATION		INSTRUCTIONS

CHECK TYPE OF MAIL
- [ ] REGULAR
- [ ] REGISTERED
- [ ] AIR
- [ ] CERTIFIED
- [ ] SPECIAL DELIVERY

CLASSIFICATION

DATE

IN REPLY REFER TO

To:

INSTRUCTIONS

1. Message type phraseology is permissible.

2. Both addresses must be appropriate for window envelope or bulk mailing, as intended. Include attention codes, when known. Use dots and brackets as guides for window envelope addresses.

3. Give priority to processing, routing, and action required. Avoid time-consuming controls.

4. In order to speed processing, a readily identifiable, special window envelope, OPNAV 5216/145A, Speedletter Envelope, is provided for unclassified speedletters where bulk mailing is not used. Other window envelopes also may be used. In bulk mail, speedletters should be placed on top of regular correspondence.

Fold STANDARD REFERENCES AND ENCLOSURES, IF ANY; TEXT AND SIGNATURE BLOCK

Fold

COPY TO

From:

⟵ ──── ADDRESS

REPLY AS SHOWN AT LEFT;
OR, REPLY HEREON AND
RETURN

CLASSIFICATION

B-17088

Figure 10-3. Naval Speedletter.

message should not be used if the necessary information or directive can reach its destination in time for proper action when transmitted by speedletter or naval letter. Messages are prepared on the form prescribed by the local communications activity. Figure 10-4 shows an example of a message form that is currently used within the fleet. Naval messages are prepared in accordance with communication instructions and related publications issued by the Chief of Naval Operations. Details on the drafting and handling of messages are furnished by local communications activities.

In the naval message, use abbreviated titles, in capital letters, of the command or activities in the "from," "to," and "info" lines. For brevity and security, the number of addressees should be limited to those who need to know only. A most useful phrase, which will become more important as you earn higher assignments (command), is "Unless otherwise directed"; this is written UNODIR in a message. It relieves your superior of the need to reply and very often influences him to do nothing and lets you do as you wish. It shows initiative on your part and is usually the mark of a good officer. Never ask permission or ask for instructions if you can use UNODIR instead, not just in naval correspondence or communications but in your day-to-day relations with your superiors.

Other Naval Correspondence

There are numerous other types of naval correspondence that you should be aware of, although it is quite unlikely that you will be originating them. Therefore, it will suffice to just briefly mention one and refer you to the *Correspondence Manual of the Navy* for details of other types of correspondence.

An endorsement is used by you to forward, with appropriate recommendation, comment, or information, correspondence which is transmitted via you before it reaches its destination. The contents of a prior endorsement also may be the subject of comment. An endorsement is most effectively used for transmission of correspondence through the chain of command.

NAVAL MESSAGE
OPNAV FORM 3110 28 (REV 3 61)

RELEASED BY			DRAFTED BY			PHONE EXT NR		PAGE	PAGES
DATE		TOR/TOD		ROUTED BY		CHECKED BY			OF
MESSAGE NR	DATE/TIME GROUP (GCT)		PRECE-DENCE	FLASH	EMERGENCY	OPERATIONAL IMMEDIATE	PRIORITY	ROUTINE	DEFERRED
			ACTION						
			INFO						

(PRECEDENCE/DTG) _____

FM _____

TO _____

INFO_____

_____

BT

(CLASSIFICATION //SSIC//) _____

(SUBJECT)_____

BT

- -
DISTRIBUTION

(PAGE ONE ONLY)

UNCLASSIFIED | DATE/TIME GROUP (GCT) |

Figure 10-4. The Naval Message Form.

Unit Directives System

It is important for you, as a division officer, to understand the Navy Directives System. As a division officer, you will be called upon to write a ship's bill or instruction. This will test both your ability to write well and to follow complex guideline and format considerations. A sample directive is illustrated in Figure 10-5.

Directives are used by commands to communicate plans and policies to subordinates. They serve as guides for controlling the decisions and actions of subordinates in the organization. For an adequate understanding of the purpose of directives, a knowledge of the definitions of policies, procedures, orders, instructions, and regulations is required (see Chapter 4, "Administration").

Directive is a comprehensive term meaning an order or instruction which prescribes policy, organization, conduct, procedures, or methods. Two types of directives that you as a division officer will be concerned with are *instructions* and *notices*. An *instruction* is a directive containing authority or information having continuing reference value or requiring continuing action. It remains in effect until superseded or otherwise cancelled by the originator or higher authority. A *notice* is a directive of a one-time or brief nature, with a self-cancelling provision, that has the same force and effect as an instruction. Usually it will remain in effect for less than six months but is not permitted to remain for longer than one year.

The basic purpose of the Navy Directives Issuance System is to establish a simple and uniform plan for issuing, maintaining, and filing directives and for making their location and reference a relatively rapid process. A directive system must provide for wide dissemination of the policies of the command. It must also provide a medium for subordinates to issue amplifying and supplementary instructions for placing those policies in effect. Finally, it must permit integration of the unit directives with those received from outside the unit, thus ensuring that policies and procedures used in administering and operating the unit are continually in keeping with the plans and policies of the Navy Department and of fleet and type commanders.

In addition to the directives already mentioned briefly above,

UNITED STATES NAVAL ACADEMY
Annapolis, Maryland 21402

USNAINST 1531.16J
3b/Registrar

October 15, 1974

USNA INSTRUCTION 1531.16J

From: Superintendent

Subj: Administration of Academic Programs

Ref: (a) USNA Regulations
(b) USNA Catalog and Supplementary Bulletins

Encl: (1) Graduation and Degree Requirements
(2) Course Enrollments and Changes of Status
(3) Academic Performance
(4) Courses, Classes and Semester Examinations
(5) Academic Reporting System
(6) Merit lists and Class standing
(7) Academic Accountability

1. Purpose. To promulgate instructions regarding academic requirements
and related matters.

2. Cancellation. This Instruction cancels USNA Instruction 1531.16H,
and 1080.3A effective immediately.

3. Scope. This Instruction and the applicable sections of references
(a) and (b) contain the guidelines for the administration of the Academic
programs at the Naval Academy.

4. Responsibilities. Specific individual responsibilities are indicated
in enclosures (1) through (7). After the choice of a major, each midshipman is assigned an Academic Adviser who is available for counseling; but
it is the responsibility of the individual midshipman to ensure that his
own academic program and performance meet the requirements outlined in
this Instruction.

5. Action. Enclosures (1) through (7) are effective this date. Approval
was voted by the Academic Board and the Objectives Review Board on 26
September 1974.

W. P. MACK

Distribution:
CC, F
Academic Dean (5)
Comdt of Midn (100)
PhysEd Dept
Library (2)
Chaplains (4)
Dir Computer Services (2)

CO, NavHosp (2)
Data Processing Div (4)
Midn Store (2)
Publications Officer
Registrar (25)

Figure 10-5. A Sample Navy Directive.

there are also directives that are not included under the Navy Directives System. A list of the most important ship's directives follows:

Plan of the Day
Captain's Night Order Book
Engineer Officer's Night Order Book
Officer of the Deck Standing Order Book

Again, you may not be required to originate any of the above-mentioned shipboard directives; however, you should become aware of what each of these contains. Shipboard directives are discussed in the *Standard Organization and Regulations Manual of the U.S. Navy.*

Bills

As a division officer it will be your responsibility to update and keep current those ship's bills which affect you and your division (see Chapter 3). A complete discussion of the types of bills that you may find on your ship can be found in Chapter 6 of the *Standard Organization and Regulations Manual of the U.S. Navy.* Regardless of the type of bill encountered, they all generally follow the same prescribed format.

A ship's bill sets forth policy for assigning personnel to duties or stations for the purpose of executing specific evolutions or accomplishing certain functions. It consists of the following sections:

1. A *Preface,* which contains a statement of the purpose of the bill, an assignment of responsibility for maintenance of the bill, and information of a background or guidance nature.
2. A *Procedure,* which contains all information and policies necessary to interpret the tabulated material and all special responsibilities of individuals with regard to planning, organizing, directing, or controlling the function or evolution to which the bill relates.

Reports

The final area of naval correspondence that you will be interested in as a division officer is that of report writing. A long report may take weeks or months of preparation and research. Hopefully, this chapter has given you new ideas as well as insights to get you started towards the goal of a well-written report. Since reports vary so much, from a one-page tabulation of asked-for figures to a 100-page report on engineering capabilities, the discussion that follows will be confined to some brief general statements applicable to most reports.

A common error in report writing, as in any writing, is to write from the standpoint of what you, the author, want to say on the subject. The results of such an approach can range from a rambling discussion to an essay on generalities—leaving your reader still hoping for an answer to his questions. A report should be written from the reader's standpoint: What does he need or want to know about a subject? Viewed in this light, modern practice puts the conclusions and recommendations at the beginning.

In some instances, your reader already knows a lot about the subject and is looking only for the figures or for a list of procedures. Or he may want to know how the conclusions or recommendations were reached; if so, then a word about method and sources should appear near the beginning of the report.

Some officers, when first called upon to write reports, find difficulty in organizing a report to focus on the conclusions and recommendations. They feel that the reader should first be prepared by all the facts and discussion before the answers are sprung on him. Or they insist that the reader see how the answers were achieved. If you fit into this category, don't feel alone. Realize, however, that most readers of reports have learned to turn directly to the recommendations whether at the beginning or at the end of the report. Usually the person who asked for the report agrees quickly with many of your conclusions. For those areas he is unsure of, or in disagreement with, he will certainly check your method of approach and compilation of information which should be included in the body of the report.

The guiding principle of report writing is: Cast your final draft in a form that immediately shows your reader the information he is seeking. Although reports may be written and organized in numerous forms and variations, the important characteristics of good writing discussed earlier in the chapter apply here as well.

Completed Staff Work

Since much of your initial writing will essentially be a form of writing drafts for seniors in the chain of command (department head, executive officer, commanding officer) it is quite appropriate to mention the doctrine of completed staff work. There may be a natural frustration on the part of a junior officer when confronted with the completed staff work concept. "What's the use of learning to write better, when the commanding officer nitpicks my stuff anyway?" The answer is twofold: (1) constructive criticism, not taken personally, will only serve to improve your writing skills; and (2) when you become the boss you will have gained the experience necessary to supervise the writing efforts of your subordinates.

The reason you are writing a particular piece of correspondence is most likely because you are the expert. You, as the first lieutenant, would have a close understanding of the requirements for an accommodation ladder, for instance, and therefore would be the logical officer to initiate correspondence for the commanding officer's signature.

You must expect your writings to be modified and edited by your superiors. However, this does not relieve you of the burden of trying to submit a flawless piece of work. If your work turns out to be perfect you will have received your reward. If it was not completely acceptable find out what was wrong so that you know how to improve your work, remembering that each individual you will write for will be a little bit different from the other.

11/Conclusion

Much of my life has been concerned with the problem of leadership, and I have already tried to explain how military leadership today needs a somewhat different approach. Two thousand years ago men obeyed automatically because of the "authority" vested in the superior. The centurion in St. Matthew's Gospel clearly thought that because he had authority his soldiers would obey, and he was right. But today the authority has got to be exercised wisely and sensibly, and, if it is not, soldiers get restless. The first thing a young officer must do when he joins the Army is to fight a battle, and that battle is for the hearts of his men. If he wins that battle and subsequent similar ones, his men will follow him anywhere; if he loses it, he will never do any real good. The centurion was dealing with regular soldiers who had made the Army their profession; with such disciplined men, the habit of obedience is strong. But in practically all armies today the bulk of the soldiers are National Servicemen. These men do not serve for long and have to be disciplined and taught obedience; some do not take too kindly to it. My experience of the British soldier, Regular or National Service, is that once you have gained his trust and confidence, and won his heart, he is easy to lead. In fact, he responds at once to good leadership and likes it.—Field Marshall Montgomery.

This chapter will deal with a number of quite unrelated, but nonetheless important, subjects that do not fit directly into any of the foregoing chapters.

Human Factors in Leadership

The first of these subjects concerns the importance of the *human factor* in military leadership. Your men are the most important assets you have; they are the one common denominator in all naval activities. Machinery can be repaired, and compartments repainted with routine ease, but tired, disheartened, or demoralized men cannot be restored to fresh energy and spirit without the employment of much time and skill. Burned-out motors or bearings are not difficult to replace, but a man deeply hurt and embittered may never regain his full usefulness to an organization. Men are profoundly vulnerable emotionally, yet they can also be inspired to prodigious labor and self-sacrifice. The greatest resource you have as a division officer lies in your men. To release this latent energy takes wisdom and skill in human relations, but the rewards can be almost immeasurable. Men will perform much more efficiently and will make many more sacrifices for a leader they respect and trust, than for one who merely drives them along with the force of his impersonal and delegated authority.

The comprehension of these truths provides a firm base on which an officer can build his professional skill and develop his professional knowledge. Most officers deal with people all their lives, and the measure of their success with people is a measure of their success in their profession. The application of this idea to a division officer's daily tasks is not difficult to see. While he must accept and operate the weapons and the machinery which are furnished to him, a division officer does not have to accept the performance of his men in using the weapons or in running the machinery. There are almost no limits to the proficiency he can develop in his men. No matter what cadmium-plated, supersonic, electronic, beam-riding gadget he is provided with, he still has to select and train men to operate it. The human factor is a constant factor in warfare. The fingers that designed, assembled, and programmed the space capsule launch rockets are the same human mechanism that released the English arrows at the Battle of Crecy.

Customs, Traditions, and Manners

Naval customs, traditions, and usages have evolved over a period of nearly two hundred years, during which time they have been time-tested and proven through usage. In fact, they are sometimes recognized in legal proceedings to the extent that they almost have the force of law.

Every naval officer should endeavor to know, understand, and follow naval customs, traditions, and usage, realizing that there is a strong reason for their existence, based on the experience in peace and in war of generations of our worthy predecessors. They should be departed from only after the most careful thought and consideration.

Young officers, new to the service and unaccustomed to life aboard ship, sometimes offend by an apparent lack of manners or respect for certain customs of the Navy. The more senior officers, with whom they work and live in close contact, have acquired a deep respect for the traditions and customs of the Navy. This may cause these officers, quite understandably, to become sensitive to matters of behavior which new officers may not even be aware of. Crowded living conditions make it particularly important for all officers to recognize those conventions of shipboard behavior and those vital traditions whose observance and recognition distinguish officers and gentlemen.

Junior officers are prone to treat the wardroom of a ship as if it were the lounge of their fraternity house at college. This behavior is understandable, but is not well received by officers who have learned that consideration for their fellow officers can make crowded ships livable and comfortable. Books, papers, charts, caps, jackets, and rain clothes should not be left in the wardroom. Neither should wardroom magazines be removed, nor feet rested on coffee tables. Coffee cups should be returned to the sideboard when empty, and ashtrays should be used when smoking. The best seats at wardroom movies (usually those nearest the screen) should be left vacant by junior officers for their seniors. Caps should never be placed on wardroom mess tables, sideboards, or buffets. These all seem to be small and obvious points, yet collectively they are important. Junior officers should be prompt for meals, especially when guests are present. When they have guests of their own, they should introduce the guests to their shipmates, particularly to the senior officer, who is normally the command duty officer.

In leaving the ship, junior officers always enter a boat first. It is natural, civilian good manners to step back and let your seniors precede you, but naval customs and tradition require you to enter a boat or automobile first. In a boat, move well forward unless the only shelter is to be found forward; in that event take the most exposed seat in the boat, leaving the sheltered seats for your seniors. In returning to the ship, the senior officers are the first to debark and the first to go up the accommodation ladder or brow.

Civilian clothes are normally worn off duty in the Navy. It has long been a custom among naval officers to wear their uniform only while on duty or when attending an official ceremony. While there is nothing wrong in not observing this custom occasionally, it is not smart to go ashore for fun and frolic in uniform. A certain formality of dress, to which you as a college man might not be accustomed, is required of commissioned officers. It is suitable to your status as a professional man and also serves to set a standard for the wearing of civilian clothes by your men. As a young executive in private industry, for example, or as a young lawyer, you would not come and go in sport clothes; you would dress the part of a professional man.

The Navy draws a firm line between official or shipboard relations and social relations. Aboard ship there must be a certain formality and dignity, particularly on the bridge or on the quarterdeck, or in the presence of a group of men. Officers of about the same rank with the same job interests tend to group together. Ashore, at a club, at a party, or at someone's home, a more informal atmosphere is appropriate. Officers' wives often make close friendships among themselves with little regard for seniority, and a first-name basis is quite normal for officers on the golf course or on the tennis court despite a disparity in rank. An officer can never go far wrong in being perfectly natural and friendly ashore, while observing a certain formality and reticence aboard ship until he gets to know his seniors.

Institutional Aspects of the Navy

In the chapter on discipline, the point was made that a division should be run in a regulation manner. In this chapter, the importance of naval customs and traditions has been stressed. There are some excellent reasons for these important points. The Navy, like any other institution, such as the church, owes much of its strength and vigor to well-established procedures and ceremonies. Men, living in groups over a period of centuries, have been conditioned to react to certain fixed symbols and formalities. The study of man in his environment (sociology) has a direct military application. The officer who is too much of an individual, who runs things his own way, who does not stress the normal, regulation way of doing things, provides a difficult problem for anyone who succeeds him. Strong individualists must recognize their role as that of only one officer in a long line of officers.

It is in this context that the official formalities of Navy life should be considered. Morning quarters, colors, and the ceremony of the quarter-deck are all important in that they are the visible evidences of the permanent spirit and tradition of the Navy. The wearing of the uniform, the manner of saluting, and correct military behavior in speech and in correspondence are all important and must be recognized, observed, and enforced by junior officers. New men and officers, fresh from civilian life, are often prone to discount and ignore many of the rules of behavior of the Navy. They sometimes believe that it is not American, not democratic, to be military. Nothing could be farther from the truth. The very survival of our American democracy in a war-threatened world depends on the strength of the armed services. These services, to be strong and effective, must be authoritative in nature. No officer, however humanitarian or idealistic his views, should feel apologetic in observing the military rules and traditions of his profession. Furthermore, an officer without real pride in the service and without a sense of obligation and duty, cannot hope to achieve success in the Navy.

The petty annoyances that are bound to occur—the last-minute schedule change that upsets your weekend plans, the hurry-up-and-wait of a fueling evolution, perhaps even an unmerited harsh word—must be taken in their proper context: The Navy, whether you are in it for a career or a short period of volunteer service, is a large and complex operation run by fallible human beings. There will always be mistakes in judgment or casualties to equipment, though perhaps to a lesser degree than in any other organization of comparable size. These must not become a preoccupation. "Keep your eyes beyond the beam of your ship," as a venerable salt once advised, and appreciate instead the power and majesty of naval tradition.

People in the Navy

Just as all commands incorporate informal organizations that differ from the formal, official ones found in those units' organization manuals, so does the Navy as a whole contain an informal organization. It might appear to you as a newly commissioned officer that the rank structure represents a constant and fixed set of values, but this is far from true. For example, the Navy warrant officers, while technically junior to ensigns and junior lieutenants, actually represent a group of seasoned, responsible, and skillful officers who exert a much greater influence than their broken stripes would indicate. Warrant officers are an exceptionally able group who have a detailed knowledge of their specialty and a wealth of experience in the Navy. A newly commissioned ensign or junior lieutenant should tread very lightly in dealing with these wise old-timers; he should solicit their advice on technical matters and their guidance in dealing with naval problems. Warrant officers, proud of their special skills and long service, are always glad to help a young officer get squared away in his new job.

There are also some ensigns and lieutenants who have had

many years of service, gained as they worked up through enlisted and warrant status. The point is that rank does not always indicate length of service or degree of skill and background. Do not judge a man by his uniform, but check into his background and experience.

It is important that you establish a good working relationship with your senior petty officers, who, in most cases, will be chief petty officers. The "chief" has traditionally been referred to as the "backbone of the Navy," and he thinks of himself as such. He is the man through whom you must translate orders into action, theory into practice. He stands at the top of his career—has proved himself through years of experience. He stays with "his gang" while division officers come and go.

Your tacit acknowledgment of these facts will amost always result in the wholehearted cooperation of your senior petty officers. They will be eager to share with you their hard-won knowledge of the Navy and of their specialties, and will take pride in the knowledge that they have had a part in your development as a professional naval officer.

New Ideas

Another characteristic of all institutions, such as the Navy, is resistance to change. Yet change, progress, and the introduction of new ideas and techniques are essential to the healthy existence and growth of any institution. Some sort of change is one of the continuous facts of life. The important and critical decisions which face us concern largely the manner and degree in which changes should be made. As the world grows older and the indefatigable, inquisitive mind of man learns more about it, there can be no logic in clinging to the good old days. Certain sentimental reasons there may be—and valid ones, too—but these should serve only to soften the transition and should not attempt to halt inevitable progress. Most laymen opposed anesthesia, when first developed, as something immoral in that it thwarted the will of Providence. Most senior naval officers clung to sail long after the steam engine had proved its reliability. But there have always been men of vision, too, who could recognize the need for progress and the value of novel ideas.

Many young men with new ideas are hurt and discouraged when they suffer the opposition that, while deplorable, is inevitable. One way to avoid this, while still trying to sell your idea, is to avoid becoming too emotionally involved with your campaign of persuasion. Try to look at the matter objectively, realizing that opposition to new ideas is to be expected and accepted. There are some interesting aspects to this pathological tendency on the part of many men to resist change. Men who appear always, and sometimes violently, to oppose change are usually men who are basically, perhaps subconsciously, insecure. They see all changes as a threat to their position; they cannot adjust their ideas and beliefs with the flexibility of mature, well-organized personalities.

A normal conservatism on the part of senior officers usually serves the worthwhile purpose of separating the sound proposals from those that are merely novel.

New ideas and techniques are one of the most important contributions an officer can make to his profession. They should be pushed with vigor and persistence tempered by patience and good sense.

How to Estimate Your Success as a Division Officer

A division officer may very well wonder how to judge his effectiveness. There is no simple rule-of-thumb, but there are several questions that a division officer can ask himself. The first is: Do I run my division in an atmosphere of approval? If the division officer likes and respects most of his subordinates, if there is very little bitterness and recrimination noticeable in the daily routine, if his subordinates like to talk things over with him, the answer is probably affirmative. While a certain amount of stress is inevitable in running any military outfit, there is no excuse for the excess of emotion that so frequently accompanies the handling of men. It is a sign of instability and immaturity on the part of the officer in charge. Complications, problems, and mistakes are all part of the normal daily routine and should not be considered by any officer to be a sort of personal affront. Men usually perform their routine tasks more efficiently when not distracted by displays of temperament.

Standards of Discipline

Another criterion of efficient division leadership is standards of discipline. A well-led outfit has few mast cases, few men absent without authority, and a minimum number of small incidents of bad behavior. The men should conform to regulations and meet the standards of appearance, performance, and behavior that have been established. They should do so because they have accepted those standards as the standards of their group. The appearance of your men, while working and when ashore, will reveal to a critical observer a great deal about the discipline of your division. Their performance can be estimated by the comments made during formal inspections. All these matters are relative, of course, and it is not reasonable to expect perfection. Comparisons can be made with other divisions which should provide a basis for your judgment.

Team Spirit

An important criterion of a division's leadership is team or group spirit. Are the men interested in the various forms of competition? Do they generate ideas and enthusiasm over a group activity such as a baseball game or a picnic? Do they really work hard before an inspection or do they just go through the motions? A highly motivated group of men will voluntarily work many hours overtime, if they must, to prepare properly for an inspection. There are dozens of other indications of team spirit—or the lack of it—in a division. There may, of course, be factors beyond your control that dampen the spirits of your men, but in general you should be able to judge their spirit in comparison to that of other divisions. The group discussions described in the chapter on training foster team spirit. The degree of enthusiasm and interest shown by your men during the discussions is a measure of their interest and of your success in guiding the discussions through a stimulating exchange of ideas to a meaningful conclusion.

Being alert to these matters may assist you in uncovering sources of irritation or confusion that would not normally be brought to your attention. For example, a leading petty officer may be going stale through overwork or may have personal problems which are reflected in his being a little rough on his men. It is possible that your first knowledge of this may be gained from observing the men in their daily tasks.

Relations with Seniors

It may have occurred to you that a junior officer not only has to be a good leader; he also must be an accomplished follower. All of us work for someone in the Navy and cannot be successful unless we please our seniors. As you will discover, this can be difficult until you learn a few basic principles and techniques. In a military organization you cannot choose your immediate superior, and your first duty is to carry out his orders.

A dual relationship usually develops between you as a division officer, and, let us say, your department head. You may even become close friends and play golf together. The important feeling, of course, is one of mutual respect; friendship can be considered a bonus. It is wise to keep these relationships separate. Enjoy his friendship ashore but be careful to treat him as your superior officer on board.

Study your senior; his habits, likes and dislikes, way of doing things. Try to see things his way; appreciate his responsibilities and his relationship with *his* boss.

If you find yourself in strong disagreement on some professional question with your senior, do not fight the problem. Do it his way—then suggest changes if you still want them.

When you present new ideas or new ways of doing things to your senior try to do it in a modest, quiet manner so as not to arouse a natural opposition to change.

The most important thing you can do for your senior is to take action on his orders. Take notes to be sure you are responsive to *all* of his ideas. Some officers rarely give a firm, clear order; they suggest or imply—it is up to you to act.

Remember the value of completed staff work. Wrap up a project if possible and present it in a positive manner. Ask as few questions as possible—it is better to say: "Unless you direct otherwise I propose to . . . ." Then all you need is a nod and you can go ahead.

Remember, your superior must do a good job for *his* boss. Keep him informed so that he is not embarrassed by being asked questions, by the commanding officer, for example, about his duties that he cannot answer.

Career Advantages

One of the most serious problems the Navy has had to solve in recent years has been that of retention of trained men. New ships have been built and advanced detection, weapons and propulsion systems have been developed, but the most sophisticated "hardware" in the world is only as good as the men who maintain and operate it. This means the Navy has to retain qualified men if it is to make effective use of the ships and equipment provided.

The reasons men give for not reenlisting are many and varied. Some of them are real and valid, many of them are imaginary. The unhappy fact is that the Navy has lost many valuable trained men, with loss in its condition of readiness and professional standards of performance. For each man so lost the cash investment in training alone runs to thousands of dollars.

Over a period of years the Navy has developed and implemented many ways to improve personnel retention. The system for advancement in rating is fair and objective and rewards the man who studies hard by allowing him to compete with his contemporaries on an equal basis through standard exams. Cash payments for reenlistment have, for some highly technical ratings, amounted to several thousand dollars. Career counseling programs instituted in all ships and shore activities are designed to inform men of the advantages of a Navy career plus the opportunities open to them. These programs have had some, but not enough, effect on retention.

Several programs which have been initiated indicate a

different attitude toward a "people-oriented" Navy. Admiral Elmo R. Zumwalt, Jr., who became Chief of Naval Operations in 1970, laid the groundwork for the new Navy by his "Z-Grams" which were intended to streamline and modernize regulations to improve the human aspect of the Navy. Typical of such modifications are those dealing with hair styles and the wearing of uniforms, which have replaced antiquated standards with more modern ones.

The "Z-Grams" were only the beginning of a new era in our Navy. The principles which they support will be the same through several CNOs and each will refine the programs until they are a smooth-running part of the overall organization. Principles of social change require constant refinements if these programs are to continue to contribute to the accomplishment of the Navy's missions.

The problem of reenlistment and retention can be partially solved at the Navy Department and political level, but probably even more significantly at the level of each man's division, and ship.

As a division officer you play a vital role in this program, on which the very effectiveness of the fleet depends. First of all, as you learn to become a good leader whom your men can respect and look up to, you must become familiar with all the actual benefits and advantages enjoyed by a career man. Many data of this sort are available in the Fleet reenlistment manuals and from the career counselors.

Secondly, you must show your dedication to the Navy by your attitude. Never, under any circumstances, talk the Navy down. Unfortunately, there are some unthinking officers and petty officers who betray their country's trust when they foolishly join in loose and inaccurate talk about the rigors of Navy life and the pleasures of a Utopian civilian existence. As rigorous and demanding as the Navy can be, there are rewards in feelings of accomplishment and pride that no civilian can comprehend, much less measure. Talk up and stress the aspects of naval life that appeal to all men. Men leaving the Navy look back with pleasure and satisfaction upon the experiences of travel and foreign cruises. Similarly, they cherish the memories of friends and shipmates, of danger and hardship faced together. Yet too many of us shy away from even mentioning these really important aspects of life.

Fundamentally, the really worthwhile men are not reenlisted merely because of what their Navy pay will be or how it compares with that of men on the outside. They will reenlist and become career men only when they are convinced by the example, attention, and interest of their leaders that what we do in the Navy is tremendously more important than how much we get paid for doing it. No worthwhile man will turn permanently to the Navy for his career unless he is convinced that the Navy not only needs him, but will make the most of his individual abilities. Your part is to convince him of that.

The Meaning of a Commission

Note the wording of an officer's commission: "Reposing special trust and confidence in the patriotism, valor, fidelity and abilities . . . I do appoint . . . by and with the advice and consent of the Senate." "Special trust and confidence" is more than a polite phrase; it means just that. A commissioned officer is assumed to be a man of honor and integrity.

It is true, of course, that in this era of huge armed forces, it is not always administratively feasible to accept an officer's word at face value. National security often requires that an officer provide proof of his actions or identity. But despite this, an officer in uniform is recognized as the custodian of his country's honor and safety.

The war in Vietnam brought a general feeling of revulsion toward things military. This is a natural, if somewhat painful, expression of public attitude toward the war, and will fade. Tomorrow's world situation will bring tomorrow's public opinion. The history of the United States shows that the military is most respected when it is most needed. An officer must appreciate his appointed position of special trust and confidence and must earn public respect by maintaining traditional standards of honor and devotion to duty.

Remember that an officer's oath of commission obligates him to support and preserve the Constitution. Since the Constitution defines the great moral and judicial principles upon which our Republic is founded it follows that an officer is, by his oath of office alone, committed to the exercise of moral leadership.

Patriotism

In this age of conflict, ideological as well as military, it is well for all officers to recall the oath they took upon receiving their commissions. Our enemies attack us with ideas that are designed to destroy our faith. This must stimulate us to affirm our faith and our pride in our country, and all that she stands for. We cannot afford to be complacent about our freedom and our prosperity.

Attitude surveys of enlisted men reveal many who do not know why large military forces are needed by the free world. Many of us assume that young men in the services are aware of their responsibilities as American citizens to defend the United States. This is not necessarily true and no officer should hesitate to counter the apparent cynicism of youth in regard to patriotism.

Remember, your men are not just employees and your role is not simply that of a manager. You and your division represent the United States in a manner in which very few are privileged to represent her. You are her strength, her commitment, and her guarantee to the world. You, and others like you, must meet the task or the whole world pays the price. Every ship that is off the line, every plane that is grounded, weakens our position. Each of us plays an important role in the maintenance of our strength. Few have a role as important as the division officer. Naval officers find themselves charged with this responsibility very early in their careers. Too often that portion of their career is over before they realize its true importance.

The quality of your leadership and performance are the measure of America's future. Seize this opportunity before it escapes you. It can bring rewards and knowledge you will treasure for your career and your lifetime.

The deterrence of nuclear confrontation, controlling free passage of the world's sea lanes, and the mobile exercise of American sea power are *your* mission. These roles embody the four missions of the Navy. Whether by use of our might or mere show of force our naval power is the key to our success. You hold the key to keeping our naval power at its peak.

As an officer whose obligation and privilege it may be to lead your men in war, you should seize every opportunity to encourage and inspire loyalty toward, respect for, and devotion to, our country. Men have always fought more effectively when fighting for something they believed in. The barbarians did not overrun Rome until her freemen had lost their faith and vigor.

War and Peace

A division officer should realize early in his career that he will never satisfy completely all the demands that are imposed upon him and upon his men. He will rarely have perfect appearance of personnel and material, and at the same time be completely prepared in all respects for wartime operations. It must be conceded that the emphasis on spit-and-polish sometimes tempts young officers to believe that appearance and smartness are the most important considerations in apportioning their time and manpower. It is a grave mistake, however, to believe seriously that any responsible senior is more interested in appearance than in combat efficiency. It may happen that ships which are outstanding in appearance will win the battle efficiency awards, but in most cases the same ships are outstanding in fighting potential, too.

A division officer must never forget that he and his men have one primary mission in life: to prepare for and to conduct wartime operations. All duties and activities should lead by some means to this end.

Index